MW00946984

ANCIENT CHRISTIANITY

The Essentials

A foundational study of the basics of Christianity

By Dwain Kitchens, D. Min.

XULON PRESS

Xulon Press
2301 Lucien Way #415
Maitland, FL 32751
407.339.4217
www.xulonpress.com

Copyright © 2013 by Dwain Kitchens
Revised 2021

Ancient Christianity: The Essentials
by Dwain Kitchens

All rights reserved solely by the author. The author guarantees all contents are original and do not infringe upon the legal rights of any other person or work. No part of this book may be reproduced in any form without the permission of the author. The views expressed in this book are not necessarily those of the publisher.

Unless otherwise indicated, Bible quotations are taken from the *English Standard Version*, Copyright © 2001. The ESV and English Standard Version are trademarks of Good News Publishers.

Other versions used are:

AMP—Scripture taken from the *Amplified® Bible*, Copyright © 1954, 1958, 1962, 1964, 1965, 1987 by The Lockman Foundation.

THE MESSAGE—Scripture taken from *THE MESSAGE*. Copyright © 1993, 1994, 1995, 1996, 2000, 2001, 2002.

NASB—Scripture taken from the *New American Standard Bible*, © 1960, 1962, 1963, 1968, 1971, 1972, 1973, 1975, 1977, 1995 by The Lockman Foundation.

NET—Scripture quoted from the *New English Translation*. Quotations designated (*NET*) are from The NET Bible® Copyright © 1996-2006 by Biblical Studies Press, L.L.C. www.netbible.org. All rights reserved.

NIV—Scripture taken from the *Holy Bible, New International Version®*. Copyright © 1973, 1978, 1984 by International Bbile Society.

NKJV—Scripture taken from the New King James Version of the Bible. Copyright © 1979, 1980, 1982 by Thomas Nelson, Inc.

NLT—Scripture quotations marked *NLT* are taken from the *Holy Bible, New Living Translation*, copyright © 1996, 2004, 2007 by Tyndale House Foundation.

Printed in the United States of America

ISBN 978-1-6250-9677-7

Table of Contents

Introduction

I have served in the position of senior pastor since the age of 23. I am now 63, and have witnessed many changes within the context of the church. Methods change, approaches to ministry change, but the message and doctrinal truths of the Scriptures must never change. In a world that is accelerating with change, the church of Jesus Christ must be careful not to deviate from the basic teachings and theological tenets of the ancient church—the church of the first century. In the epistle of Jude we read these words, "Beloved, although I was very eager to write to you about our common salvation, I found it necessary to write appealing to you to contend for the faith that was once for all delivered to the saints" (Jude 3). If Jude felt it necessary to write about this in the first century, how much more so in the twenty-first century!

Though my theological position has changed slightly through the years, particularly on the subject of the Holy Spirit, I would consider myself a mainstream conservative evangelical. I have written this resource for two purposes. First, to provide a Spirit-filled foundational resource for new believers and mature Christians alike that is solidly grounded in the Scriptures. Second, to provide a resource for the people I serve that is personal, from my heart, and that addresses those topics I feel are essential to provide a good foundation. It is my prayer that others will find this as a resource in establishing a solid theological foundation. May the Lord use it to bless you, your ministry, and the equipping of His saints (Eph. 4:11-14).

Dedication

I dedicate my first book to my wife, Pam, an incredible pastor's wife who has stood by me, supported me, been my confidant, my best friend, my encourager, and the love of my life. She has given me two wonderful sons of whom I am extremely proud. She is an excellent mother and now grandmother. When the Lord brought us together as husband and wife 44 years ago. He matched us perfectly and gave me the perfect help mate. I am truly blessed to have her in my life!

Acknowledgments

I want to thank my Executive Administrative Assistant, Mrs. Joyce Phillips for reading through the manuscript and assisting me with corrections. She has served me for over twelve years and is by far the best administrative assistant I have had the privilege of serving with. I also want to thank Ms. Sanny Rider for doing an excellent job in serving as my editor. She has been a pleasure to work with. Thank you to Mrs. Joanne Sargent for cross-checking my biblical references. She is one of our precious volunteers in our church office and emulates the life of Jesus through her servanthood. And a special thank you to my Tabernacle Church family for their prayers, support, and encouragement during the project.

Endorsements

W hen Dwain sent me the manuscript on his new book to read, I had already been asked by a couple of others to read theirs and write a foreword for them and I thought this is another book which will take up my precious little time. But Dwain is a friend so I printed it off and began to wade through it, wow! I found this is not just another book.

Whether the explanation he gives on the deity of Christ, basics of salvation, Holy Spirit baptism, End Times or apostasy, Dwain's solid Southern Baptist Bible training is evident. This book not only has relevant information, but a clear, firm, balanced theology with excellent Hermeneutics and Exegesis of the Bible that is very rare in today's light, shallow preaching. This book on Christianity is a book on time and I would go further and say it must be read by all Leaders and congregations alike.

Some may feel a little uncomfortable because it challenges a programmed mindset which we all have after a period of years, but you cannot fault the solidity of the research and Biblical guidelines that Dwain has followed.

Dwain, well done, I will recommend this book to Charismatics, Pentecostals, Evangelicals and Traditionalists and hope that all our fixed mind sets do not hinder the truths in this book.

Colin J Cooper
Leader of Cathedral House (Huddersfield Christian Fellowship)
Chairman of Ministers Fellowship Europe

This book is a masterpiece on the fundamental doctrines of Christianity. It makes the truths of the Bible come alive and easily understood. I recommend it to be read by those new to the Christian faith, those who are established in the faith, and to any who might be searching. While it is possible you may not agree with everything the author states, it is laid out sincerely and clearly and will challenge you in your Christian beliefs with truths that are hard to reject.

Dick Iverson
Founder Ministers Fellowship International
A foundation is the first and most important stage of a building process. Every wise builder understands the significance and necessity of laying a solid base. Whatever else is built must rest upon it; the greater the building, the stronger the foundation must be.

Doctrines are the foundational truths of Christianity. We build our lives and ministries upon them. They shape destinies by framing what we believe about God, sin, redemption, the Holy Spirit, the Church, evangelism and more. I highly recommend *Ancient Christianity: The Essentials*, Dwain has done a masterful job making the basics beautiful while providing a great discipling resource for pastors and leaders and meaningful read for those wanting to grow in their faith.

Pastor Mike Servello,
Founding Pastor Redeemer Church Utica, New York
Founder & CEO of Compassion Coalition Utica, New York

When I received the manuscript of *Ancient Christianity: The Essentials* from my friend Dr. Dwain Kitchens, I thought it would be a boring book dealing with issues of the past and not so interesting or relevant to the postmodern generation. But as I turned the pages and read them chapter by chapter I found it more than interesting or relevant to the people of the 21st century. This book talks about the past, the present and the future. It's very broad and yet very specific. It raises many questions, and provides solid philosophical and theological answers. It's a well-researched piece of work. His statements are well supported by the Bible and many credible scholars and writers of our generation.

Once I started reading I had a hard time putting it down. I wanted to read more and more because it deals with the basics of the human quest for spiritual answers. The questions at the end of each chapter help the reader carefully ponder and make personal reflection. In every chapter Dr. Kitchens deals with the subject matter carefully and objectively. It's clear that he writes with personal conviction from the heart.

I have travelled to speak in many nations and met with people of all walks of life, Christians and non-Christians. While reading this book I saw many faces in my mind, thinking that this book will answer some of their basic questions about the reliability of the Scripture and God's answer to the deepest need of the human heart.

This book will bring faith to the skeptics, conviction to sinners, hope for the hopeless and a renewed passion for the cold-hearted, backslidden Christians. I strongly recommend to those who are in the church and the unchurched. The contents and insights of this book will help affirm your faith and help you defend your faith.

Chin Do Kham, D.Min., Ph.D.
President, Global Outreach and Community Development
Church Consultant

Chapter One

The Bible: Our Authority

"The Bible." Those simple words release multiple emotions. Many people love and adore the Bible, but there are those in whom the very word 'Bible' causes immediate anger, animosity, and divisiveness. No other book on the planet has been so loved while at the same time creating hostile and antagonistic reactions. I think a critical question that should be asked and explored is: why? Why does the Bible, the most quoted and influential book ever written, produce such vehement responses? What is it about the Bible that causes groups like the ACLU to send their lawyers to courts across a nation or to challenge the placement of the Ten Commandments in schools and public halls and seek to have them removed? Why are some school districts now placing restrictions on The Gideons (an International Christian ministry that publishes and gives out Bibles for free), prohibiting them from providing Bibles to students, as has been their practice for many years?

These are questions that need to be answered by people who are willing to explore the Bible. What other religious book has generated such an aggressive attack in history? None! This fact alone should be reason enough to create a sufficient level of curiosity and cause a person to read and examine its contents.

Though there may be several answers to the questions above, I believe the key answer to all questions about the Bible's impact has to do with the nature and authority of the Bible. The Bible confronts people with their sin and with the message of Jesus Christ. It teaches that man is a sinner and needs a Savior. You cannot read and examine the Bible without being confronted with this message. It clearly teaches that man has a sin problem, and that the answer to that problem is surrendering one's life to the Lordship of Christ.

The Bible also makes clear that there are not many ways or paths to God, but only one way, and that way is Jesus. This is not a politically correct message in the twenty-first century. We live in a pluralistic society that prides itself in being tolerant of other people's belief systems including their religious beliefs. And being tolerant has taken on new meaning.

At one time being tolerant simply meant recognizing that people have a right to their beliefs and opinions, including their religious beliefs, and they also should have the freedom to practice those beliefs. This is an American value with which I wholeheartedly agree.

The *new* definition of tolerance is that not only do people have the right to their own beliefs, but also that their beliefs are just as valid and correct as yours. That is, you have no right to say that Christianity is the *only* true way to experience God. You have no right to say that certain lifestyles are sinful and unacceptable. You have no right to say that other religions and practices will not all lead to the same place. If you show any intolerance to this way of thinking, you will be labeled a bigot. The interesting thing is that those who espouse this position become intolerant of your point of view by saying it is unacceptable, which is the very thing their philosophy of intolerance is not supposed to do!

The real issue here comes down to one's source of authority. People can have all kinds of opinions and speculations about ideas, philosophies, lifestyles, and religion. But the crux of the matter is: what is their authority? Upon what do they base their opinions and make their assumptions? My contention is that if people do not have an authoritative source to validate their opinions and espoused opinions of acceptable behavior, then they have no basis for their conclusion about any given matter.

People have been filled with various thoughts, opinions, and philosophies since the inception of time. There is a plethora of books advocating those philosophies. But the issue at hand is: on what basis do they make their claims? What is their source for making authoritative statements and drawing conclusions about life? What is right and what is wrong? People can discuss morality and ethics all they want, but based on what? Many people may say to you, "I just think this is right. I just think this is okay." But there are multiple opinions on various issues and topics and all of them cannot be right or correct. Therefore I contend that there must be an authoritative standard to juxtapose with our system of beliefs in order to see if they are consistent to that standard. For Christians, that standard is the Bible, which we believe to be the inspired and infallible Word of God.

You may say, "Well, I don't believe the Bible" to which I would say, "Why not? Have you ever read it? Have you ever studied it? If not, why not?" The Bible has been the best-selling book on the planet for hundreds of years. If a particular book was on the best-sellers list of the *New York Times* for ten straight years, would that not be a possible reason to read it? Yet, we have the Bible, which has been the number one seller for several hundreds of years, along with being the most published book on the planet. Yet for all that, people still refuse to pick it up and read it! This is astounding and beyond rational thinking to me. Apologist Josh McDowell writes:

> A professor once remarked to me, "If you are an intelligent person, you will read the one book that has drawn more attention than any other, if you are searching for the truth." The Bible certainly qualifies as this one book. As Theodore

Roosevelt once observed, "A thorough knowledge of the Bible is worth more than a college education."[1]

So why are so many people unwilling to read and explore the Bible? Why is this the case? How can this be? I again submit to you the reason has to do with the nature and the authority of the Bible. People do not want to be confronted with anything that may challenge their lifestyle, their belief system, or more specifically cause them to face or deal with their sin. So they avoid it. They criticize it. They castigate it. They belittle and make fun of it. They call it antiquated or claim that it is full of contradictions and mistakes. Yet they have never bothered to examine or read it for themselves.

Dr. R.A. Torrey was once confronted by a young man who attacked the Bible. Insightfully, Torrey asked the question, "Is your life right?" The young man abandoned the conversation and quickly excused himself. Like this young man, most people have not rejected Christianity on intellectual grounds but on spiritual grounds.[2]

The reason I begin this chapter with "The Bible, Our Authority" is because the Christian faith has *no other* authority. Let me point out that I do not accept the Bible as being authoritative out of blind faith or wishful thinking. I have reasons for believing the Bible is the very Word of God. As believers in Christ, we need to have confidence that when we read the words in the Bible, we are reading the very words of God. When we discuss our beliefs (doctrines) concerning God, Jesus, sin, salvation, the Holy Spirit, morality, prayer, heaven and hell, and other subjects, we need to know that we can trust our source, the Bible, and we need to be confident that it is authoritative on all matters pertaining to what it says and reveals.

Everything that is taught in this study concerning our Christian beliefs and lifestyle is based on the teachings of the Bible, so it is critical that this is our beginning point.

Throughout our entire lives, you and I will need to make decisions on a variety of issues, including moral ones. Upon what will we base our decisions? On our feelings about a particular subject? On what our gut seems to be telling us? On what society embraces as right and wrong? Remember: we are sinful creatures and our understanding and thinking capacity has been adversely affected by our sin nature. Everything we seek to process must go through an imperfect filter. It is critical that we have a trustworthy and reliable authority on which to base our decisions. That authority is the Bible.

My goal in this chapter is to build your faith in the Bible as the Word of God. I want to establish and place this foundation firmly under you so that you never question its veracity and truthfulness. I want to fortify your belief in the Bible as God's Word so that your faith will not be shaken or undermined. And I want to ensure that you will not lose confidence in the Bible's authority. All Christian teaching is based on the teachings of the Bible, and this is why I have purposely chosen to place this first in our understanding of Christianity.

As I build my case for the authority of the Bible, I want to focus on its *uniqueness*. Let's get started by considering the many ways that the Bible is unique.

Unique in being quoted

There is no other book quite like the Bible! It is the most quoted book in history. Not only have preachers and Christians quoted it, but kings, presidents, governors, congressmen and congresswomen, senators, and other governmental officials alike have quoted and made use of the Bible in speeches and addresses. The founding fathers of the United States quoted the Bible extensively and etched its words on the monuments and historical sites that characterize the nation's capitol. Why? Because it is recognized to be a unique, special book, and a book that has influence.

Unique in its circulation

There is no other book that has such wide-spread circulation. Christian apologist Josh McDowell writes:

> It's not unusual to hear about books that have hit the bestseller list, selling a few hundred thousand copies. It's much rarer to come across books that have sold more than a million copies, and rarer still to find books that have passed the ten-million mark in sales. It staggers the mind, then, to discover that the number of Bibles sold reaches into the billions. That's right, billions. More copies have been produced of its entirety as well as selected portions than any other book in history. As *The Cambridge History of the Bible* states, "No other book has known anything approaching this constant circulation."[3]

Why is this? The reason is because it is the Word of God. The Holy Spirit has ensured that the Bible would be circulated to all peoples of every nation. The Bible is a book in which God reveals who He is, where life originated, the purpose and destiny of humanity, and the answers to the deepest questions and yearnings of the human heart. Though God speaks through His creation and through His Holy Spirit, He speaks primarily through His Word, the Bible. Thus, through the Holy Spirit, He made certain that the Bible would be translated into the many languages of the world and circulated among the nations.

According to Wycliffe Bible Translators, the Bible has been translated into 2,696 languages. "The Bible Society of the United Kingdom calculates that the number of Bibles printed between 1816 and 1975 was 2,458,000,000. By 1992 the estimated number rose to nearly six billion. Furthermore, worldwide sales of the Bible number more than a staggering 100 million each year, far outpacing any other book in history. Without a doubt, the Bible is the best-selling book of all time. This means that as of 2007 approximately 7.5 billion Bibles have been distributed throughout world—with the vast majority still available for use! And these figures do not include the various digital versions of the Bible being used today by millions on computers, Blackberries and iPhones."[4] Another source says, "The New Yorker confirms that it is the best-selling book in history and outsells all other books every year, and that The Amusing Facts Website estimates that approximately 50 Bibles are sold each minute around the world."[5]

How can anyone say that the Bible is just *another* book? These facts and statistics concerning the Bible point to the hand of God. God is sovereignly circulating His Word to the ends of the planet!

"The numbers of translation of the Bible are every bit as impressive as its sales numbers. Most books are never translated into another tongue. Among the books that are, most are published in just two or three languages. Far fewer books see translation figures rise into the teens. According to the United Bible Societies, the Bible (or portions of it), has been translated into more than 2,200 languages … Worldwide, no other book in history has been translated, retranslated, and paraphrased more than the Bible."[6]

Unique in its transmission and preservation

It is a miracle that the Bible still exists! Even though the Bible has been attacked more than any other book in history, it has not only survived, but it also has flourished throughout the centuries. The question needs to be asked, "Why has it survived?" The answer is because it has been supernaturally preserved by God. The Holy Spirit's protection hovered over the ancient documents of Scripture to guarantee its accuracy and survival during and after its transmission.

"Although it was first written on perishable materials and had to be copied and recopied by hand for hundreds of years before the invention of the printing press, the Scriptures have never diminished in style or correctness, nor have they ever faced extinction. Compared with other ancient writings, the Bible has more manuscript evidence to support it than any ten pieces of classical literature combined. Bernard Ramm speaks of the Bible's accuracy and number of biblical manuscripts: "Jews preserved it as no other manuscript has ever been preserved. With their *massora (parva, magna,* and *finalis*) they kept tabs on every letter, syllable, word and paragraph. They had special classes of men within their culture whose sole duty was to preserve and transmit these documents with practically perfect fidelity—scribes, lawyer, massoretes. Who counted the letters and syllables and words of Plato or Aristotle? Cicero or Seneca?"[7]

The meticulous care with which the Scriptures were copied is amazing. This was no accident. It was the providential hand of God. The supernatural oversight of the Holy Spirit not only ensured that the Scriptures would be preserved, but it also guaranteed that the copyist would transcribe the Scriptures with great accuracy in order to protect the Scriptures' trustworthiness. There are literally hundreds of accurate copies of the Scriptures that demonstrate unquestionably their reliability.

Dr. Frank Harber, an atheist studying to become a lawyer, was challenged by some Christian friends to investigate the claims of Christianity. Wanting to disprove the existence of God, Harber took them up on their challenge. His careful examination of the historicity of the Scriptures led him not to disproving God's existence, but to a passion for Christ. He left law school and enrolled in Southwestern Baptist Theological Seminary, earning a PhD in a record-setting two and one half years. He is now a Christian apologist and leader in defending the Christian faith. In his book, *Sherlock's Faith*, he writes:

> The original autographs of the Old Testament were written
> on papyrus. Papyrus deteriorates at a very rapid rate. Because
> of this, scribes were employed to copy the books of the Old
> Testament. These scribes believed the Scriptures to be the
> Word of God and went to great lengths to eliminate error.
> They followed strict Jewish traditions which even dictated
> how many columns and lines could be on a page, counting
> every line, word, and letter to find any mistakes. Any copy
> with even one mistake was destroyed. Because of this, the
> Old Testament has been preserved in its original form. Prior
> to 1947 the oldest existing Old Testament copy was the
> Massoretic Text which is dated about A.D. 900. In 1947 the
> Dead Sea Scrolls were found at Qumran. Many of the scrolls
> dated back to around 150 B.C. making them almost 1,000
> years older than the Massoretic Text. The Dead Sea Scrolls
> read identical to the Massoretic Text, both of which are iden-
> tical to the Hebrew translations in our own Bibles. Only a
> small percent of variation can be found, all of which can be
> attributed to variations in spelling. [8]

The Bible is reliable and trustworthy! There will always be critics who seek to undermine the reliability of the Bible, but I would submit to you once again that the issue is not if it is reliable and trustworthy. The issue is its authority and how to respond to its message. Dr. Harber continues:

> The reliability of the New Testament is also beyond reproach.
> More than 24,000 partial and complete copies of the New
> Testament are available today. No other document of antiquity
> can even come close to such large numbers. Homer's *Iliad* is
> a second with a mere 643 existing manuscripts. So sparse are
> copies of ancient classical works that 20 copies would be a

lofty number of manuscripts. In addition to the New Testament manuscripts, there are over 86,000 quotations of the New Testament from the Early Church fathers. So thorough are these quotations that all but 11 verses of the New Testament can be reconstructed from this material, which dates less than 200 years after the coming of Jesus....Not only are the New Testament documents superior because of their great numbers, but also because of the time span existing between the original autographs and their copies. Unlike Buddha, whose sayings were not recorded until 500 years after his death, all the books of the New Testament were probably written within 30 years of the death of Jesus. The earliest copies of our existing New Testament begin at A.D. 125. In comparison, Homer's *Iliad* has a time span exceeding over 500 years between the time of writing and the oldest manuscript. No book in antiquity can compare with the New Testament in the number of manuscripts or in the interval of time between the originals and the copies. The New Testament in comparison to other ancient manuscripts is virtually free from any corruption. Textual critics have found only one-half of one percent differs. Thus, 99.5 percent of the New Testament has no variation. These variations for the most part deal with matters of spelling or word order. Not one single variant has any bearing on a doctrine of faith. In any case, the Church has in its possession 100 percent of the New Testament. Such confidence cannot be attributed to any other piece of classical literature.[9]

As was stated, the fact that the Bible and its numerous copies have been preserved through the ages is in itself miraculous. This is in spite of the numerous persecutions. Hatred for the Bible is not a new development of the twenty-first century, as the Bible has been attacked throughout the centuries. In times past and in our present century, the Bible continues to be the most persecuted and attacked book on the planet. But again, this is not new. From its very inception there have been those who have sought its destruction.

Most of my ministry to this point has been spent serving as a pastor in Southern Baptist churches. Though I am no longer a Southern Baptist, I treasure the impact and influence the churches have made on my life, particularly in reference to the Bible. I deeply appreciate their zeal for evangelism and their commitment to the Scriptures. One of my favorite preachers (who is now with the Lord) was Dr. W. A. Criswell, the beloved pastor of the historic First Baptist of Dallas, Texas. He was an anointed and fiery preacher and a leading pastor in the Southern Baptist Convention throughout his ministry. In the midst of a long and embattled controversy in the Southern Baptist Convention concerning the inerrancy of the Scriptures, Dr. Criswell was one of the prophetic voices defending the inerrancy of the Bible and warning about a liberal drift in the Convention. In his book, *Great Doctrines of the Bible*, he writes:

> In A.D. 303, Diocletian, Emperor of the Roman Empire, decreed that every Bible in the world should be destroyed, and that the people who possessed Bibles should be slain. So effective was that horrible, cruel onslaught that in about a year or two the persecutors supposed that they had eradicated the Bible from the face of the earth. Myriads of Christians laid down their lives when they were discovered with the Word of God. Diocletian was told that Christians were a people of the Book, and that if the Book were destroyed, the faith would cease to exist. So he sought to destroy the Book. He considered his drive of extermination so successful that over a burned and extinguished Bible he built a column, and on it wrote these triumphant Latin words: *Extincto nomene Christianorum: The name of Christian is extinguished*. Christians were drowned in blood, consumed by fire, martyrdom, death. But who succeeded the cruel Diocletian? The Emperor Constantine. He declared himself to be a Christian, though he was the Caesar of the Roman Empire. He took the pagan symbols from off the standards of his Roman army and the shields of his marching soldiers, and he placed on them the symbol of the cross of Jesus Christ. That marvelous transformation happened in A.D. 312. How many years was that after Diocletian had erected his column over a burned and destroyed Bible, saying that the very name of the Christians was extinct? Less than ten![10]

Again, does not common sense and reason demand that we ask why the Bible has been viciously attacked through the centuries? This is not true of other books of antiquity. Why the Bible? Could one reason be that the god of this age, Satan, knowing that the Bible is the Word of God, has through the ages sought to bring about its destruction? From the beginning, Satan has sought to undermine and to place in question the authority of God's Word. Notice part of the dialogue and appeal that Satan made to Eve in the garden:

> Now the serpent was more crafty than any other beast of the field that the LORD God had made. He said to the woman, *"Did God actually say*, 'You shall not eat of any tree in the garden'?" And the woman said to the serpent, "We may eat

of the fruit of the trees in the garden, but God said, 'You
shall not eat of the fruit of the tree that is in the midst of the
garden, neither shall you touch it, lest you die.'" But the serpent said to the woman, "You will not surely die. For God
knows that when you eat of it your eyes will be opened, and
you will be like God, knowing good and evil." (Gen. 3:1-5,
emphasis mine)

Notice I italicized the words "Did God actually say." From the beginning,
Satan's key strategy is to get us to undermine and question the authority of
the Word of God. He wants to cast doubt in our minds concerning its veracity,
because once we question its veracity, we will automatically question its
authority. So no one should be surprised that through the centuries there has
been an aggressive assault on the Bible. But the Word of God is indestructible!
The prophet Isaiah said, "The grass withers, the flower fades, but the word of
our God will stand forever" (Isa. 40:8). Jesus said: "For truly, I say to you, until
heaven and earth pass away, not an iota, not a dot, will pass from the Law until
all is accomplished." (Matt. 5:18)

But although the Bible is indestructible, there will always be critics and
skeptics attacking its credibility. One of the more colorful accounts of an attack
on the Bible recorded in history is that of the renowned atheist Voltaire of the
eighteenth century, who died in 1778. He was one of the noisy critics who
thought he had the gift of prophecy when it came to the demise of Christianity
and the Bible. He proclaimed that the Christian faith and the Bible would cease
to exist in 100 years.

"But what has happened? Voltaire has passed into history, while the Bible
continues to increase in circulation in almost every part of the world, carrying
blessing wherever it goes. Concerning Voltaire's prediction of the extinction
of Christianity and the Bible in 100 years, Geisler and Nix point out that "only
fifty years after his death the Geneva Bible Society used his press and house to
produce stacks of Bibles."[11] Quite the turn of events.

The enemies of Christianity and the Bible always rise up but do not prevail.
Jesus' words are true: "Heaven and earth will pass away, but my words will not
pass away." (Mark 13:31) I love the words of theologian Bernard Ramm:

A thousand times over, the death knell of the Bible has been
sounded, the funeral procession formed, the inscription cut
on the tombstone, and committal read. But somehow the
corpse never stays put. No other book has been so chopped,
knived, sifted, scrutinized, and vilified. What book on philosophy or religion or psychology or *belles letters* of classical or modern times has been subject to such a mass attack
as the Bible? With such venom and skepticism? With such

thoroughness and erudition? Upon every chapter, line and tenet? The Bible is still loved by millions, read by millions, and studied by millions.[12]

Unique in its unity

Though the Bible was written by various authors over hundreds of years, it is unified in its theme and focus, free from any contradictions. Dr. Harber writes:

> The Bible towers above all other books as the all-time best seller in history. Over 40 authors combined to write the 66 books found in the Bible. It was written over a span of 1,500 years, in three languages, and was composed in 13 countries on three continents. The Bible was written by men from all walks of life including kings, peasants, herdsmen, tax collectors, philosophers, statesmen, fishermen, poets, and scholars. It uses various literary forms such as history, poetry, proverbs, preaching, prophecy, parables, allegories, biography, drama, exposition, law, and letters. Yet, in spite of all this diversity, the Bible contains a vast unity. This unity is so unique that the books of the Bible form a unit, such that the Bible is not a mere collection of books, it is just one book.... Some have proposed that the Bible is just the invention of men. However, such a theory of human conspiracy is ruled out by the vast time span involved. Not only would such a conspiracy require someone who could make up the fictitious story, it would require legions of actors and civilizations to act out the story in history.[13]

What is the reason for the Bible's unity? The Bible was written under the inspiration of the Holy Spirit. Even though there were over forty authors writing in different centuries and cultures, there is uniformity. As the various authors held their pens and wrote, inscribing the words we read today on ancient parchments, their very thoughts and words were being directed by the Holy Spirit of God. Though they were given the freedom to use their own vocabularies in relaying the message, their contemplations and expressions were placed within them through the inspiration of the Holy Spirit.

The true author of the Bible is God. Substantiating that claim, the apostle Peter writes these words in his second epistle: "Knowing this first of all, that no prophecy of Scripture comes from someone's own interpretation. For no prophecy was ever produced by the will of man, but men spoke from God as they were carried along by the Holy Spirit" (2 Pet. 1:20-21). Frank Harber writes:

To read the words of Scripture is not to read the words of men but the words of God. This is clearly taught by the Scriptures themselves. The prophets were conscious of this as they repeatedly uttered the phrase "thus says the Lord" and "the word of the Lord came to me." Writers of the New Testament believed the entire Old Testament to be the very Word of God (Rom. 3:2). The New Testament writers often quoted an Old Testament author such as Moses using phrases such as "God said" (Gen. 2:24).[14]

The apostle Paul, writing to young Timothy says:

And how from childhood you have been acquainted with the sacred writings, which are able to make you wise for salvation through faith in Christ Jesus. All Scripture is breathed out by God and profitable for teaching, for reproof, for correction, and for training in righteousness, that the man of God may be competent, equipped for every good work. (2 Tim. 3:14-17)

What does it mean exactly when we say the Bible was written under the inspiration of God? What does the word "inspiration" mean?

"The Greek word most nearly equivalent to our word "inspiration" is found in 2 Timothy 3:16. It is *theopneustos*. It means, literally, "God-breathed." By divine breath and power the Holy Spirit moved the (human) authors of the Bible with such precision that the product accurately reflects the intention of God himself. As God spoke through prophets and apostles, the original documents the writers produced bear the special marks of divine inspiration. This means that the 66 books in the canon, which make up the Bible, in their original expression are entirely trustworthy as the voice of the Holy Spirit."[15]

It was through the inspiration of the Scriptures that the Bible was transmitted and preserved. But how do we know that the Bible in its present form is accurate? How can we know that the Bible doesn't contain mistakes? We have thousands of manuscripts today and not one copy of the originals. What if through the centuries the manuscripts were added to or distorted by copyists who wanted to insert their own thoughts and opinions? These are valid questions.

The good news is that there are several thousands of ancient manuscripts of the Bible and we can compare those manuscripts with each other word for word and see if anything was changed or manipulated. Scholars and linguists have done just this, and the remarkable thing is that they have found very few variations among texts. Therefore, we can be assured with certainty that our copies of the Scriptures today are reliable and trustworthy.

Dr. Criswell confirms and substantiates the reliability of ancient manuscripts.

About 1,500 years after Herodotus had written his history, there was only one copy of it left in the world. And 1,200 years after Plato wrote his glorious classics, there was only one manuscript in existence. To the present day, there is only one manuscript of the Greek anthology. We have just a few manuscripts of Sophocles and Euripedes, of Thucydides, of Virgil, and of Cicero. But there are thousands and thousands of copies of the Word of God, which can be compared one against the other in order to arrive at the most accurate reading.

One of our Greek scholars has estimated that there are more than 4,105 ancient Greek manuscripts of the New Testament. Another one says that there are 15,000 to 30,000 ancient Latin versions of the Holy Scriptures. Another says that there are more than 1,000 ancient versions (the translation of the Scriptures into other languages), besides the papyri they are daily discovering in archaeological excavations, and besides the quotations found in the Church Fathers. By comparing these thousands of manuscripts, it is easy to discover the original that God has inspired in heaven. If one copyist made an error, God prevented other copyists from making that error.[16]

One of the renowned Spirit-filled pastors and authors of our day is Dr. Jack Hayford, who served for many years as senior pastor of Church on the Way in Van Nuys, California. He is an excellent teacher, a prolific author, and theologian. I appreciate his balanced approach to Scriptures, which has made a significant impact on my theological journey. In his book, *Grounds for Living*, he speaks of the reliability of our Bible and corroborates what others have said as related to ancient manuscripts.

Evidenced by the number of existent manuscripts

Many of the most well known works of antiquity, such as the writings of Plato and Aristotle, are known from only 25-40 manuscripts – that is 25-40 copies of their writings made by *others* and dating to within a few hundred years of the author's writing, but not the original writings of the men themselves. In contrast, there are more than 6,000 manuscripts or parts of the New Testament, many from within the first two centuries AD, that are available for us to compare. This large number from scattered locations, from early yet varied dates, provides a base for comparison that would give every reason to expect a high degree of variance between manuscripts. Yet notably, although not surprisingly, if the Bible really is the Word of God, there is an incredibly high level of consistency and continuity between them.

Evidenced in the reliability of the text

Because of the fact that manuscripts were hand-copied, one might well assume that errors and mistakes could easily creep in. The *Iliad* by Homer, for instance, contains 15,600 lines of which literary scholars question the accuracy of 746 lines (due to errors or omissions). According to literary scholars (and it is important to stress here that these are not necessarily Christian believers, but people pursing the New Testament solely as an historical Greek manuscript) there are 20,000 lines, only 40 lines of which have given their most critical eye any reason to question the accuracy. Even more profoundly, and significant to every believer in the Bible, even among these few contested "lines", *not one* relates to a major doctrinal issue.

Evidenced by the discovery of the Dead Sea Scrolls

Before the Dead Sea Scrolls were discovered, the oldest Old Testament manuscripts dated to the tenth century AD (known as the Masoretic text). Given that the book of Malachi is estimated to have been written around the fourth century before Christ, and the Masoretic text is dated around the tenth century after Christ, there existed a hiatus of about 1,400 years between the time of the last writer in the OT and the oldest existing copy of the Hebrew Scriptures.

Then - the discovery of the Dead Sea Scrolls in 1948! This find has been categorically described as the greatest archaeological discovery of the entire twentieth century. Significant for us is that, for example, a scroll of the complete text of the book of Isaiah was found (a copy dated to 125 BC, almost one thousand years earlier than the Masoretic text). With a millennium having transpired between the two, scholars expected to find that many changes and mistakes had been introduced into the Masoretic text when comparing them to the Scrolls. But they found almost none – the integrity of the text was remarkably well preserved, a full thousand years' passage giving evidence for our believing the Bible we have in hand today is indeed what was written long ago."[17]

More than any other book of antiquity, the Bible can be trusted! The transmission and preservation of His Word throughout the centuries once again attests to the uniqueness of the Bible and how the Holy Spirit ensured that it would be available throughout all generations for those who desire to know and experience God.

Unique in its influence on literature

In *The Greatest English Classic*, Cleland B. McAfee writes, "If every Bible in any considerable city were destroyed, the Book could be restored in all its essential parts from the quotations on the shelves of the city public library. There are works, covering almost all the great literary writers, devoted especially to showing how much the Bible has influenced them."[22] The Bible has had a profound impact on literature throughout time!

Unique in its fulfilled prophecies

Dr. Harber shares several examples of fulfilled prophecies.

> The Old Testament contains well over 2,000 predictive prophecies which are very specific and detailed. One of the main reasons the Bible contains so many prophecies is so that in their fulfillment, the divine origin of the Scriptures may be established.

> The Bible records many instances of specific detailed prophecies which were given hundreds of years in advance of the fulfillment. One example is Isaiah predicting that a man named Cyrus would rebuild the temple (which was still standing in his day!) in Jerusalem (Isa. 44:28). Cyrus, the Persian king, was born 150 years later. He released the Jews from their 70 years captivity in order that they might return to their homeland for the rebuilding of Jerusalem and the temple.

> In many of these prophecies, the exact details of the destruction were predicted. More than 100 specific prophecies exist detailing the destruction of Babylon. Babylon was the greatest city of the ancient world. The historian Herodotus records that its walls were 200 feet tall and 87 feet thick. Three hundred-foot towers extended above the walls which enclosed an area of 196 square miles. The Bible not only predicted its destruction, but prognosticated that because of the wrath of God, it would become desolate and uninhabitable (Jer. 50:13). Today Babylon lies in a heap of ruins in the middle of the desert.

It was prophesied that the Jews would be scattered but would preserve their identity. For 1,900 years Jews wandered the earth being scattered and persecuted, yet Jesus predicted that the Jewish race would be intact when He comes again. So why does one never hear of Hittites, Philistines, Hivites, Moabites, Jebusites, or Ammonites? Consider the truth of the Scriptures: the Jewish people are still here today.

The Bible also predicted that though they would be scattered, they would one day return to their homeland (see Ezek. 36; Amos 9). For years people said this would be impossible, yet in 1948 the Jews returned to their homeland from all parts of the earth.[19]

Who can predict the future in such detail except the one who knows the future? But for one to know the future, one must have omniscience. The only person I am aware of who has this ability is God. God orchestrated the numerous prophecies in the Bible and He oversaw their fulfillment. If He can arrange the recording and fulfillment of the hundreds of prophecies in the Bible, He can be trusted as the ultimate source of authority in our lives.

His Word, recorded in the Scriptures, are supernatural and authoritative. They are inspired and they can be trusted. As we read the many fulfilled prophecies in the Bible, we can increase our faith to believe that God's Word is true.

Up to this point, I have been focusing on the uniqueness of the Bible; but let me give you a few additional thoughts to consider.

First, if you believe that Jesus was the Son of God, God in the flesh, and the Savior of the world, you must necessarily affirm what He personally affirmed concerning the Scriptures. Of the 66 books in the Bible, the 39 Old Testament books would be the most controversial, written over hundreds of years and filled with numerous supernatural happenings. Events such as the creation of the universe from *nothing* except God's spoken Word, the creation of Adam from the dust of the ground and Eve from a rib from Adam's side, their temptation and fall through a serpent who spoke, Noah and the ark, the Exodus of the children of Israel from Egypt with the Ten Plagues, Jonah and the great fish, and the many miraculous events performed by the hands of the prophets – these and other supernatural events and occurrences in the Old Testament Scriptures for many people seem too far-fetched and quite preposterous to be true.

Some who deny the historicity of the events in the Old Testament say they themselves are believers, and that they believe Jesus is their Savior, the Son of the living God. They just cannot from an intellectual point of view embrace all of the events in the Old Testament as being valid and true. But can you have it both ways? Can you say you believe in Jesus as your personal Lord and Savior, believe that He was God in the flesh, and the redeemer of mankind, and still refuse to believe what Jesus said about the Old Testament Scriptures? I find this extremely difficult and irrational to say the least. You cannot have it both ways. The reason? Jesus placed *His stamp of approval* on the entirety of Old Testament Scriptures and based His life and ministry on them. He believed and affirmed that the Old Testament Scriptures were the very words of God. Dr. Frank Harber writes:

One of the greatest reasons for believing that the Bible is true is that Jesus believed in the truthfulness of the Scriptures. To reject Scripture is in essence to reject Jesus. It would be very unusual for someone to believe in Jesus as Savior and Lord and yet believe that Jesus was wrong on the issue of the Scriptures. Jesus used the Old Testament to validate who He was (Luke 24:27, 44; John 6). He believed that the Scripture could not be broken (John 10:35). Jesus held that every word and letter was important (Matt. 5:17-19).

In controversies, Jesus simply quoted the Scripture to end the debate (Matt. 4:4-10; John 8:17). Jesus authoritatively answered His critics with questions like: "It is written," "Have you not read," and "Search the Scriptures." Jesus even used Scripture to overcome the temptations of Satan (Matt. 4:4).

The writings of the New Testament make it clear that Jesus did not believe the Old Testament to be a collection of legends. Jesus never questioned the integrity of any Old Testament book. He believed the writers were those whose names were on the writings.

The New Testament verified the historicity of over 40 Old Testament people, not counting the genealogical lists. It is difficult to say that one could accept the New Testament as historical but not the Old Testament. If one truly believes the New Testament, one cannot reject any of the Old Testament. Jesus believed in the accuracy of the Old Testament and believed it to be the Word of God.[20]

It is inconsistent and incongruous to say that Jesus was God in the flesh and to deny the authenticity of the Old Testament Scriptures. Notice the words of Jesus:

"Then he said to them, 'These are my words that I spoke to you while I was still with you, that everything written about me in the Law of Moses and the Prophets and the Psalms must be fulfilled.'" (Luke 24:44)

In this brief statement, Jesus authenticated every word in the Old Testament Scriptures. The "Law of Moses and the Prophets and the Psalms" includes *every* book of the Old Testament. Jesus even based the most critical event of His life, His resurrection, on what many liberal scholars refer to as nothing but myth or fiction: Jonah being swallowed by a huge fish. But notice Jesus' words to the religious leaders of His day, the Pharisees, in this passage from the book of Matthew:

Then some of the Pharisees and teachers of the law said to him, "Teacher, we want to see a sign from you." He answered, "A wicked and adulterous generation asks for a sign! But none will be given it except the sign of the prophet Jonah. For as Jonah was three days and three nights in the belly of a huge fish, so the Son of Man will be three days and three nights in the heart of the earth. The men of Nineveh will stand up at the judgment with this generation and condemn it; for they repented at the preaching of Jonah, and now something greater than Jonah is here." (Matt. 12:38-41)

Jesus never gives one hint that the account of Jonah's extraordinary journey is fable, fiction, or myth. Would Jesus base the most significant event of His life on a myth? Would He really refer to some mythological story in referencing His resurrection? Absolutely not! It is absurd to give this one trace of consideration. If Jesus had not been resurrected from the dead, everything we believe about Jesus and the Christian life would be in vain (see 1 Cor. 15). Jesus clearly viewed the Old Testament Scriptures as the inspired, inerrant, and authoritative Word of God, and so should we.

Dr. Frank Harber gives this insight into the New Testament Scriptures:

The Bible contains no traces of being a forgery. If the Bible was the invention of human minds, the characters of the Bible would have been cast in a favorable light. A forged Bible would have tried to cover up all negative elements.

However, the writers of the Bible did not try to cover up the facts. One finds the prominent disciples arguing, struggling with doubts, and giving up hope. The New Testament writers were committed to telling the truth as eyewitnesses. They wrote their writings in the same generation as the actual events. If they did not tell the truth, there were plenty of people around that could refute them. Because most of the New Testament was written between A.D. 40 and 70, there was not enough time for myths about Christ to be told without being refuted.

The New Testament writers had nothing to gain by falsifying information. Even when subjected to persecution and martyrdom, they maintained that what they had preached and taught was truth. No atheist would be willing to die for such an elaborate religious sham. Why would the disciples risk eternal damnation over a religious enterprise from which they would not receive material or financial benefits? Only men of great spiritual integrity would have maintained their position of the Scriptures under such intense life-threatening pressures.[21]

17

Though there are many other things I could say about the uniqueness of the Bible, I will mention one last thought. Throughout the centuries, literally millions of lives across this planet, of every people and from very nation, have experienced life transformation because of the words they have read from the Bible.

The Bible has the power to transform people from a life of hopelessness and despair to a life of joy, peace, and purpose, and to give them an exciting and wonderful future. People from all walks of life, from the poorest of the poor to the wealthy billionaire, have experienced life change through the message of the Bible. Factory workers, clerks, construction workers, maids, cashiers, waiters and waitresses, school teachers, government workers, doctors, lawyers, scientists, business magnates and entrepreneurs—and yes, even several presidents have professed their personal faith in Jesus Christ and have experienced supernatural transformation. There is power in the Word of God!

I go back to one of my premises. The majority of people don't accept the Bible not because it lacks credibility, but because its message and authority speaks into people's lives who read it. I fully concur with Dr. Harber's words:

> The Bible is at the same time the most loved and most hated book of all time. Why has the Bible generated so much animosity? Precisely for the simple reason that the Bible reveals the guilt of men and holds them accountable for their sins. The problems most people have with the Bible are not its alleged difficulties, but with its teachings on how sinful man is reconciled to a Holy God. Mark Twain spoke of this problem when he commented, "Most people are bothered by those passages in Scripture which they cannot understand. The Scripture which troubles me the most is the Scripture I do understand."[22]

I am convinced that if anyone studies and explores the Bible with an open mind, being objective in one's study, one will come to the conclusion that it is a special and unique book, indeed, that it is like no other book on the planet. I feel it is without argument the most unique, influential, and powerful book in print. Read it, study it, memorize it, and assimilate it into your hearts and minds and you will be transformed and strengthened by its power. In making decisions for your life and family, know that it can be trusted. What it says about God is true. What it says about Jesus is true. What it says about morality is true. Though our culture may change along with a society's belief system, I assure you the Word of God does not change. Stand upon the Word with every conviction of your heart. Let it be your compass and guide. You will be eternally blessed!

"The grass withers, the flower fades, but
the word of our God will stand forever."
(Isaiah 40:8)

Discussion Questions

1. Do you feel the Bible is a controversial book? If so, why?

2. Why is it important to have an authoritative source on which to base one's opinions?

3. As a Christian, why is the Bible such an important book?

4. How is the Bible a unique book?

5. Since the beginning, Satan sought to question God's Word. Why?

6. What was Jesus' viewpoint concerning the Old Testament Scriptures? Why is His viewpoint significant?

7. On the last page, in the opinion of the author, what is the main reason for people rejecting the Bible? Do you agree?

8. How has the Bible personally impacted your life?

Chapter Two

The Deity of Jesus Christ

T he most controversial as well as the most influential person that has ever lived is Jesus. In the first chapter, I made a similar claim about the Bible: No other book on the planet has been so loved while at the same time has created hostile and antagonistic reactions. A critical question that should be asked and explored is why?" Likewise, Jesus is one of the most loved persons who has ever walked on earth - loved by literally millions of people - and He is also one of the most despised and hated.

I can understand hostility towards someone like an Adolf Hitler, but Jesus? Again, I ask, "Why?" Try talking about Him in a crowd of people. Just mention His name and watch how people become uncomfortable. Or try starting a conversation about Jesus with non-believers and you'll probably find that many of them will not enter the discussion but simply walk out of the room. Why is that? Like the song says, "There's just something about that name!"

Yes, it is true that the most quoted and influential name on the planet, Jesus, has a way of causing an emotional stir. It did so in Jesus' day and it does so in ours. I believe that the reason for such contention is that His message confronts us at the deepest level of need, which is also our most resistant level. Jesus and His message confront us with the truth of our sin problem, yet He also provides the answer to our problem. Unfortunately, many people stop where they are convicted of their sin and consequently resist Jesus, rather than turning to Him for help in overcoming sin.

Only Jesus can meet our deepest need of freedom from sin. That also means that mankind's enemy, Satan, and his demonic hosts are doing everything within their diabolical power to keep people from receiving Jesus and His teachings. Satan wants to keep people bound in their sin, so he devises schemes to keep people away from the source of freedom. This is why Jesus, more than any other religious teacher, has been incessantly attacked through the centuries. This is also the reason why anyone who is open to the truth and sincerely desires to find truth has no other option but to encounter His words and teachings.

Hostilities toward Jesus are not restricted to His name, but also to symbols that represent Him. The symbol of the cross has been vehemently attacked.

Presently, anti-Christian groups such as the American Civil Liberties Union (ACLU) are doing their best to have crosses removed from national cemeteries, parks, and any other public properties where a cross is erected. The same is true of manger scenes depicting the birth of Jesus. Why are people so eager to remove reminders of Jesus from the public view? If Jesus is who He said He is, then people can leave Satan's domain and cross over into freedom in Christ. Thus, it is understandable that Satan would try everything in his power to limit the influence and message of Jesus the Christ, the Son of the living God.

Christianity is first and foremost about the person and life of Jesus. Christians not only believe that Jesus was the Son of God, but also that He was and is God Himself, alive today and present in the world through the person of the Holy Spirit. The teaching of Christianity is that God is the Trinity. He is one being, but He exists in three distinct persons. Not three gods, but one God who exists in three distinct persons, whom the Bible refers to as God the Father, God the Son, and God the Holy Spirit, thus three in one.

You may ask, "How can this be?" Theologians have tried to intellectually wrap their minds around this for centuries but to no avail. It is beyond comprehension. It is beyond our finite minds. We accept the existence of the Trinity by faith because it is clearly taught in the Bible and by Jesus Himself. Some people try to rationalize it in their minds and say He simply "appeared" in three different forms, but this is inconsistent with the Scriptures and with the teachings of the Church throughout its history. He is three, but one.

If you can't quite comprehend this, do not allow this to trip you up in your faith. We are speaking about Creator God. To expect our finite minds to grasp the fullness of the Godhead (Father, Son, and Holy Spirit) is simply unrealistic. It is beyond our ability to comprehend. We believe and affirm the concept of the Trinity because it is taught in the inspired Scriptures and by the Lord Jesus Christ. The Bible is our authority for all theology and teachings concerning Christ and Christianity. (That is why we started this book talking about the Bible.)

Before I give you the biblical evidence concerning the deity of Jesus, that is, that Jesus was and is God in human form, I want to examine one of the best apologetic resources (books that defend the Christianity) written. Josh McDowell has written a powerful book entitled *New Evidence that Demands a Verdict*. It is filled with various topics concerning the Christian faith and it gives a defense, an argumentation, as to why Christianity is true and other religions false.

McDowell makes it clear that there are but three options concerning the identity and person of Jesus that one can intellectually and rationally accept. McDowell calls it "The Trilemma." But before we get into the heart of his argument concerning his propositions in the "Trilemma," let's examine what he writes about the person we know as Jesus:

Throughout history, people have given a variety of answers to the question, "Who is Jesus of Nazareth?" Whatever their answer, no one can escape the fact that Jesus really lived and that His life radically altered human history forever.

The world-renowned historian Jaroslav Pelikan makes this clear: "Regardless of what anyone may personally think or believe about him, Jesus of Nazareth has been the dominant figure in the history of Western culture for almost twenty centuries. If it were possible, with some sort of supermagnet, to pull up out of that history every scrap of metal bearing at least a trace of his name, how much would be left? It is from his birth that most of the human race dates its calendars, it is by his name that millions curse and in his name that millions pray."

How influential has Jesus been? In their book *What If Jesus Had Never Been Born?*, D. James Kennedy and Jerry Newcombe attempt to answer this question, at least partially. They begin with the assumption that the church - the body of Christ - is Jesus' primary legacy to the world. From that assumption, they examine what has happened in history that displays the influence of the church. Here are "a few highlights" they cite:

- Hospitals, which essentially began during the Middle Ages.
- Universities, which also began during the Middle Ages. In addition, most of the world's greatest universities were started by Christians for Christian purposes.
- Literacy and education of the masses.
- Representative government, particularly as it has been seen in the American experiment.
- The separation of political powers.
- Civil liberties.
- The abolition of slavery, both in antiquity and in modern times.
- Modern science.
- The discovery of the New World by Columbus.
- Benevolence and charity; the Good Samaritan ethic.
- Higher standards of justice.
- The elevation of the common man.
- The high regard for human life.
- The civilizing of many barbarian and primitive cultures.

- The codifying and setting to writing of many of the world's languages.
- The greater development of art and music; the inspiration for the greatest works of art.
- The countless changed lives transformed from liabilities into assets to society because of the gospel.
- The eternal salvation of countless souls!

Considering the basic facts about Jesus' life, the vast impact He has had is nothing short of incredible. A nineteenth-century preacher put it this way:

He [Jesus] was born in an obscure village, the child of a peasant woman. He grew up in another village, where He worked in a carpenter shop until He was thirty. Then for three years He was an itinerant preacher. He never wrote a book. He never held an office. He never had a family or owned a home. He didn't go to college. He never visited a big city. He never traveled two hundred miles from the place where He was born. He did none of the things that usually accompany greatness. He had no credentials but Himself.

He was only 33 years old when the tide of public opinion turned against Him. His friends ran away. One of them denied Him. He was turned over to His enemies and went through the mockery of a trial. He was nailed to a cross between two thieves.

While He was dying, His executioners gambled for His garments, the only property He had on earth. When He was dead, He was laid in a borrowed grave through the pity of a friend. Nineteen centuries have come and gone, and today He is the central figure of the human race.

All the armies that ever marched, all the navies that ever sailed, all the parliaments that ever sat, all the kings that ever reigned, put together, have not affected the life of man on this earth as much as that one solitary life.

C.S. Lewis, a professor of English literature at Cambridge University and a former agnostic, captures the truth of Jesus' impact on history in his book *Mere Christianity*. After surveying some of the evidence regarding Jesus' identity, Lewis writes:

I am trying here to prevent anyone saying the really foolish thing that people often say about Him: "I'm ready to accept Jesus as a great moral teacher, but I don't accept His claim to be God." That is the one thing we must not say. A man who was merely a man and said the sort of things Jesus said would not be a great moral teacher. He would either be a lunatic – on a level with the man who says he is a poached egg – or else he would be the Devil of Hell. You must make your choice. Either this man was, and is, the Son of God or else a mad man or something worse. You can shut Him up for a fool, you can spit at Him and kill Him as a demon; or you can fall at His feet and call Him Lord and God. But let us not come up with any patronizing nonsense about His being a great human teacher. He has not left that open to us. He did not intend to.[1]

Christian apologist Josh McDowell writes, "Jesus' claim to be God must be either true or false. If Jesus' claims are true, then He is the Lord, and we must either accept or reject the lordship. We are 'without excuse'.

If Jesus' claims to be God were false, then there are just two options: He either knew His claims were false, or He did not know they were false. Let's look at each alternative separately and then consider the evidence."[2]

Earlier I referred to what Josh McDowell calls "The Trilemma: Lord, Liar, or Lunatic." In this he argues there are only three options or possibilities that any reasonable person can conclude about the person of Jesus. The first conclusion is that Jesus was who He said he was, Lord, God in human form. Second, Jesus was a liar who deceived the disciples and the rest of the world with His teachings. Or third, He was a lunatic, who genuinely thought He was God, and He was delusional in thinking this. There are no other options. I whole-heartedly agree with McDowell's "Trilemma" scenario!

The following is the case McDowell makes for the Trilemma and the conclusion that Jesus is Lord.

WAS JESUS A LIAR?

If when Jesus made His claims, He knew He was not God, then He was lying. But if He was a liar, then He was also a hypocrite, because He told others to be honest, whatever the cost, while He, at the same time, was teaching and living a colossal lie.

More than that, He was a demon, because He deliberately told others to trust Him for their eternal destiny. If He could not back up His claims and knew they were false, then He was unspeakably evil.

Last, He would also be a fool, because it was His claims to deity that led to His crucifixion.... If Jesus was a liar, a con man, and therefore an evil, foolish man, then how can we explain the fact that He left us with the most profound moral instruction and powerful moral example that anyone ever has left? Could a deceiver - an imposter of monstrous proportions - teach such unselfish ethical truths and live such a morally exemplary life as Jesus did? The very notion is incredulous.

John Stuart Mill, the philosopher, cynic, and adversary of Christianity admitted that Jesus was a first-rate ethicist supremely worthy of our attention and emulation. As Mill expressed it:

About the life and sayings of Jesus there is a stamp of personal originality combined with profundity of insight in the very first rank of men of sublime genius of whom our species can boast. When this pre-eminent genius is combined with the qualities of probably the greatest moral reformer and martyr to that mission who ever existed upon earth, religion cannot be said to have made a bad choice in pitching upon this man as the ideal representative and guide of humanity; nor even now would it be easy, even for an unbeliever, to find a better translation of the rule of virtue from the abstract into the concrete than to endeavor to live so that Christ would approve of our life.

Throughout history Jesus Christ has captured the hearts and minds of millions who have strived to order their lives after His. Even William Lecky, one of Great Britain's most noted historians and a dedicated opponent of organized Christianity, noted this in his *History of European Morals from Augustus to Charlemagne:*

It was reserved for Christianity to present to the world an ideal character which through all the changes of eighteen centuries has inspired the hearts of men with an impassioned love; has shown itself capable of acting on all ages, nations, temperaments and conditions; has been not only the highest pattern of virtue, but the strongest incentive to its practice....The simple

25

record of [Jesus'] three short years of active life has done more to regenerate and soften mankind than all the disquisitions of philosophers and all the exhortations of moralists.

When the church historian Philip Schaff considered the evidence for Jesus' deity, especially in light of what Jesus taught and the kind of life He led, Schaff was struck by the absurdity of the explanations designed to escape the logical implications of this evidence. Stated Schaff:

This testimony, if not true, must be downright blasphemy or madness. The former hypothesis cannot stand a moment before the moral purity and dignity of Jesus, revealed in His every word, and work, and acknowledged by universal consent. Self-deception in a matter so momentous, and with an intellect in all respects so clear and so sound, is equally out of the question. How could He be an enthusiast or a madman who never lost the even balance of His mind, who sailed serenely over all the troubles and persecutions, as the sun above the clouds, who always returned the wisest answer to tempting questions, who calmly and deliberately predicted His death on the cross, His resurrection on the third day, the outpouring of the Holy Spirit, the founding of His Church, the destruction of Jerusalem—predictions which have been literally fulfilled? A character so original, so complete, so uniformly consistent, so perfect, so human and yet so high above all human greatness, can be neither a fraud nor a fiction. The poet, as has been well said, would in this case be greater than the hero. It would take more than a Jesus to invent a Jesus.[3]

Now, I don't think any reasonable person would give any credibility to the position that Jesus was a liar. Even the enemies of Christianity see this as an unrealistic possibility. If the premise that Jesus was a liar is not plausible, we move to a second consideration.

WAS JESUS A LUNATIC?

Again, McDowell presents the case that concluding Jesus was a lunatic is a considerable stretch of the imagination:

If it is inconceivable for Jesus to have been a liar, then could He have thought He was God but have been mistaken? After all, it is possible to be both sincere and wrong.

26

But we must remember that for someone to think he was God, especially in a culture that was fiercely monotheistic, and then to tell others that their eternal destiny depends on believing in him, was no slight flight of fantasy but the thoughts of a lunatic in the fullest sense. Was Jesus Christ such a person? Christian philosopher Peter Kreft presents this option, and then shows why we must reject it:

A measure of your insanity is the size of the gap between what you think you are and what you really are. If I think I am the greatest philosopher in America, I am only an arrogant fool; if I think I am Napoleon, I am probably over the edge; if I think I am a butterfly, I am fully embarked from the sunny shores of sanity. But if I think I am God, I am even more insane because the gap between anything finite and the infinite God is even greater than the gap between any two finite things, even a man and a butterfly.

Well, then, why (was not Jesus a) liar or lunatic? . . . Almost no one who has read the Gospels can honestly and seriously consider that option. The savviness, the canniness, the human wisdom, the attractiveness of Jesus emerge from the Gospels with unavoidable force to any but the most hardened and prejudiced reader....Compare Jesus with liars...or lunatics like the dying Nietzsche, Jesus has in abundance precisely those three qualities that liars and lunatics most conspicuously lack: (1) his practical wisdom, his ability to read human hearts; (2) his deep and winning love, his passionate compassion, his ability to attract people and make them feel at home and forgiven, his authority, "not as the scribes"; (3) his ability to astonish, his unpredictability, his creativity. Liars and lunatics are all so dull and predictable! No one who knows both the Gospels and human beings can seriously entertain the possibility that Jesus was a liar or a lunatic, a bad man.

Even Napoleon Bonaparte went on record as saying:

I know men; and I tell you that Jesus Christ is not a man. Superficial minds see a resemblance between Christ and the founders of empires, and the gods of other religions. That resemblance does not exist. There is between Christianity and whatever other religions the distance of infinity.... Everything

27

in Christ astonishes me. His spirit overawes me, and His will confounds me. Between Him and whoever else in the world, there is no possible term of comparison. He is truly a being by Himself. His ideas and sentiments, the truth which He announces, His manner of convincing, are not explained either by human organization or by the nature of things... The nearer I approach, the more carefully I examine, everything is above me—everything remains grand, of a grandeur which overpowers. His religion is a revelation from an intelligence, which certainly is not that of man.... One can absolutely find nowhere, but in Him alone, the imitation or the example, of His life.... I search in vain in history to find the similar to Jesus Christ, or anything which can approach the gospel. Neither history, nor humanity, nor the ages, nor nature, offer me anything with which I am able to compare it or to explain it. Here everything is extraordinary.

Philip Schaff, the noted historian, wrote: "Is such an intellect— clear as the sky, bracing as the mountain air, sharp and penetrating as a sword, thoroughly healthy and vigorous, always ready and always self-possessed—liable to a radical and most serious delusion concerning His own character and mission? Preposterous imagination!"[4]

If Jesus was a lunatic, we are all in trouble! The person whose words have given such comfort, hope, assurance, peace, inspiration, and have literally transformed millions of lives throughout the centuries—a lunatic? Never!

JESUS IS LORD!

This brings us to the wonderful conclusion that Jesus is exactly who He said he was—creator, redeemer, healer, sustainer, and yes, the Lord of the universe! McDowell writes:

If Jesus of Nazareth is not a liar or a lunatic then He must be Lord.... Other self-proclaimed gods and saviors have come and gone upon history's stage, but Jesus is still here, standing head-and-shoulders above them all.... Who you decide Jesus Christ is must not be an idle intellectual exercise. You cannot put Him on the shelf as a great moral teacher. That is not a valid option. He is a liar, a lunatic, or the Lord. You must make a choice, "But", as the apostle John wrote, "these have been written that you may believe that Jesus is the Christ, the Son of

God"; and more important "that believing you may have life in His name" (John 20:31 NASB).... The evidence is clearly in favor of Jesus as Lord. However, some people reject the clear evidence because of the moral implications involved. There needs to be a moral honesty in the above consideration of Jesus as either liar, lunatic, or Lord and God.[5]

Josh McDowell makes an extremely credible case for the deity and Lordship of Jesus Christ. The prior quotes definitely lead towards affirming the Lordship of Jesus Christ. But our authority does not lie in the opinions of men, but the Bible, the inspired Word of God. Over the next several pages, I want to present to you references from the Bible that teach and affirm the deity and Lordship of Jesus.

Jesus, God in Flesh (Human form)

When Christians speak of the "Deity of Christ," they are typically referring to the belief that God took on human flesh through the process of being born a human being through the miraculous conception of the Holy Spirit upon a virgin by the name of Mary, and though born fully human, He was fully God. He had no earthly father, but was conceived through a miracle when the Holy Spirit came upon Mary (see Matthew 1:8). Therefore, Jesus is God walking on the planet in human form - a physical body of real flesh and blood.

One of the clearest presentations of the deity of Christ is found in the gospel of John. The author, John, was one of Jesus' twelve apostles for over 3 years. He writes his gospel from the unique perspective of one who was in Jesus' inner circle and eyewitness to Jesus' amazing life, supernatural miracles, and life changing teachings.

In the very first chapter of John's gospel, we read the following words of this beloved apostle: In the beginning was the Word, and the Word was with God and the Word was God. He was in the beginning with God. *All things were made through him, and without him was not any thing made that was made.* In him was life, and the life was the light of men.... *And the Word became flesh* and dwelt among us, and we have seen his glory, glory as of the only Son from the Father, full of grace and truth." (John 1:1-4;14, emphasis mine)

The apostle John states clearly in verse one of this chapter that "the Word was God." Then in verse fourteen, he says, "the Word became flesh," that is, the Word took on human form. This marvelous truth has been affirmed throughout the centuries. Since the first century, theologians have repeatedly made the case that the God of the universe became a human being and was destined to die on a cross in order to offer mankind the opportunity to be forgiven of its sins and receive the gift of eternal life by faith in Him.

Notice John points out that, "all things were made through him, and without him was not any thing made that was made" (John 1:3). John is telling us that all creation, everything that exists, was made through Jesus. That statement speaks

29

of Him as creator and affirms His preexistence. The apostle Paul also affirms Christ as creator and sustainer of the universe in his letter to the Colossians:

> He is the image of the invisible God, the firstborn of all cre-
> ation. For *by him* all things were created, in heaven and on
> earth, visible and invisible, whether thrones or dominions or
> rulers or authorities—all things were created through him and
> for him. *And he is before all things*, and in him all things hold
> together. And he is the head of the body, the church. He is the
> beginning, the firstborn from the dead, that in everything he
> might be preeminent. For in him all the fullness of God was
> pleased to dwell, and through him to reconcile to himself all
> things, whether on earth or in heaven, making peace by the
> blood of his cross. (Col. 1:15-20; emphasis mine)

Paul not only agrees with the apostle John on the preexistence of Christ, saying "he is before all things," but also says that "in him all things hold together," that is, it is through Jesus' power that the universe and all that exists are held in place. Who has the power to hold the universe and creation together? Who can sustain the universe and keep it from disintegrating and flying into a chaotic state? Only God!

The writer of the book of Hebrews assents the very same thing, that it is Jesus who is holding things together:

> Long ago, at many times and in many ways, God spoke to our
> fathers by the prophets, but in these last days he has spoken
> to us by his Son, whom he appointed the heir of all things,
> through whom also he created the world. He is the radiance
> of the glory of God and the exact imprint of his nature, *and he
> upholds the universe by the word of his power*. After making
> purification for sins, he sat down at the right hand of the
> Majesty on high. (Heb. 1:1-3, emphasis mine)

If Jesus is creator, then He is God. There is no other conclusion.

Jesus Affirms His Deity

Jesus Himself makes it clear that He eternally existed prior to taking on human form. On one occasion when the Pharisees and other Jews were questioning Jesus, He talked about the Pharisees' need to be set free by the truth (the gospel message). Jesus also discussed His relationship with His Father (God). The Jews said their father was Abraham, and they did not need to be set free. They then accused Jesus of having a demon. In His discussion with them Jesus said the following: "Your father Abraham rejoiced that he would see my day. He saw it and was glad." So the Jews said to him, "You are not yet fifty years old, and have you seen Abraham?" Jesus said to them, "Truly, truly, I say to you, *before Abraham was, I am* ." So they picked up stones to throw at him, but Jesus hid himself and went out of the temple" (John 8:56-59, emphasis mine).

Notice Jesus said, "before Abraham was, I am." Jesus is clearly referring to His existence *prior* to Abraham. He also used the phrase, "I am," the same name God used of Himself when Moses asked whose name he should give people when he was asked who sent him. Notice what God said: "God said to Moses, '*I AM WHO I AM.*' And God said, 'Say this to the people of Israel, "*I AM* has sent me to you"'" (Exod. 3:14, emphasis mine).

Jesus purposely used "I am" statements to reveal that He is God. Notice the following statements by Jesus:

- "*I am* the bread of life" (John 6:35)
- "*I am* the light of the world" (John 8:12)
- "*I am* the door" (John 10:9)
- "*I am* the good shepherd" (John 10:14)
- "*I am* the resurrection and the life" (John 10:25)
- "*I am* the way, the truth, and the life" (John 14:6)
- "*I am* the true vine" (John 15:1,5)

Jesus uses these "I am" statements to show the interrelatedness of Him and the I AM, the God of Abraham, the God of Isaac, and the God of Jacob. That is, Jesus is the eternal God of their fathers who has always existed. He used His words and deeds to declare to the people that He is that very God who is alive in human form. The religious leaders understood exactly what He was saying, and that is why they picked up stones to kill Him (see John 8:59).

One of the most conclusive claims that Jesus made concerning His deity is found in a discussion Jesus had with His disciples. Jesus was explaining that it was necessary to leave them and prepare a place in heaven for them. In this discussion about His leaving, He once again mentioned His relationship with His Father. Philip asked, "...Lord, show us the Father, and it is enough for us" (John 14:8). Notice Jesus' reply:

> Jesus said to him, "Have I been with you so long, and you still do not know me, Philip? Whoever has seen me has seen the Father. How can you say, 'Show us the Father'? Do you not believe that I am in the Father and the Father is in me? The words that I say to you I do not speak on my own authority, but the Father who dwells in me does his works. Believe me that I am in the Father and the Father is in me, or else believe on account of the works themselves." (John 14:9-11)

31

Jesus makes it absolutely clear. There is no room for question or debate when we take His words at face value. He categorically states that when you are looking upon Him (Jesus), you are looking into the face of the Father (God). He and the Father are one. Though the disciples were seeing and talking to Jesus, they were talking with and to God the Father because He is God who took upon Himself human flesh. You cannot escape this conclusion. Jesus was clearly making Himself equal with God His Father and placing Himself on the exact same level with no distinction except He was in human form.

Another example of Jesus' oneness with His Father is found in the tenth chapter of John's gospel. Once again, the Jews were questioning Jesus concerning His identity. They wanted Him to speak plainly concerning who He was. Notice Jesus' words:

> Jesus answered them, "I told you, and you do not believe. The works that I do in my Father's name bear witness about me, but you do not believe because you are not among my sheep. My sheep hear my voice, and I know them, and they follow me. I give them eternal life, and they will never perish, and no one will snatch them out of my hand. My Father, who has given them to me, is greater than all, and no one is able to snatch them out of the Father's hand. *I and the Father are one.*" (John 10:25-30, emphasis mine)

Again, those listening to His words clearly understood what He was saying. They knew He was claiming equality with God. This is why they accused Him of blasphemy and picked up stones to kill Him.

The Jews picked up stones again to stone him. Jesus answered them, "I have shown you many good works from the Father; for which of them are you going to stone me?" The Jews answered him, "It is not for a good work that we are going to stone you but for blasphemy, because you, being a man, *make yourself God*." (John 10:31-33, emphasis mine)

These Jews knew that Jesus was claiming to be God. Jesus was constantly revealing Himself as God, not only with the supernatural miracles He was performing, but also with His very words. In light of His actions and teachings, one must conclude that Jesus taught He was God.

Jesus Accepted Worship

Jesus was worshiped and He accepted worship, which is reserved for God alone. Notice the following Scriptures:

- "And going into the house they saw the child with Mary his mother, and they fell down and *worshiped* him. Then, opening their treasures, they offered him gifts, gold and frankincense and myrrh." (Matt. 2:11, emphasis mine)

- And those in the boat *worshiped* him, saying, "Truly you are the Son of God." (Matt. 14:33, emphasis mine)
- "And behold, Jesus met them and said, "Greetings!" And they came up and took hold of his feet and *worshiped* him." (Matt. 28:9, emphasis mine)
- "And when they saw him they *worshiped* him, but some doubted." (Matt. 28:17, emphasis mine)
- "And they *worshiped* him and returned to Jerusalem with great joy." (Luke 24:52, emphasis mine)
- He said, "Lord, I believe," and he *worshiped* him." (John 9:38, emphasis mine)

Jesus never once refused to accept worship. In contrast, angels refuse worship. When the apostle John received the revelation of Jesus on the Isle of Patmos, an angel often showed him incredible visions and John would prostrate himself before the angel in an act of worship. But instead of receiving John's worship, the angel would instruct John to get up because he wasn't God, just a messenger (see Rev. 19:10).

Yet, in the fifth chapter of Revelation, in a futuristic heavenly scene, Jesus is clearly worshiped by the host of heaven and receives it. The context of this chapter makes it clear that this is Jesus, the one who was slain (a reference to the cross), but who is now alive and is receiving worship from the elders and living creatures falling before Him:

> And between the throne and the four living creatures and among the elders I saw a Lamb standing, as though it had been slain, with seven horns and with seven eyes, which are the seven spirits of God sent out into all the earth. And he went and took the scroll from the right hand of him who was seated on the throne. And when he had taken the scroll, the four living creatures and the twenty-four elders fell down before the Lamb, each holding a harp, and golden bowls full of incense, which are the prayers of the saints. And they sang a new song, saying, "Worthy are you to take the scroll and to open its seals, for you were slain, and by your blood you ransomed people for God from every tribe and language and people and nation, and you have made them a kingdom and priests to our God, and they shall reign on the earth." Then I looked, and I heard around the throne and the living creatures and the elders the voice of many angels, numbering myriads of myriads and thousands of thousands, saying with a loud voice, "Worthy is the Lamb who was slain, to receive power and wealth and wisdom and might and honor and glory and

blessing!" And I heard every creature in heaven and on earth and under the earth and in the sea, and all that is in them, saying, "To him who sits on the throne and to the Lamb be blessing and honor and glory and might forever and ever!" And the four living creatures said, "Amen!" and the elders fell down and worshiped. (Rev. 5:6-14)

Here the risen Lord Jesus is being worshiped and given praise, honor, and exaltation as the Lamb of God who provided redemption and forgiveness through His shed blood on the cross. The hosts of heaven proclaim His worthiness to receive glory and praise for the salvation He has provided through His sacrifice on the cross for mankind. One day all of humanity along with the heavenly hosts will fall on their knees proclaiming Jesus as the supreme potentate and the sovereign Lord of the universe. The apostle Paul, writing to the Philippians says emphatically that Jesus is Lord and that one day every creature will bow in His presence and make this proclamation:

And being found in human form, he humbled himself by becoming obedient to the point of death, even death on a cross. Therefore God has highly exalted him and bestowed on him the name that is above every name, so that at the name of Jesus every knee should bow, in heaven and on earth and under the earth, and every tongue confess that *Jesus Christ is Lord*, to the glory of God the Father. (Phil. 2:8-10, emphasis mine)

The Demons Acknowledged His Lordship

One of the interesting aspects of Jesus' encounters with the demonic is that every demon knew who Jesus was and also acknowledged that Jesus was the Son of God. They never challenged Him, knowing that He had the power and authority to send them to their eternal destiny at any time He wished, simply with a command. Notice the two following encounters Jesus had with the demonic:

They came to the other side of the sea, to the country of the Gerasenes. And when Jesus had stepped out of the boat, immediately there met him out of the tombs a man with an unclean spirit. He lived among the tombs. And no one could bind him anymore, not even with a chain, for he had often been bound with shackles and chains, but he wrenched the chains apart, and he broke the shackles in pieces. No one had the strength to subdue him. Night and day among the tombs and on the mountains he was always crying out and cutting himself with stones. *And when he saw Jesus from afar, he ran and fell down before him. And crying out with a loud voice, he said, "What have you to do with me,*

34

Jesus, Son of the Most High God? I adjure you by God, do not torment me." For he was saying to him, "Come out of the man, you unclean spirit!" And Jesus asked him, "What is your name?" He replied, "My name is Legion, for we are many." And he begged him earnestly not to send them out of the country. Now a great herd of pigs was feeding there on the hillside, and they begged him, saying, "Send us to the pigs; let us enter them." So he gave them permission. And the unclean spirits came out and entered the pigs; and the herd, numbering about two thousand, rushed down the steep bank into the sea and drowned in the sea. (Mark 5:1-3, emphasis mine)

Again, notice the response of the demon:

And he went down to Capernaum, a city of Galilee. And he was teaching them on the Sabbath, and they were astonished at his teaching, for his word possessed authority. And in the synagogue there was a man who had the spirit of an unclean demon, and he cried out with a loud voice, "Ha! What have you to do with us, Jesus of Nazareth? Have you come to destroy us? I know who you are—the Holy One of God." But Jesus rebuked him, saying, "Be silent and come out of him!" And when the demon had thrown him down in their midst, he came out of him, having done him no harm. And they were all amazed and said to one another, "What is this word? For with authority and power he commands the unclean spirits, and they come out!" And reports about him went out into every place in the surrounding region. (Luke 4:31-37)

Clearly, demons recognized and acknowledged the Lordship and deity of Jesus. They also knew that one day He would judge them severely. They didn't question His authority or power. He was Lord and they knew that one day, He would put an end to their hellish scheming, deception, and destruction and send them and Satan to a tormenting hell. It wasn't a matter of if He would, but when He would.

Not only do demons acknowledge Jesus' authority, but also the prophets do. There are many Old Testament references concerning Christ, but let me share the words of the prophet Isaiah, recorded several hundreds of years before Christ's first coming. Notice the titles given to the one who is to come:

For to us a child is born, to us a son is given; and the government shall be upon his shoulder, and his name shall be called Wonderful Counselor, *Mighty God, Everlasting Father,* Prince of Peace. Of the increase of his government and of peace there will be no end, on the throne of David and over his kingdom, to establish it and to uphold it with justice and with righteousness from this time forth and forevermore. The zeal of the LORD of hosts will do this. (Isa. 9:6-7, emphasis mine)

Isaiah is revealing the attributes of the one who is to come, the Messiah, the Lord Jesus. Notice the names given are names that point to His deity. "Mighty God" and "Everlasting Father" are names that can be used only to describe God, and they are referring to the Messiah, our Lord Jesus Christ.

As I bring this chapter to a close, there is so much more that I could say and demonstrate from the Scriptures to show that Jesus is God. There are scholars and theologians who have written extensively on this subject, and I have simply shared just enough to equip you with a solid foundation that Jesus was not just a great teacher, a prophet, a healer, a miracle worker, or a deliverer; but He was who He professed to be—God!

Now, the implications of this truth are huge!

- Everything He revealed about Himself and God is true.
- Every promise He gave is trustworthy.
- He is worthy of our worship and praise.
- He has come to offer us forgiveness and eternal life.
- Our salvation is secured in Him.
- He is with us today in the presence of the Holy Spirit.
- One day He is coming again.
- We will stand in His presence and give an account of our lives.

Let me close with a verse from Paul's letter to his young protégé Timothy:

"Great indeed, we confess, is the mystery of godliness: He was manifested in the flesh, vindicated by the Spirit, seen by angels, proclaimed among the nations, believed on in the world, taken up in glory."
(1 Timothy 3:16)

Discussion Questions

1. Do you agree with the author that Jesus is the most controversial person that has ever lived on the planet? If you agree, why?

2. Why is it difficult to understand the Trinity? Why is belief in the Trinity important?

3. How influential has the message of Jesus been in the world? What is the evidence of Jesus' influence?

4. Jesus taught only three to three and one half years. In relationship to His global influence, why is this a significant point?

5. Why would it be inconsistent to admire Jesus and His teaching and then conclude that He was not who He claimed to be?

6. Josh McDowell presents what he calls "The Trilemma." What does he mean by this phrase and what are the implications?

7. What Scriptural references support the doctrine that Jesus was God in the flesh?

8. Did Jesus affirm that He was God? Based on what Scriptures?

9. What is the significance of the "I Am" statements of Jesus?

10. Is worship something that belongs exclusively to God? How did Jesus respond to those who worshiped Him?

11. How did the demonic world respond to Jesus?

12. What are the implications of Jesus being who He claimed to be: the Son of God?

Chapter Three

Salvation Basics

W hat do we mean when we use the word *salvation*? Or, when we ask the question, "Are you saved?" what do we mean by the term *saved*? "Saved from what?" may be the normal response when someone is asked this question today.

One thing that is becoming increasingly evident in our post-modern world is that many people are not familiar with the terminology we use as Christians. Words and phrases like redemption, justification, sanctification, repentance, atonement, the New Birth, and the like are not understood by the average person living in today's society. This is why when I use these terms in preaching or teaching, I do my best to use other words to further explain and amplify their meaning.

This chapter is entitled, *Salvation Basics*. What does this title mean? The word *salvation* is used by Christians to refer to what they receive when they make a decision to accept Christ by faith into their lives. The word *salvation* means a person has been saved, delivered, and rescued from a state of condemnation. He or she was headed for an eternal destiny in a place the Bible calls "hell," a real and horrific place where one is separated from God. Jesus often referred to hell and described it in detail as a truly frightening and isolated place. I can assure you that no one wants to experience it.

So when Christians say a person has been saved (referring to Jesus' salvation), they are saying that the person's sins are forgiven and that person also has received a new life that is wonderful, glorious, abundant, and eternal. Because of our faith in Christ, we as Christians have received salvation, forgiveness of sins, and new purpose and direction in life. Instead of an eternal destiny in hell, we will go to a place the Bible refers to as heaven after our physical death. Heaven is a place of peace, love, no hatred, no suffering, no crime, no discouragement, no worry, incredible joy, and - praise the Lord - no more death! It is a place of experiencing and living in the very presence of God and enjoying His presence forever!

Now we have an understanding of the term "salvation." The other half of this chapter is the word "basics." By "basics," I am referring to the basic or elementary concepts and teaching that evangelical Christians have embraced since the beginning of Christianity. Basics are those fundamental essentials of what the Bible teaches concerning salvation and the implications of those essentials for those who believe in Christ. So in this chapter, I want to share some *basic* concepts from the Bible of what it means to be a Christian, how to become a Christian, and what becoming a Christian (receiving salvation) means now and in the future.

We have a problem

I begin with this statement because it is the beginning or initial step in coming to Christ. Until we see our need and acknowledge we have a problem, we will not be willing to deal with it. The problem is a three letter word the Bible calls sin. It is really an "I" problem. Right in the middle of that little word *sin* is an "I." Mankind's basic problem is that we want to live independently from God. That is, we want to do our own thing have no accountability, and live life as we please. This is the root of our problem. And, as the Bible teaches, regardless of who we are, our family heritage, our nationality, our education, or position in life, we are all sinners in the need of a Savior. That's the bad news. The good news is that a Savior has been provided and is available to all people of all nations and His name is Jesus!

Yet, many people don't quite understand that we are all sinners in need of forgiveness, but the Bible makes this clear. Notice the following Scripture: "None is righteous, no, *not one*" (Rom. 3:10, emphasis mine). Whether one is the Pope, Billy Graham, or Mother Teresa, every person who has lived on the planet (except Jesus) is a sinner and is in need of forgiveness if he or she wants to go to heaven following their death. The Bible is very clear in this matter. The apostle Paul makes it obvious in the above verse that "none," "not one" person on earth is righteous. This means that there is not a single person who can stand before God and make any claim or argument for his or her being righteous. "Not one!"

Paul continues his writing and restates the same conviction that there are no righteous people: "For *all* have sinned and fall short of the glory of God" (Rom. 3:23, emphasis mine).

This verse once again points out that every person who has ever lived fails to meet the standard set by a holy and righteous God. It means that even our very best when offered to God does not meet His standard. All of us are helpless to achieve, earn, or merit forgiveness based on our attempts at righteousness. This brings us to a second key truth that the Bible reinforces:

Performing good works or deeds cannot merit salvation

Regardless of how many good deeds (good works) we do in life, nothing we do can earn us entrance into heaven. Many people feel as if they can perform enough kind deeds or acts of goodness or kindness to earn a spot in heaven. Therefore, they try to be a good person, keep the Ten Commandments, attend a church, give money to the church, and help others in need. They conclude that their good deeds will outweigh their bad deeds and that when God examines them, He will forgive them and give them entrance into heaven. *The problem with that reasoning is that it is not biblical.* As a matter of fact, the Bible teaches the exact opposite. Notice this verse:

> For by grace you have been saved through faith. And this is *not your own doing*; it is the gift of God, not a result of works, so that no one may boast. (Eph. 2:8-9, emphasis mine)

This is a key verse which teaches that it is not what we do (good deeds or works) or how we perform that saves us; but it is simply God's grace and our faith in Christ that releases salvation. Notice Paul says that salvation is the "gift of God." You can't work for a gift. A gift is not something you earn, but something you receive. If you have to work for the gift, then it becomes something you can boast or brag about, or say you deserve it. But notice Paul says in this verse "so no one can boast." When I stand in the presence of God, I cannot say I should be allowed entrance into heaven because I deserve it, worked for it, or earned it, but solely because I believed in Christ can I be admitted. This takes away all basis for boasting in one's achievements.

There are many Bible passages that teach this principle, but let me give you two more:

> Who saved us and called us to a holy calling, *not because of our works* but because of his own purpose and grace, which he gave us in Christ Jesus before the ages began. (2 Tim. 1:9, emphasis mine)

> He saved us, not *because of works done by us in righteousness*, but according to his own mercy, by the washing of regeneration and renewal of the Holy Spirit. (Titus 3:5, emphasis mine)

Again, it is not our good works, good deeds, or our performance that secures our entrance into heaven, but simply the righteousness of Jesus that we receive when we place our faith in Him. This brings me to a third basic truth:

Salvation is a matter of placing our faith in Jesus

Why did Jesus come to the planet in the first place? Why did He die such a humiliating and agonizing death on a cross? The answer to both of these questions is that Jesus came to provide a cure for our sin problem. He came to provide us the ability to be forgiven so our relationship with God can be restored and so we can experience salvation. If we could have saved ourselves by doing good works or deeds, why would He have ever submitted Himself to be nailed to a cross? He could have avoided all the humiliation, suffering, and pain. The cross was His destiny and the only means to procure our salvation.

Jesus never sinned. He kept every God-given commandment, lived a perfect and righteous life, and willingly died on a cross for *our* sins. We could not die on the cross for ourselves because we have sinned. But Jesus, who was without sin, could redeem mankind from sin by offering His perfect, sinless life as a sacrifice to God. That is exactly what He did on the cross.

"For while we were still weak, at the right time Christ died for the *ungodly*." (Rom. 5:6, emphasis mine)

"For our sake he made him to be sin *who knew no sin*, so that in him we might become the righteousness of God." (2 Cor. 5:21, emphasis mine)

"For Christ also suffered once for sins, *the righteous for the unrighteous,* that he might bring us to God, being put to death in the flesh but made alive in the spirit." (1 Pet. 3:18, emphasis mine)

Our sins had to be paid for, and because God is a fair God, justice had to be executed. Sin could not be ignored. For this reason, God sent His Son Jesus to become the payment for our sin. Theologians call this the *substitutionary atonement,* meaning that Jesus' death on the cross became the substitute for our sin so that we could be delivered from His wrath. Again, because God is a just God and could not simply ignore our sins, a payment (price) was required to meet the demands of God's holy law. That payment was the sacrifice of Jesus offered on the altar of the cross. His life satisfied God's demand for righteousness due to our sins. When we by faith surrender our lives to Christ, the righteousness of the life of Jesus is *transferred* to our account. It is as if we never sinned!

When I say we surrender our lives *by faith*, I am referring to our *believing* (trusting) that Jesus died for our sins on the cross, was resurrected, and forgives our sins when we give control of our lives to Him by faith. Placing our *faith* in Jesus and *believing* in Jesus are synonymous. Notice the words of Jesus who was approached by a religious leader named Nicodemus:

For God so loved the world, that he gave his only Son, that whoever *believes* in him should not perish but have eternal life. For God did not send his Son into the world to condemn the world, but in order that the world might be saved through him. Whoever *believes* in him is not condemned, but whoever does not believe is condemned already, because he has not believed in the name of the only Son of God. (John 3:16-18, emphasis mine)

Believing (placing our faith in Christ) is what provides forgiveness and eternal life. *Faith* is the key that unlocks heaven's door. The Bible teaches that because of our faith in Him, we are justified, made right in our relationship with God. Let me share the following Scriptures:

> ...The righteousness of God *through faith* in Jesus Christ for all who believe. For there is no distinction: for all have sinned and fall short of the glory of God, and are justified by his grace as a gift, through the redemption that is in Christ Jesus, whom God put forward as a propitiation by his blood, to be received *by faith* . This was to show God's righteousness, because in his divine forbearance he had passed over former sins. It was to show his righteousness at the present time, so that he might be just and the justifier of the one *who has faith* in Jesus. Then what becomes of our boasting? It is excluded. By what kind of law? By a law of works? No, but *by the law of faith*. (Rom. 3:22-27, emphasis mine)

God's holy demands for righteousness were satisfied when Jesus, the sinless Son of God, died on the cross on behalf of our sins. Notice the above text stresses it is through "*faith in Jesus*." It is through the "propitiation by his blood," that is, the satisfaction of His innocent blood being shed for those who are guilty that salvation comes. Notice the text also says as a "gift," something you don't earn but receive. Once again, this excludes any "boasting" because the gift of salvation is not anything we have earned by performance, but rather have received by faith.

Let me give a few additional Scriptures (emphasis mine):

> For in it the righteousness of God is revealed from faith for faith, as it is written, "The righteous shall live *by faith*." (Rom. 1:17)

> Therefore, since we have been justified *by faith*, we have peace with God through our Lord Jesus Christ. Through him we have also obtained access *by faith* into this grace in which we stand, and we rejoice in hope of the glory of God. (Rom. 5:1-2)

> Yet we know that a person is not justified by works of the law but *through faith* in Jesus Christ, so we also have believed in Christ Jesus, in order to be justified *by faith* in Christ and not by works of the law, because by works of the law no one will be justified. (Gal. 2:16)

42

> And the Scripture, foreseeing that God would justify the Gentiles *by faith*, preached the gospel beforehand to Abraham, saying, "In you shall all the nations be blessed." (Gal. 3:8)

> But the Scripture imprisoned everything under sin, so that the promise *by faith* in Jesus Christ might be given to those who believe. (Gal. 3:22)

> So then, the law was our guardian until Christ came, in order that we might be justified *by faith*. (Gal. 3:24)

Notice that we are *justified*, given a right standing before God, by our faith in Christ. This means we are no longer in a position of hostility with God, but we are at peace with God because we have placed our faith in Christ. Before we believed in Christ, we were dead in our sins and faced the wrath of God. We were God's enemies, which placed us in a hostile position. Not a good place to be. Notice the following Scriptures:

> And you were dead in the trespasses and sins in which you once walked, following the course of this world, following the prince of the power of the air, the spirit that is now at work in the sons of disobedience—among whom we all once lived in the passions of our flesh, carrying out the desires of the body and the mind, *and were by nature children of wrath*, like the rest of mankind. (Eph. 2:1-3, emphasis mine)

> For if while *we were enemies* we were reconciled to God by the death of his Son, much more, now that we are reconciled, shall we be saved by his life. (Rom. 5:10, emphasis mine)

It is by our faith in Christ that we are forgiven, that we come into a relationship of peace with God. Faith in Christ allows us to stand as righteous in front of God, our sins covered with His blood. "Since, therefore, we have now been justified *by his blood*, much more shall we be saved by him from the wrath of God." (Rom. 5:9, emphasis mine).

Jesus' suffering and death on the cross involved the sacrifice of His blood. Through the entire Old Testament we read of sacrifices of animals being made for the sins of the people. These were temporary solutions for a permanent problem. They all pointed to the ultimate sacrifice of Jesus pouring out His blood on the cross to cover our sins. When we place our faith in Christ, His blood is applied to our sin, covers our sins, and provides forgiveness.

When I stand before God on the Day of Judgment, I will stand justified, having my sins covered by the blood of Jesus. I am saved by believing (having faith) that through His sacrifice on the cross, His blood being shed for my sins, my sins are covered and forgiven in the sight of God. Notice the following Scriptures:

> In him we have redemption *through his blood*, the forgiveness of our trespasses, according to the riches of his grace. (Eph. 1:7, emphasis mine)

> But now in Christ Jesus you who once were far off have been brought near *by the blood of Christ*. (Eph. 2:13, emphasis mine)

> And through him to reconcile to himself all things, whether on earth or in heaven, making peace *by the blood of his cross*. (Col. 1:20, emphasis mine)

> He entered once for all into the holy places, not by means of the blood of goats and calves but *by means of his own blood*, thus securing an eternal redemption. (Heb. 9:12, emphasis mine)

> How much more will *the blood of Christ*, who through the eternal Spirit offered himself without blemish to God, purify our conscience from dead works to serve the living God." (Heb. 9:14, emphasis mine)

> And they sang a new song, saying, "Worthy are you to take the scroll and to open its seals, for you were slain, *and by your blood* you ransomed people for God from every tribe and language and people and nation." (Rev. 5:9, emphasis mine)

> Knowing that you were ransomed from the futile ways inherited from your forefathers, not with perishable things such as silver or gold, but *with the precious blood of Christ*, like that of a lamb without blemish or spot. He was foreknown before the foundation of the world but was made manifest in the last times for the sake of you who through him are believers in God, who raised him from the dead and gave him glory, so that your faith and hope are in God. (1 Pet. 1:18-21, emphasis mine)

Praise the Lord for the forgiveness of our sins through the precious blood of Jesus! His blood has the power to cover our past, present, and future. There is no sin that cannot be cleansed by the power of the blood of Jesus. Place your guilt, your shame, and your condemnation under His blood and begin walking by faith and enjoying the peace and presence of God in your life!

Surrendering our lives to the Lordship of Christ

Now, I want to make it clear that it isn't just a belief in God that brings salvation, but it is faith in the Lord Jesus and His death on the cross for our sins that saves. Many people say they are Christians because they believe in God. But the Bible makes it clear that it isn't just *believing in God* that gets a person to heaven.

The apostle James says that believing in God is a good beginning point, but mere belief in the existence of God does not result in salvation. James says that even the demons believe in God! "You believe that God is one; you do well. Even the demons believe—and shudder" (Jas. 2:19)! So, it isn't simply believing in God that results in salvation.

Salvation comes as a result of believing the right message about God. It is believing in His life, death, and resurrection to such an extent that you are willing to place your faith in Him, turn from your sins, and surrender your life to His Lordship. In other words, you are turning from your sins and making a definitive decision to follow Christ, thus committing your life to Him.

The act of turning from a sinful direction and pursuing life in Christ is called *repentance*. The word *repent* means a change of mind that leads to a change in direction. Before coming to Christ, a person lives for the self, lives independent of God, and seeks only to please the self. But when people come to Christ, they make a decision to turn from their sins, embrace life in Jesus, and surrender their lives to Christ. They confess and agree that He is Lord. This belief (faith) in Him as Lord is what brings forgiveness and transformation in their lives. Notice what the apostle Paul says in his letter to the Romans:

> Because, if you confess with your mouth that *Jesus is Lord* and believe in your heart that God raised him from the dead, you will be saved. For with the heart one believes and is justified, and with the mouth one confesses and is saved. (Rom. 10:9-10, emphasis mine)

Both belief and confession of Jesus' Lordship activates salvation. Again, James says the demons believe that God exists and they tremble; but there is not going to be one demon in heaven. It is a belief that leads you to surrender to the Lordship of Jesus Christ that will give you access to heaven. You receive Christ not only as your Savior, but as your Lord.

WHAT DOES THIS MEAN?

What does *all* this mean? It means that when you by faith surrender your life to Christ, you have entered a brand new relationship with God. Your past is forgiven and a new life begins. Let me touch on few implications of being a Christian:

You have been reborn

Earlier, I alluded to Jesus speaking to a Jewish religious leader by the name of Nicodemus. Nicodemus came to Jesus inquiring how to receive eternal life. Jesus' response was that receiving eternal life requires experiencing a new birth. A person has to be born again, that is, experience a spiritual birth. The phrase "born again" literally means *born from above*. It is a heavenly or spiritual experience. Just like a person has a *physical* birth to enter the world, a person must experience a *spiritual* birth to enter heaven. Notice the account in John's gospel:

> Now there was a man of the Pharisees named Nicodemus, a ruler of the Jews. This man came to Jesus by night and said to him, "Rabbi, we know that you are a teacher come from God, for no one can do these signs that you do unless God is with him." Jesus answered him, "Truly, truly, I say to you, unless one is *born again* he cannot see the kingdom of God." (John 3:1-3, emphasis mine)

Notice the emphatic words of Jesus: "Truly, truly, I say to you, unless one is born again he cannot see the kingdom of God." The rest of this passage makes it clear that the new birth takes place by believing in Jesus and His death on the cross for your sins. When you become a follower of Jesus, you experience what Jesus referred to as being "born again," that is, you experience a spiritual birthing.

If you want to enter heaven, you must be spiritually born. Jesus leaves no option. New birth is a divine imperative if you want to experience Jesus' salvation that brings you into a radically new life with a new beginning!

You have a new beginning

The wonderful news about the new birth is that you have a new beginning. There are many people who wish they could have a new beginning. In Christ, a new beginning is a reality. All your sins, your past, and your previous life without God have been forgiven and you are brand new in Christ.

A new life, a new beginning, and a glorious future are yours! "Therefore, if anyone is in Christ, he is a new creation. The old has passed away; behold, the new has come" (2 Cor. 5:17). The King James Version translates this verse this way: "Therefore, if any man be in Christ, he is a new creature; old things are passed away; behold, all things are become new" (2 Cor. 5:17, *KJV*).

From these verses, we can conclude that because of your faith in Christ, you are a *brand new* person in Christ! Notice the King James translation says you are a "new creature." A radical spiritual transformation takes place when you become a Christian. Both translations say, "the old has passed away, behold, the new has come." Many people live with guilt, shame, and condemnation over their past and their past sins; but the Bible says the old life is gone. Spiritually, in the eyes of God, it doesn't exist. A brand new life has begun. Your old life has been covered by His blood. You have a new life, a new beginning, a new relationship, a new hope, a new peace, a new power, and an awesome future!

You are adopted into God's family and given a new identity

One of the amazing things that I think few of us can really comprehend is our new position (identity) in relationship with God. The Bible teaches that when we come to Christ and experience the new birth, we are not only made brand new, but we are also adopted by God and have become *His children*. Think of it: children of God! A Christian should never again have any feeling of insignificance. You are special and significant because you are a child of the living God. You have a personal relationship with God and are now part of His extended family. Notice the words of John:

> But to all who did receive him, who believed in his name, he
> gave the right to become *children of God*, who were born, not
> of blood nor of the will of the flesh nor of the will of man, but
> of God. (John 1:12-13, emphasis mine)

As children of God, we not only receive eternal life because we belong to our eternal Father, but we also receive His Spirit, His character, His heart, His mind, and one day His very image.

> For all who are led by the Spirit of God are sons of God. For
> you did not receive the spirit of slavery to fall back into fear,
> but you have received the Spirit of adoption as sons, by whom
> we cry, 'Abba! Father!' The Spirit himself bears witness with
> our spirit that *we are children of God*, and if children, then
> heirs—heirs of God and *fellow heirs* with Christ, provided we
> suffer with him in order that we may also be glorified with
> him. (Rom. 8:14-17, emphasis mine)

Now, not only are we God's children when we accept salvation, but we are also "fellow heirs with Christ." Because we are now part of God's family, we will inherit the very things that belong to Jesus. I am not sure of all of the implications of this statement, but I do know this—it is going to be awesome! That I, a sinner, saved by grace, will inherit things belonging to the Lord Jesus is absolutely amazing to me, but this is exactly what the Bible says. Glory to God!

Also notice that we as children of God cry, *"Abba! Father."* The term *Abba* is an endearing term of a child that literally means *Daddy*. As a child, Daddy was a person who loved me, a person I could trust, who watched over me and protected me, who provided for me, and who cared for me. Because I am a child of God, I have a new relationship with God that is intimate and personal. I don't have to approach Him in fear, but as His child I can approach Him, my loving father. I have the assurance that He loves me and has my best interest in mind.

You have entered a new domain

Prior to coming to Christ, we lived in a realm the Bible refers to as *darkness*. We lived and operated in a realm that was spiritually alienated from God, indifferent and opposed to Him - a kingdom that had no desire for God. By coming to Christ, we are taken out of this sphere of darkness and placed into a new sphere called the kingdom of God. It is a kingdom of spiritual illumination, insight, understanding, of righteousness, power, and peace. Instead of running from God or living in opposition to God, our new desire is to love God, serve God, and advance His kingdom.

We have literally been transported into a new kingdom, a new domain, which is spiritual. This positional change is explained by Paul in his letter to the Colossians: "He [God] has delivered us from the domain of darkness and transferred us to the kingdom of His beloved Son". (Col. 1:13). Notice the word "transferred." We have entered a new dimension.

We have entered a spiritual existence that we had not known before coming to Christ. Within this new domain, we have new resources at our disposal. We have a new understanding of life and our purpose and destiny. We have new desires, new aspirations, and a gravitational pull toward the things of God. We develop new appetites and establish new goals and priorities in life. Why? We are no longer living in the old domain but have been transferred into a new one that is eternal, powerful, and filled with joy and the presence of the Holy Spirit.

> For the kingdom of God is not a matter of eating and drinking
> but of righteousness and peace and joy in the Holy Spirit.
> (Rom. 4:17)

You have a new destiny

For the children of God, this planet is our temporary residence. It is not our final home. It is not our final destination. If we would just *believe* this truth, our life would be a whole lot less complicated. We fret, worry, and become anxious and fearful over the prospects of this life. But it is only our temporary dwelling. The early believers knew this, believed this, understood this, and embraced this. I am not saying that they didn't have difficulties, challenges, and worries in life - they did. But they faced them with the ever present reality that this world and this life was not their home. There was a better place of unlimited possibilities and joy in their ultimate destination called heaven. Let me share some key Scripture passages that reinforce this:

> So we do not lose heart. Though our outer self is wasting
> away, our inner self is being renewed day by day. For this light
> momentary affliction is preparing for us an eternal weight of

glory beyond all comparison, as we look not to the things that are seen but to the things that are unseen. For the things that are seen are transient, but the things that are unseen are *eternal*. (2 Cor. 4:16-18, emphasis mine)

For we know that if the tent that is our earthly home is destroyed, we have a building from God, a house not made with hands, *eternal* in the heavens. (2 Cor. 5:1, emphasis mine)

These all died in faith, not having received the things promised, but having seen them and greeted them from afar, and having acknowledged that they were strangers and exiles on the earth. For people who speak thus make it clear that they are seeking a homeland. If they had been thinking of that land from which they had gone out, they would have had opportunity to return. But as it is, they desire a better country, that is, a heavenly one. Therefore God is not ashamed to be called their God, for he has prepared for them a city. (Heb. 11:13-16)

Blessed be the God and Father of our Lord Jesus Christ! According to his great mercy, he has caused us to be born again to a living hope through the resurrection of Jesus Christ from the dead, to an inheritance that is imperishable, undefiled, and unfading, kept in heaven for you, who by God's power are being guarded through faith for a salvation ready to be revealed in the last time. In this you rejoice, though now for a little while, if necessary, you have been grieved by various trials, so that the tested genuineness of your faith—more precious than gold that perishes though it is tested by fire—may be found to result in praise and glory and honor at the revelation of Jesus Christ. (1 Pet. 1:3-7)

Beloved, I urge you as sojourners and exiles to abstain from the passions of the flesh, which wage war against your soul. (1 Pet. 2:11)

Notice these words of Jesus:

Let not your hearts be troubled. Believe in God; believe also in me. In my Father's house are many rooms. If it were not so, would I have told you that I go to prepare a place for you? And if I go and prepare a place for you, I will come again and

will take you to myself, that where I am you may be also. And
you know the way to where I am going. (John 14:1-4)

Much of our time and energy is expended in this world and on things that
have no eternal significance. Our focus and priorities need to be heavenward,
not here below. How much time and resources do we waste on things that have
nothing to do with the kingdom? That's why Paul writes to the Colossians
saying these words:

> If then you have been raised with Christ, seek the things that
> are above, where Christ is, seated at the right hand of God. Set
> your minds on things that are above, not on things that are on
> earth. For you have died, and your life is hidden with Christ
> in God. (Col. 3:1-3)

Jesus stresses:

> Do not lay up for yourselves treasures on earth, where moth
> and rust destroy and where thieves break in and steal, but lay
> up for yourselves treasures in heaven, where neither moth
> nor rust destroys and where thieves do not break in and steal.
> For where your treasure is, there your heart will be also.
> (Matt. 6:19-21)

Paul writing to Timothy said:

> But godliness with contentment is great gain, for we brought
> nothing into the world, and we cannot take anything out of the
> world. But if we have food and clothing, with these we will be
> content. But those who desire to be rich fall into temptation,
> into a snare, into many senseless and harmful desires that
> plunge people into ruin and destruction. For the love of
> money is a root of all kinds of evils. It is through this craving
> that some have wandered away from the faith and pierced
> themselves with many pangs. (1 Tim. 6:6-10)

I want to challenge you to discipline your mind to constantly have an
eternal perspective. Such discipline will change how you think, your priorities
and ambitions in life, how you face trouble and heartaches, how you respond
to difficult and challenging times, and every other experience you have in life.
Why? Because you know that this world is not your final destiny and that like
a pilgrim, you are just passing through. Strive through the power and anointing
of the Holy Spirit to develop a mindset with a *default* eternal perspective. That
way, regardless of what you're facing, your mind automatically reverts to the

eternal perspective default, reminding you that this world is not your home. You are just passing through!

You have purpose, significance, and were created for relationship
God created you for *relationship*. Life is not the result of an accidental cosmic explosion. To those who believe in the Big Bang Theory, my question is, "When has there ever been an explosion that has brought about design and order?" Our universe is meticulously ordered. Even what was thought to be a simple cell has been discovered to be incredibly complex and designed with precision to function. (If you have not seen Ben Stein's film, *Expelled,* you need to watch it. The film is a must-see that will catapult your faith to a new dimension.) There is an awesome and divine design to the universe, and you have been uniquely designed as the focus of that grand plan. God created mankind for relationship, for communion, for love, and to express His glory.

The Bible teaches that we were made in the image of God. We are the only creatures that were created in His image. Theologians have given various interpretations of what this means, but I think the meaning of why we were created in God's image is much deeper than what we can imagine. Possibilities may include our capacity to build relationships, think creatively, design and plan for the future, and experience emotions.

Not only are we like God in our physical image, but we are also imitators of God because we have a spirit. Because we have a spirit, we are designed to have a relationship with God, who the Bible teaches is Spirit. God is a triune being (Father, Son, and Holy Spirit) and we also are triune beings, having a body, a soul, and a spirit. I am not sure of the depth of what it means to be created in the *image of God*, but I do know that it means that of all creatures on the planet, we are unique, special, dearly loved by our Creator, and we can have a personal relationship with Him.

In Genesis, the first book of the Bible, we read these words:

> Then God said, "Let us make man in our image, after our likeness. And let them have dominion over the fish of the sea and over the birds of the heavens and over the livestock and over all the earth and over every creeping thing that creeps on the earth." So God created man in his own image, in the image of God he created him; male and female he created them. And God blessed them. And God said to them, "Be fruitful and multiply and fill the earth and subdue it, and have dominion over the fish of the sea and over the birds of the heavens and over every living thing that moves on the earth." (Gen. 1:26-28)

It is not my intention to give you an extended teaching on man and His relationship to God, but I do want to point out that you are so significant, special, unique, and loved by God, that He sent His Son Jesus to die for you in order to restore your relationship with Him. He designed you to personally know Him, to love Him, and to experience Him.

I say this to emphasize that you were not saved to simply sit back and wait for the Lord to return at His Second Coming or to simply exist and wait to die and go to heaven. He wants you to pursue Him, seek Him, come to know Him intimately, love Him, communicate with Him, lead others to Him, enjoy His presence, and bring glory and honor to His name. He wants you to be part of a body (a local church) where you can participate with other believers in worshipping Him, glorifying Him, and bringing edification to others within the kingdom. His work is active, ongoing, and He wants you to become engaged in the process and enter into partnership with Him. For this you were created and uniquely designed!

CONCLUDING THOUGHTS

In this chapter, I have tried to convey a basic understanding of salvation and its implications, along with touching on a few of the blessings of knowing Christ. The wealth and richness of our inheritance as partakers in Christ's life are far more than I can write in this chapter. They are beyond description. I am begging you to please never take for granted your salvation or your significance to Christ.

I am convinced that we will never understand or comprehend with our minds the full implication of our salvation or the depth of the cross until we stand in the majestic presence of our Lord and Savior Jesus Christ, receive the full revelation of who He is and what He has provided for us through His grace, and see the eternal provision that He has given us in Christ that will be ours for all eternity.

What we receive in heaven will be so utterly glorious that we will wonder why we ever thought the life of a Christian involved any degree of sacrifice. In essence, grasping this eternal perspective was Paul's prayer for the saints in Ephesus. It was his desire that they would come to comprehend the depth of their salvation in Christ. Read these words carefully:

> For this reason, because I have heard of your faith in the Lord Jesus and your love toward all the saints, I do not cease to give thanks for you, remembering you in my prayers, that the God of our Lord Jesus Christ, the Father of glory, may give you the Spirit of wisdom and of revelation in the knowledge of him, having the eyes of your hearts enlightened, that you may know what is the hope to which he has called you, *what are*

the riches of his glorious inheritance in the saints, and what is the immeasurable greatness of his power toward us who believe, according to the working of his great might that he worked in Christ when he raised him from the dead and seated him at his right hand in the heavenly places, far above all rule and authority and power and dominion, and above every name that is named, not only in this age but also in the one to come. And he put all things under his feet and gave him as head over all things to the church, which is his body, the fullness of him who fills all in all. (Eph. 1:15-23, emphasis mine)

As I bring this chapter to a close, let me make one thing clear. There is only one way to God, one way to be saved, and it is through Jesus. There are not multiple plans to get to heaven. There is not an A Plan, a B Plan, a C Plan and so forth. There is but one plan. Some may say this is narrow minded and exclusive thinking. It is no more narrow minded than Jesus and His Word.

Again, the issue goes back to our authority, the Bible. Either it is the true and inspired Word of God or it is not. You do not have the freedom to pick and choose what is true in the Bible and what is false. The Bible clearly teaches that Jesus is the only way to eternal life. I know in a day that promotes tolerance there is the temptation to say that there are many ways to God and all religions are equal. But the problem with that reasoning is that it is not biblical. It is totally inconsistent and diametrically opposite of what Jesus and the Bible teaches. Notice these words of Jesus: "Jesus said to him, 'I am the way, and the truth, and the life. *No one* comes to the Father except through me.'" (John 14:6, emphasis mine).

Luke in his book of Acts writes: "And there is salvation in no one else, for there is *no other name* under heaven given among men by which we must be saved." (Acts 4:12, emphasis mine)

That's pretty emphatic. "No other name" is speaking about the name of Jesus. It is an affront to a holy God who commissioned His only Son to die an agonizing and humiliating death on a cross to say, "There is some other way besides Jesus." If there is another way, why did He allow His Son to suffer and die in this horrific way? There wasn't, so He did.

I cannot end this chapter without making an appeal. Just in case you are reading this chapter and you are unsure of your salvation, why not take a minute and pray this prayer? I admonish you to do so before it is eternally too late.

"Dear Jesus, thank You for dying on the cross for my sins. I believe You died for me, were resurrected, and will be coming again. Forgive me for all of my sins. I ask for Your forgiveness based on Your death for my sins on the cross. I turn from my sins and surrender my life to Your Lordship. From this day forward, I make the decision to follow Jesus all the days of my life. Thank You for saving me, forgiving me, and giving me a brand new life in Christ. Fill me with Your Holy Spirit and power. In Jesus' name, Amen."

If you prayed that prayer, and were sincere in praying these words, you are saved and can know it!

"I write these things to you who believe in the name of the Son of God that
you may *know* that you have eternal life."
(1 John 5:13, emphasis mine)

BASIC GLOSSARY OF
SALVATION TERMS

- **Faith**

     The Greek word for *faith* is πιστεύω; the AV translates as "believe" 239 times, "commit unto" four times, "commit to (one's) trust" once, "be committed unto" once, "be put in trust with" once, "be commit to one's trust" once, and "believer" once. Enhanced Strong's Lexicon states: "to think to be true, to be persuaded of, to credit, place confidence in."

     Faith in the Bible as related to salvation implies trusting in, relying upon, being convinced of, and placing total confidence in. In reference to Christ and salvation, faith is believing that Christ died for your sins, was raised from the dead, and that by confessing your sins (admitting to Him you are a sinner) and asking Him for forgiveness based on His death on the cross for your sins, He not only forgives your sins, but also transfers His righteousness (by His sinless life) to you, thus providing you with eternal life, salvation.

     Scripture references: Romans 1:16-17; 3:21-28; 5:1-2; Galatians 2:16; 3:7-14,22,26; Ephesians 2:8-12; Philippians 3:9; Colossians 2:12; 2 Timothy 3:15; 1 John 5:4

- **Repentance**

     The Greek word repentance is μετάνοια, the AV translates as "repentance" 24 times. The Enhanced Strong's Lexicon's definition is "a change of mind, as it appears to one who repents, of a purpose he has formed or of something he has done."

     Repentance in the Bible as related to salvation implies that the sinner has changed his or her mind in relation to his or her sin, admitting that the committed sins are an offense to God and that sinful behavior is wrong. The sinner feels compelled to turn from a sinful life and make a decisive decision to follow Christ and His teachings.

Scripture references: Luke 5:32; 15:17; 24:47; Acts 5:31; 11:18; 20:21; 2 Corinthians 7:10, 2 Timothy 2:25; 2 Peter 3:9

- **Justification**

   The Greek word for *justification* is **δικαίωσις**, the AV translates as "justification" twice. The Enhanced Strong's Lexicon's definition is: "**1)** the act of God declaring men free from guilt and acceptable to him; **2)** abjuring to be righteous, justification."

   Justification in the Bible means having been made right in your relationship with God. It means you are no longer considered His enemy, but His child. Justification is based on the righteousness that was transferred to you by your belief in Christ's death for you on the cross. It means that when you stand in God's presence on the Day of Judgment, you will stand there without any condemnation, but totally accepted as His child.

   Scripture references: Romans 3:24,28,30; 4:25; 5:1,9,16,18; 10:10; 1 Corinthians 6:11; Galatians 2:16-17; 3:8,11,24; Titus 3:7

- **Sanctification**

   The Greek word for sanctification is **γιασμός**, the AV translates as "holiness" five times, and "sanctification" five times. Enhanced Strong's Lexicon gives this definition: "**1)** consecration, purification; **2)** the effect of consecration. 2ᴀ sanctification of heart and life."

   Sanctification in the Bible is a process of increasing levels of holiness and purity in one's life. It is *progressive*, meaning that we grow and develop in our sanctification, setting ourselves apart exclusively for God and His kingdom. We never reach a state of sinless perfection, but we do advance in our sanctification as we yield to the Holy Spirit and His influence in our lives. When we go to heaven and receive our new glorified bodies, we then become totally sanctified, receiving a body like Jesus, which in salvation terms is called *glorification*.

   Scripture references: Romans 6:19,22; 1 Corinthians 1:30; 1 Thessalonians 4:3; 5:23; 2 Thessalonians 2:13; Hebrews 13:12; 1 Peter 1:2

- **Redemption**

   The Greek word for *redemption* is **πολύτρωσις**, the AV translates as "redemption" nine times and "deliverance" once. Enhanced Strong's Lexicon defines as: "**1)** a releasing effected by payment of ransom. 1ᴀ redemption, deliverance. 1ʙ liberation procured by the payment of a ransom."

The word *redemption* in the Bible refers to Christ paying a price to purchase us (redeem us) as His unique, own possession. He paid for us with the sacrifice of His body on the cross and by shedding His innocent blood for us. All the sacrifices in the Old Testament pointed to His supreme sacrifice on the cross. When we accept Christ as our personal Lord and Savior, we become His possession by virtue of the payment He made.

By surrendering our lives to Christ, we are no longer our own, but now we belong to Him. Our bodies, minds, material possessions, and all that we have are His. This is not a negative thing for the believer because we become joint heirs with Christ. In reality, we receive when we surrender and give our lives over to Him. We receive eternal life, a home in heaven, a new body, peace and joy—and it will last forever!

Scripture references: Galatians 4:5; Ephesians 1:7; 4:30; Colossians 1:14; Titus 2:14; Hebrews 9:12

- **Atonement (Reconciliation)**

  The Greek for *atonement* is **καταλλαγή**, the AV translates as "reconciliation" twice, "atonement" once, and "reconciling" once. Enhanced Strong's Lexicon defines as: "**1)** exchange. 1A of the business of money changers, exchanging equivalent values. **2)** adjustment of a difference, reconciliation, restoration to favor. 2A in the NT of the restoration of the favor of God to sinners that repent and put their trust in the expiatory death of Christ."

  The word *atonement* is inextricably connected to Christ's death, particularly the payment He made by dying on the cross. In the Old Testament it refers to cover, or to wipe clean. It is because of His atonement (the sacrifice of His death and the pouring out of His blood) that He was able to redeem us (purchase us), and on that basis bring us back into a proper relationship with God. We are now presentable to God because the blood of Jesus has covered our sins.

  Scripture references: Romans 5:10-11, 2 Corinthians 5:18-19, Ephesians 2:14-16; Colossians 1:20-22

Discussion Questions

1. What is meant by the term "salvation?" How do others interpret this term?

2. What is the main reason we are in need of salvation?

3. Define the word "sin" and "sinners." How many people would fall into this category? What Scriptures support your answer? Is this a relevant term today?

4. What is the relationship between works and a person's salvation?

5. Can a person perform enough good deeds to earn his or her way into heaven? If your answer is no, why not?

6. When we stand before God, on what basis will He allow us to enter heaven?

7. What part does our personal faith have in our salvation? What does it mean to place one's faith in Christ? What do we mean by a *personal* faith?

8. What does it mean to repent?

9. What does it mean to surrender our life to the Lordship of Christ?

10. What actually took place when Jesus died on the cross?

11. What is the purpose of the *law*?

12. What do the following terms mean: New Birth, justification, sanctification, redemption, and atonement?

13. What is our new identity after the New Birth?

14. What are the implications of our new identity?

15. What does eternal life mean to you?

Chapter Four

The Person of the Holy Spirit

T he topic of the Holy Spirit is one that is experiencing a new passion and
emphasis. I am glad that several books have been written on the Holy
Spirit recently. The church of the twenty-first century is coming to the reali-
zation that in these last days, we need a fresh move of the Holy Spirit to fill
our churches.

Today, what evangelicals refer to as the "Pentecostal," "charismatic," and
the "Spirit-filled" movements within Christianity all have one key element
in common: the pursuit of the empowerment and presence of the Holy Spirit.
The fastest growing arm of Christianity across the planet is those who identify
themselves in one of the above categories. This is in keeping with the prophetic
words of the prophet Joel who wrote:

> And it shall come to pass afterward, that I will pour out my
> Spirit on all flesh; your sons and your daughters shall prophesy,
> your old men shall dream dreams, and your young men shall
> see visions. Even on the male and female servants in those
> days I will pour out my Spirit. And I will show wonders in
> the heavens and on the earth, blood and fire and columns of
> smoke. The sun shall be turned to darkness, and the moon to
> blood, before the great and awesome day of the LORD comes.
> (Joel 2:28-31)

This prophecy was fulfilled on the day of Pentecost as recorded by Luke in
his Acts of the Apostles:

> When the day of Pentecost arrived, they were all together in
> one place. And suddenly there came from heaven a sound like
> a mighty rushing wind, and it filled the entire house where
> they were sitting. And divided tongues as of fire appeared to
> them and rested on each one of them. And they were all filled
> with the Holy Spirit and began to speak in other tongues as
> the Spirit gave them utterance.... But this is what was uttered

through the prophet Joel: "'And in the *last days* it shall be, God declares, that I will pour out my Spirit on all flesh, and your sons and your daughters shall prophesy, and your young men shall see visions, and your old men shall dream dreams; even on my male servants and female servants in those days I will pour out my Spirit, and they shall prophesy.'" (Acts 2:1-4,16-18, emphasis mine)

According to this Scripture, the "last days" had their *beginnings* with the outpouring of the Holy Spirit. The apostle Peter explained to the crowd that what they were seeing and experiencing was that which the prophet Joel said would take place in the *end times*. According to the apostle Peter, we have been living in the last days (end times) *since* Pentecost. The Bible teaches that a day to the Lord is like a thousand years (see 2 Pet. 3:8). What is exciting about this is that believers living in the twenty-first century are not only living in the *last days*, but also like the early disciples, they are living within the full operation of the Holy Spirit within their lives and His church. Today, we have His power!

In the Old Testament, the Holy Spirit would come upon individuals to accomplish a particular task that required supernatural enablement. The Spirit did not live *within* them, but occasionally came *upon* them, giving them the ability to operate supernaturally. The Bible teaches that since Pentecost, all people who believe in Jesus have the Holy Spirit living within them. That is, the Holy Spirit *literally* takes up residence within our physical bodies. We'll explore more about this later, but simply put, this is the uniqueness of living as believers since the day of Pentecost.

The Holy Spirit is a Person
Notice that the chapter is entitled, "The Person of the Holy Spirit." I want to ensure that you understand the Holy Spirit is not simply a force or just an expression of God's power, but is God Himself. In a previous chapter, I mentioned that God is Trinitarian, that is, God exists as God the Father, God the Son, and God the Holy Spirit. They are three persons, but o*ne Being*. They are not three different Gods, or three different manifestations of the same God; but they are three *separate* persons who are nonetheless o*ne* God.

As mentioned earlier, the Trinity is difficult to understand. We are trying to understand the infinite God with our finite minds. But we can be assured that the Bible teaches the truth of an infinite, triune God and the Church has affirmed the Trinity's existence throughout the ages. I say this to emphasize that even though the Holy Spirit was not poured out until the day of Pentecost, He has eternally existed with the Father and the Son. He was present and active in the beginning of creation.

Notice Genesis 1:1-2: "In the beginning, God created the heavens and the earth. The earth was without form and void, and darkness was over the face of the deep. *And the Spirit of God* was hovering over the face of the waters."

The Holy Spirit is God and has eternally existed with the Father and the Son. Theologians refer to the Holy Spirit as the third person of the Trinity. As a person (not simply a force), the Bible teaches that the Holy Spirit has emotions. He can be grieved (see Ephesians 4:30) and quenched (see 1 Thess. 5:19). Because He is God, being one with the Father and the Son, He loves us, cares for us, extends compassion toward us, and encourages us.

He is omnipotent, omnipresent, and omniscient. In addition, He not only lives within us, but also provides His supernatural presence and releases gifts within us to empower, lead, and strengthen us individually as believers and His church corporately around the world.

Jesus, Holy Spirit, and His Promise

The Holy Spirit came upon Jesus and filled Him when He was baptized in water by John the Baptist (see Matt. 3:13-17). The Spirit rested upon Him and empowered Him for His ministry while on the earth (see Luke 4:18). Jesus taught His disciples that it was necessary for Him to go away, and that He was going to send someone to them who would be with them forever. He was speaking about the Holy Spirit. What is remarkable is that Jesus says it will be *better* if He does go away and that it will be to the disciples' advantage.

> But I have said these things to you, that when their hour comes you may remember that I told them to you. I did not say these things to you from the beginning, because I was with you. But now I am going to him who sent me, and none of you asks me, "Where are you going?" But because I have said these things to you, sorrow has filled your heart. Nevertheless, I tell you the truth: *it is to your advantage that I go away*, for if I do not go away, the Helper will not come to you. But if I go, I will send him to you. (John 16:4-7, emphasis mine)

Why was it more advantageous for Jesus to leave them instead of remaining with them? The Spirit was not only going to be *with them*, but also He was going to take up residence *in them* and empower them for ministry. While Jesus was in His physical body, He could not be everywhere at the same time. He placed limitations upon Himself in human form. But the Holy Spirit is not limited to a body, time or space, but is everywhere at all times. Regardless of where we are, His presence is not only *with* us but *in* us.

> If you love me, you will keep my commandments. And I will ask the Father, and he will give you another Helper, to be with

61

you forever, even the Spirit of truth, whom the world cannot receive, because it neither sees him nor knows him. You know him, for he dwells with you and will be in you. I will not leave you as orphans; I will come to you. Yet a little while and the world will see me no more, but you will see me. Because I live, you also will live. In that day you will know that I am in my Father, and you in me, *and I in you.* (John 14:15-20, emphasis mine)

One of the most amazing and mind blowing truths to me is that God, through the presence of the Holy Spirit, has literally taken up residence within me. As believers in Christ, the Holy Spirit actually indwells our physical bodies. Our bodies are *literally* the temple of the Holy Spirit. His presence dwells within us.

Or do you not know that your body is the temple of the Holy Spirit who is in you, whom you have from God, and you are not your own? For you were bought at a price; therefore glorify God in your body and in your spirit, which are God's. (1 Cor. 6:19-20, *NKJV*, emphasis mine)

Notice our physical bodies are the temple in which the Holy Spirit makes His home. This is why it is so critical to be careful of how we care for our bodies, what we put inside our bodies, and what activities we participate in with our bodies. As Christians, our bodies no longer belong to us. They belong to God. Paul says in the above passage that we (as believers) have been bought (purchased) with a price. What price? The blood of Jesus, the Son of the living God. And a dear price it was!

The Spirit Within You

When does the Holy Spirit come into us? He does so the very instant that we surrender our lives to Christ. In other words, the very moment we became Christians, the Holy Spirit energizes (makes alive) our spirits within us, and makes His abode within us. This happens when we are *born again.* Remember, the new birth experience is a spiritual birthing by the Holy Spirit that happens when you place your faith in Christ. Jesus said you must be born not only of the flesh (natural birth), but also of the Spirit (spiritual birth).

Jesus answered, "Truly, truly, I say to you, unless one is born of water and the Spirit, he cannot enter the kingdom of God. That which is born of the flesh is flesh, and that which is born of the Spirit is spirit. Do not marvel that I said to you, 'You must be born again.' The wind blows where it wishes, and you hear its sound, but you do not know where it comes from or where it goes. So it is with everyone who is born of the Spirit." (John 3:5-8, emphasis mine)

Every person has a spirit within them, but it is dead because of sin. Paul writes in chapter two of Ephesians, "And you were dead in the trespasses and sins" (Eph. 2:1). What was dead? Our spirits. We were not dead physically, but spiritually. Prior to coming to Christ, we had no desire to serve Christ, live for Christ, or please Christ; but when we received Christ as our Lord and Savior, our desires, goals, and ambitions changed. Why the change? Because the Holy Spirit took up residence within us, gave life to our dead spirit, enlightened us to God and His kingdom, and gave us a heart to pursue God. "But God, being rich in mercy, because of the great love with which he loved us, even when we were dead in our trespasses, *made us alive* together with Christ—by grace you have been saved—and raised us up with him and seated us with him in the heavenly places in Christ Jesus." (Eph. 2:4-6, emphasis mine)

We have a body, a soul, and a spirit (see 1 Thess. 5:23). When we placed our faith in Christ, the spirit within us experienced a type of resurrection by which the Holy Spirit made us alive to God. This is true of every person who has ever received Christ as personal Lord and Savior. As a matter of fact, you cannot be a Christian if the Holy Spirit is not living within you. Notice the words of Paul:

> You, however, are not in the flesh but in the Spirit, if in fact
> the Spirit of God *dwells in you. Anyone who does not have*
> *the Spirit of Christ does not belong to him.* But if Christ is
> *in you*, although the body is dead because of sin, the Spirit is
> life because of righteousness. If the Spirit of him who raised
> Jesus from the dead *dwells in you*, he who raised Christ Jesus
> from the dead will also give life to your mortal bodies through
> his Spirit *who dwells in you*. (Rom. 8:9-11, emphasis mine)

This is an amazing passage of Scripture. First, notice Paul says "Anyone *who does not have the Spirit of Christ does not belong to him*" (v. 9). He speaks about the Spirit living or dwelling in us three times in these few sentences and speaks of Christ "in you" once. How is Christ in us? Because the Father, Son, and Holy Spirit are one, so the *Spirit* dwelling in us is synonymous with *Christ* dwelling in us.

Second, don't miss the phrase, "If the Spirit of him who raised Jesus from the dead *dwells in you.*" Don't read over these words lightly. The very same Spirit (the Holy Spirit) that raised Jesus' cold, dead, lifeless body from the grave dwells and lives within us! The *same* power that raised Jesus from the dead is inside of us.

If you and I could grasp the depth of that truth, our lives would be revolutionized. Our way of thinking would change, our vision expanded, and our thoughts and dreams would dare to believe for the impossible. I want you to understand that regardless of who you are or what your educational level is, your financial portfolio, or your status or position in life, you have incredible potential because of the Spirit of God that lives within you. That is how the disciples who were fishermen and common men could speak with such boldness, wisdom, and power. The religious leaders and Pharisees could not believe the power and wisdom by which they spoke! "Now when they saw the boldness of Peter and John, and perceived that they were *uneducated, common men*, they were astonished. And they recognized that they had been with Jesus" (Acts 4:13, emphasis mine).

We must never underestimate our potential because the Spirit of God lives within us. We can accomplish great exploits for God and His kingdom. Regardless of what comes our way or whatever situation we find ourselves in, we must never surrender to our circumstances or be overwhelmed with a feeling of helplessness or hopelessness. The very same Spirit that raised Jesus from the dead lives within us and is ready to empower and equip us as we look to Him!

This is another reason we should never have an inferiority complex or feeling of insignificance. We are God's children and His Spirit attests to this fact. The Bible says that the presence of His Spirit in us is one way we can know that we are Christians, because His Spirit affirms (gives evidence and confirmation) with our spirit that we are His children. "For all who are led by the Spirit of God are sons of God. For you did not receive the spirit of slavery to fall back into fear, but you have received the Spirit of adoption as sons, by whom we cry, 'Abba! Father!' The Spirit himself *bears witness* with our spirit that we are children of God" (Rom. 8:14-16, emphasis mine).

It is God's Spirit within us that produces a radical transformation - so radical, that we are no longer the same person because we have been born again by His Spirit.

When I gave my life to Christ, I experienced a radical transformation. My lifestyle changed, my language changed, my interests changed, my music changed, and my worldview changed. Why? The Holy Spirit made my dead spirit alive to Him and began the transformational process of making me more like Christ. My prayer to receive Christ lasted about a minute, but the transformation was immediate, profound, radical, and life altering. My entire destiny and path in life was eternally changed in an instant! Try explaining that one apart from the supernatural!

I know for some people the transformation is more extensive and radical than others because of a previous lifestyle and choices made; but regardless of your past, there is a definite change that takes place when you receive Christ because of the Holy Spirit within you. How can the God of this universe take up residence in our human bodies without something far-reaching taking place? It must and it does!

The Spirit, Our Source of Power

Now that we have established who the Spirit is, and that all believers have the Spirit living within them, let me now share that He is our only source of power to live victoriously as believers in the world. We may be Christians, but that doesn't mean that life will be easy. Let's face it—life is filled with challenges, difficulties, discouraging situations, and at times all those pressures can prove to be quite depressing. *We are not in heaven yet.* We live in an imperfect world filled with imperfect people. At any given moment our circumstances, relationships, health, employment, and the list can go on—can change.

Our faith in Christ is not to keep us from hardships or problems, but rather to get us through them. Jesus said we can expect to have trials and tribulations: "I have said these things to you, that in me you may have peace. In the world you will have tribulation. *But take heart; I have overcome the world*" (John 16:33, emphasis mine).

The good news is that the *overcomer* lives within us. He will give us the power and the ability to endure, press through, and press on as we depend on Him. We need His help, His assistance, His guidance, His strength, and His power. The key to tapping into His help is recognizing that the power source provided for us is the Holy Spirit. There is no other source.

Pastor Jack Taylor made this statement while preaching at our church: "The Holy Spirit is the only God you have on the planet. So you had better get acquainted with Him and get used to Him." When he first made that comment, my spirit recoiled within me. But the more I thought about it in relation to the Scriptures, I understood that theologically he was right. That's exactly what Jesus said. He said He was *leaving*. He would *no longer* be here on the planet. But He did say that in His absence, He would send "another *Helper*."

Jesus ascended and is at the right hand of the Father in heaven; yet He is with us in the presence of the Holy Spirit. Greek scholars tell us that the word "another" means of the *same* kind. Jesus was saying that the *Helper* would be exactly like Him. Even though He would be different, He would be identically the same. How can this be? The Holy Spirit is one with the Father and the Son. I shared these words of Jesus earlier, but look at them again:

> If you love me, you will keep my commandments. And I will ask the Father, and he will give you *another* Helper, to be with you forever, even the Spirit of truth, whom the world cannot receive, because it neither sees him nor knows him. You know him, for he dwells with you and will be in you. I will not leave you as orphans; I will come to you. (John 14:15-18, emphasis mine)

Notice what Jesus says in the last five words of this passage, *"I will come to you."* You may be asking, "I thought Jesus was leaving and sending the Holy

Spirit in His place?" Yes, that's correct; but again, they are one. The Person of the Spirit is one with the Father and one with the Son. Therefore, in sending the Holy Spirit, Jesus could say, "I will come to you." So yes, the Father is present on the planet. Jesus is present on the planet - but present through the third person of the Trinity, the Holy Spirit. The Holy Spirit is not some impersonal force or a mystical being that cannot be experienced; but He is the very presence of God in the Person of the Holy Spirit.

One of the criticisms of Spirit-filled (Charismatic or Pentecostal) believers is that they place too much emphasis on the Holy Spirit. Some Evangelicals might say, "You shouldn't be talking about the Holy Spirit so much. You're supposed to be glorifying Jesus." Is this correct? Do Charismatics place undue emphasis on the Holy Spirit? Are they guilty of exalting or elevating the Holy Spirit above that of Jesus, as some say?

Let me point out that the Lord Jesus definitely elevated the Person of the Holy Spirit when He gave the following warning:

> Therefore I tell you, every sin and blasphemy will be forgiven people, but the blasphemy against the Spirit will not be forgiven. And whoever speaks a word against the Son of Man will be forgiven, but whoever speaks against the Holy Spirit will not be forgiven, either in this age or in the age to come. (Matt. 12:31-32)

Notice the elevation that Jesus places on the Holy Spirit! If you speak against Jesus, you can be forgiven; but if you speak against the Holy Spirit, this is an unforgiveable sin. In this context, Jesus is speaking about attributing clear and verifiable manifestations of the Holy Spirit to Satan. And even though Jesus is speaking specifically about the sin of blasphemy, He makes it clear that it is more serious to be critical of the Holy Spirit than Jesus Himself.

Let me share with you a passage of Scripture that is sometimes used to make a case that the Holy Spirit should not be talked about in such an eminent way. As a matter of fact, I was taught that this Scripture opposed emphasizing the Holy Spirit when I was in my earlier years of ministry and I used this same passage as a proof text to say that we should not be speaking about the Holy Spirit too much.

The problem was that I did not understand the text or the correct meaning of the passage. Part of my misunderstanding is misinterpretation of the King James Version of the text. Not that the version is wrong, but it is difficult to understand. Here is the passage of Scripture in the King James Version:

> "Howbeit when he, the Spirit of truth, is come, he will guide you into all truth: *for he shall not speak of himself*; but whatsoever he shall hear, that shall he speak: and he will shew you things to come" (John 16:13, *KJV*, emphasis mine).

The key phrase from this text is "for he shall not speak of himself" which has been misinterpreted to mean that the Holy Spirit would not speak *about* Himself. But this is not what the text means. What Jesus meant was that the Holy Spirit, in and of Himself, that is, by Himself, will not speak on His own authority. He will only speak what He hears in council with the Father and the Son.

Other translations make this clear. Notice the following translations of John 16:13:

> When the Spirit of truth comes, he will guide you into all the truth, *for he will not speak on his own authority,* but whatever he hears he will speak, and he will declare to you the things that are to come. (*ESV*)

> But when he, the Spirit of truth, comes, he will guide you into all the truth. He will not speak on his own; he will speak only what he hears, and he will tell you what is yet to come. (*NIV*)

> When the Spirit of truth comes, he will guide you into all truth. He will not speak on his own but will tell you what he has heard. He will tell you about the future. (*NLT*)

> However, when He, the Spirit of truth, has come, He will guide you into all truth; for He will not speak on His own *authority,* but whatever He hears He will speak; and He will tell you things to come. (*NKJV*)

In the New King James Version, the editors make an effort to clarify the translation so that it is in line with other translations. It is not that the original King James Version is wrong, but if it is read quickly rather than carefully, it can lead to misinterpretation.

The verse directly after this one is often used to say that the Holy Spirit will not speak of Himself. Notice the words of Jesus: "He will glorify me, for he will take what is mine and declare it to you" (John 16:14).

Some teach that placing too much emphasis on the Holy Spirit is *glorifying* the Holy Spirit and not Jesus. Well, how does the Holy Spirit glorify Jesus? Jesus says the Spirit glorifies Him by taking what belongs to Him and "declaring it to you." This definitely does not mean the Holy Spirit can't be talked about or emphasized. I don't know of any Spirit-filled believers or fellowships that do not strive to exalt, magnify, and glorify the Lord Jesus. Jesus is our theme, our Savior, our Redeemer, our Healer, and our soon coming King. He is to be preeminently exalted in every way. But this text does not mean we can't speak about or emphasize the work and ministry of the Holy Spirit.

A look at the book of Acts will reveal that it is permissible to emphasize the ministry of the Holy Spirit. In Luke's account of the lives of the earlier believers and the first church, it becomes rather clear that they placed significant emphasis and focus on the Holy Spirit and the ministry of the Holy Spirit. Everything they did was through the Holy Spirit. Their preaching, their prayer meetings, appointing of leadership, and discovering God's will were all done by looking to and relying upon the Holy Spirit. I think the problem with the church today is not too much emphasis on the Holy Spirit, but on the contrary, too little emphasis on the Holy Spirit. It seems as if we depend on everything except the Spirit, which is diametrically opposite of what the early church practiced.

When I was completing my Doctor of Ministry degree, I had to read several hundred of pages on the subject of church growth. Today there is a plethora of books written on this subject of church growth, but authors rarely focus on the power and the anointing of the Holy Spirit or the necessity of His being integrated in the life of the church. *The book of Acts is the account of the early church.* If there is anything we should be doing today, we should be emulating the life of the early church.

I would submit to you that to emulate the church as described in the book of Acts is to acknowledge, pursue, seek, and thirst for the power and anointing of the Holy Spirit upon our individual lives and the church corporately as the body of Christ. He was *their source* and He should be *our source*! If you doubt me on this statement, I simply challenge you to read through the book of Acts and underline the words *Holy Spirit* and *Spirit*. You will see that He was intertwined in everything they did!

The Holy Spirit, Our Source

Let me share just a few closing thoughts concerning our source. Jesus said the following about the Holy Spirit:

> On the last day of the feast, the great day, Jesus stood up and cried out, "If anyone thirsts, let him come to me and drink. Whoever believes in me, as the Scripture has said, 'Out of his heart will flow rivers of living water.' Now this he said about the Spirit, whom those who believed in him were to receive, for as yet the Spirit had not been given, because Jesus was not yet glorified." (John 7:37-39)

Jesus provides a profound metaphor of the Holy Spirit's presence in these words: "rivers of living water." It is clear that Jesus is speaking about the Holy Spirit because He immediately says, "Now this he [Jesus] said about *the Spirit*."

Rivers continually flow and become a life-giving source leading to an abundance of life, both for plants and animals. But here Jesus is referring to giving spiritual nourishment, life, abundance, and refreshment to believers through the presence and power of the Spirit. Think of His words "will flow rivers of living water!" There is a river within us: the Holy Spirit. When released, He fills us, controls us, empowers us, overflows from within us, and takes us to spiritual depths that will advance to a deeper awareness and intimacy with Christ.

In this passage, Jesus is speaking about the Spirit's ability to provide spiritual nourishment, power, enablement, and every spiritual resource we need to live a life of spiritual abundance and victory. We do not have to be overwhelmed and defeated by our circumstances or the enemy. We can overcome the various trials and challenges in life and the various temptations that come our way as we surrender and yield to the Holy Spirit. The key is yielding, surrendering, relinquishing control, and submitting to the Spirit's leadership in our lives. When we yield to His influence within our lives, He takes control and gives us the victory.

When writing to the church of Galatia, the apostle Paul said:

> But I say, *walk by the Spirit*, and you will not gratify the desires of the flesh. For the desires of the flesh are against the Spirit, and the desires of the Spirit are against the flesh, for these are opposed to each other, to keep you from doing the things you want to do. *But if you are led by the Spirit*, you are not under the law. Now the works of the flesh are evident: sexual immorality, impurity, sensuality, idolatry, sorcery, enmity, strife, jealousy, fits of anger, rivalries, dissensions, divisions, envy, drunkenness, orgies, and things like these. I warn you, as I warned you before, that those who do such things will not inherit the kingdom of God. *But the fruit of the Spirit* is love, joy, peace, patience, kindness, goodness, faithfulness, gentleness, self-control; against such things there is no law. And those who belong to Christ Jesus have crucified the flesh with its passions and desires. *If we live by the Spirit*, let us also *keep in step with the Spirit*. Let us not become conceited, provoking one another, envying one another. (Gal. 5:16-26, emphasis mine)

Paul is talking about the practicalities of living out the Christian life. He says, "walk by the Spirit," "be led by the Spirit," "live by the Spirit," and "keep in step with the Spirit." This is how we gain victory over the flesh and its desires. Paul also mentions the "fruit of the Spirit," which is the *byproduct* of walking in the Spirit, being led by the Spirit, and keeping in step with the Spirit. It should be obvious in reading these verses that the Spirit is our life source and the key to living our faith and emulating the Lord Jesus in our lives.

The Spirit forms His character and passions within us, and our lifestyle becomes Spirit-filled, Spirit-led, and Spirit-controlled. We are commanded to be Spirit-filled on a continual basis. It's not an option, but a command from the

Word of God. Paul writes to the Ephesians, "And do not get drunk with wine, for that is debauchery, but be filled with the Spirit" (Eph. 5:18).

The Greek tense of "be filled" is continuous, meaning an ongoing action. In other words, we are to *keep* being filled with the Spirit. It is not a onetime event but an ongoing and daily necessity for us if we expect to live the victorious Christian life. The Amplified translation, which focuses on bringing out the tenses of the original language, translates this verse as follows: "And do not get drunk with wine, for that is debauchery; but ever be filled and stimulated with the [Holy] Spirit" (Eph. 5:18, *AMP*).

To be "filled with the Spirit" is to be controlled by the Spirit. It is a little unusual that Paul compares being filled with the Spirit to being drunk with wine. He is simply conveying that just as alcohol controls a person under its influence, He is saying that the Spirit is to control us. When people are "drunk with wine," their speech, moods, emotions, thinking, behavior, and even their physical bodies become controlled and influenced by the substance they consumed. Paul is saying in like manner, don't allow alcohol to control you, but let the Spirit of God control you. When you do, your speech, moods, emotions, thinking, behavior, and physical bodies will be controlled and directed by the Spirit. Again, this is the key to experiencing victory in your walk with Christ.

Notice the emphasis in the Amplified, "ever filled." Again, the emphasis is to *keep on* being filled. Don't expect to live and be sustained on one filling of the Spirit. We need continual fillings of His Spirit to be recharged and refueled. It is like our automobiles: one tank of gas will take us a certain distance but then the tank runs out. We need to refuel the tank, refill it. The same is true of our spiritual gas tank. This world with its system, its challenges and difficulties, along with its influence and temptations has a way of draining our spiritual power. We need a refilling to provide us with a constant source of power and strength to advance and progress throughout our lives.

Therefore, we need not one filling, but literally several hundreds of fresh fillings throughout our lives from the Source—His Spirit.

Jesus told us in chapter seven of John's gospel that we are to "drink" of the Spirit. Just like our physical bodies need replenishing with water to energize and sustain our lives, so do our inner spiritual beings, that is our spirits, need replenishing to energize and sustain our spiritual lives. Many believers are going though life in a state of spiritual dehydration simply because they have not appropriated the refreshment of the Spirit by drinking from His river. We must drink from the Spirit and drink often!

Let me point out that even though the Spirit provides the power, it is our responsibility to appropriate His power as we yield our wills. In other words, we are not going to experience the fullness of the Spirit without taking some initiative. We have a will, meaning, we can make a choice concerning the infilling of the Spirit. Notice in the Galatians passage above that Paul says, "let *us* also keep in step with the Spirit" (5:25, emphasis mine). That is, we also have the responsibility to take steps to enable Him to take control of our lives. When we

70

make a decision to yield to His influence, He will fill us with His power and strength. Notice what Paul says in his epistle to the Romans:

> For those who live according to the flesh set their minds on the things of the flesh, but those who live according to the Spirit *set their minds* on the things of the Spirit. For to set the mind on the flesh is death, but to set the mind on the Spirit is life and peace. For the mind that is set on the flesh is hostile to God, for it does not submit to God's law; indeed, it cannot. Those who are in the flesh cannot please God. You, however, are not in the flesh but in the Spirit, if in fact the Spirit of God dwells in you. Anyone who does not have the Spirit of Christ does not belong to him. But if Christ is in you, although the body is dead because of sin, the Spirit is life because of righteousness. If the Spirit of him who raised Jesus from the dead dwells in you, he who raised Christ Jesus from the dead will also *give life* to your mortal bodies through his Spirit who dwells in you. (Rom. 8:5-11, emphasis mine)

The "setting of our minds" is a decision that we must make. There are many things we can allow to occupy and control our minds, but our minds need to be set, fixed, and riveted to the things of the Spirit. Again, we have a responsibility. We cannot just sit back passively or idly and expect that we will be filled and controlled by the Spirit. We must put forth some effort on our part, and when we do, He will do His part in a glorious way.

Writing to the Galatians, Paul writes: "For the one who sows to his own flesh will from the flesh reap corruption, *but the one who sows to the Spirit* will from the Spirit reap eternal life" (Gal. 6:8, emphasis mine).

Notice again that we have a responsibility and an obligation to do the sowing. If we expect to reap the benefits of the Spirit-filled life, we must be actively engaged in sowing in the realm of the Spirit.

What are the practical steps to experiencing the continual infilling of the Holy Spirit? You will notice the title of chapter eight is *Spiritual Disciplines*. It is there that I will be providing practical steps that will lead you to experience not only the Spirit-filled life, but also to grow and develop in your personal walk with the Lord. And though you as a believer have the Holy Spirit living within you, the *power* to activate the benefits of spiritual discipline comes through the baptism of the Holy Spirit. The next two chapters will focus on the baptism of the Holy Spirit and what that means for you!

Discussion Questions

1. According to the Scriptures, what sign confirms that we have entered the "last days?"

2. What is the difference between the way the Holy Spirit interacts with New Testament saints and the way He interacts with Old Testament saints?

3. Why is it important to refer to the Holy Spirit as a Person of the Godhead?

4. What is the relationship of the Holy Spirit to God the Father and God the Son?

5. What *promise* did Jesus give concerning the Holy Spirit?

6. Why was it better for Jesus to leave the planet and send the Holy Spirit?

7. Does every believer in Christ have the Holy Spirit living within them?

8. What are the implications of the Holy Spirit living within us?

9. What are the implications of our bodies being the temples of the Holy Spirit?

10. How does the Holy Spirit provide power to the believer?

11. Why do some Christians feel that Spirit-filled people place too much emphasis on the Holy Spirit? Are they justified in their criticism?

12. What does it mean to be *filled* by the Spirit?

13. How often should we be filled by the Holy Spirit?

14. Who is ultimately responsible for staying filled with the Spirit?

Chapter Five

The Baptism in the Holy Spirit!
Part 1: Introduction

I was 43 years old and serving as senior pastor of a sizeable downtown Southern Baptist church in Bradenton, Florida. Our worship attendance was averaging between 1,200 and 1,400 people during the fall and spring. In Florida, we have a tremendous influx of winter visitors, who we affectionately refer to as *snowbirds*. The arrival of snowbirds is why our attendance fluctuated during these months. Serving as the pastor of a relatively large influential church was quite fulfilling at 43, but something was missing. I enjoyed preaching, reading, and studying the Scriptures, but the joy and passion for ministry was not at the level I desired. A spiritual hunger and desire for God began to increase in my life. I started wondering if there could be more. My brother-in-law and mother-in-law had been Spirit-filled believers for years, being part of an Assemblies of God church. I thought to myself, "Have I been wrong about this all these years?"

It was during this time frame that I read Pastor Jim Cymbala's book, *Fresh Wind, Fresh Fire*. This book is an incredible account of the power of prayer and of prayer's impact on his church, The Brooklyn Tabernacle. Reading about the miraculous testimonies and radical conversions happening in his church through prayer and the power of the Holy Spirit really began to stir a hunger within me for something fresh and new.

One day, Pam (my wife) was listening to the Moody Radio station and heard that Cymbala was coming to Tampa for a *Fresh Wind, Fresh Fire* pastor's conference. She mentioned it several times before I made a decision to attend. The conference was held in a ballroom at a motel in Tampa. As the conference began with worship and singing, I looked around and began to realize that the majority of people were from churches with a charismatic or Pentecostal background. Cymbala and the praise team led us in worship and encouraged us to lift our hands in praise to the Lord. The raising of hands was an expression of worship that I was uncomfortable with, but at Cymbala's continual prompting, I gave in. Once I did, as my hands went into the air to worship God, something was released in me.

For the first time in my life, I felt I was experiencing genuine worship. There was a new level of intimacy in my worship that I had never experienced before. God had to deal with my pride, and as I surrendered my pride and raised my hands in worship, I experienced worship that was refreshing, moving, powerful, and stirring to my spirit!

During the conference, I listened to several preachers including Warren Wiersbe. Each of the speakers was excellent and their messages were thoroughly biblical. Cymbala's topic was "The Baptism in the Holy Spirit." I listened intently, with a hunger in my spirit, hanging on to his every word and evaluating every Scripture he shared to back up his position. He progressively took us through a study in the book of Acts and demonstrated that not only was the Holy Spirit weaved into the very fabric and life of the early church, but also that their experience (called the baptism in the Holy Spirit) was real, powerful, life changing, and available to every believer.

As I listened, I kept thinking to myself that Cymbala wasn't strange, weird, didn't look like the typical Pentecostal preacher on television, but that he resonated a spirit that was genuine, authentic, and filled with humility. Cymbala quoted preachers I had become familiar with while in seminary: Charles Finney, D.L. Moody, John Wesley, and R.A. Torrey. Cymbala shared how each of these men believed in the baptism in the Holy Spirit.

When he concluded his message, Cymbala gave an altar call and invited people to come forward if they desired to be baptized in the Holy Spirit. I immediately went forward. With tears streaming down my face, I made my way to the front and stood, raising my hands in the air in worship to God. I remember thinking, "I wish someone would lay hands on me and pray for me to receive the baptism in the Holy Spirit." Instantly, one of his staff pastors laid his hands on my head and began praying for me to receive the baptism in the Holy Spirit. That prayer radically changed my life, my theology, and eventually led me to pursue association with a more Pentecostal group of churches. I would never be the same man or the same preacher. Glory to God!

Attending this conference changed my life and my destiny! I went home from the conference and immediately made some changes in my spiritual journey. First, I started worshipping with my wife in the evenings. We didn't pray together, but we practiced our devotional life individually, not together as husband and wife. We did not intend for this to happen – it just did. I never really felt comfortable praying out loud with Pam, that is, just the two of us praying together.

This might sound a little strange coming from a pastor, and it is even a bit embarrassing to admit, but it is a reality that many men and pastors also face. For some reason, it was just out of my comfort zone. But as soon as I came home from the conference, I told Pam that I wanted us to worship and pray together.

I received a worship CD of the Brooklyn Tabernacle Choir at the conference. The album had several slow and worshipful songs, which were different from the Southern gospel music I mostly had. I told Pam I wanted to lie down, turn out the lights and listen to the worship music. I said that if she felt comfortable, she could raise her hands in praise to God. She was more than willing to participate in this new worship experience, albeit a little surprised and in a quandary as to what was going on in my life. As we worshipped, something special happened and a new chapter opened in our spiritual journey. Our worship unlocked a deeper sense of awareness and intimacy with God that, up until that time, we had not known. But that night, something special happened and a new chapter opened in our spiritual journey. Our worship unlocked a deeper sense of awareness and intimacy with God that, up until that time, we had not known.

I share my personal journey with you to let you know that seldom does someone in mid-life choose to leave his theological comfort zone. I had been a Southern Baptist since my conversion, graduated from three Southern Baptist institutions, had pastored only Southern Baptist churches—and at age forty-four, I not only left my church, but also my denomination.

Let me hasten to say that I love Southern Baptists. I still listen to many Southern Baptist pastors and feel some of the most gifted and anointed preaching is from godly men who pastor churches in the Southern Baptist Convention (SBC). Southern Baptist pastors such as Charles Stanley, Adrian Rogers (who is in heaven now), David Jeremiah, Jack Graham, and others are excellent preachers doing great things for the kingdom of God. I appreciate the SBC who, because of their evangelistic zeal, have reached literally thousands for Christ.

One other point I would like to make clear is that I was not asked to leave the Southern Baptist Church I was pastoring. They were very gracious and accommodating regarding my new theological posture. But, I was no longer Southern Baptist theologically, especially in my position on the Holy Spirit. Thus I felt that I had an ethical responsibility to leave the church and the denomination that had blessed me throughout the years. They hadn't changed, I had. So I chose to leave, and it was a cordial and sweet departure. I still appreciate how they treated me in my spiritual journey at that time.

What is the Baptism in the Holy Spirit?

Now that I have given you a little of my personal story of transitioning into the Spirit-filled life, let me get to the heart of the issue concerning the baptism in the Holy Spirit. What is the baptism in the Holy Spirit? How is it defined? My answer to these questions is the reason why I left my previous denomination and now serve in a Spirit-filled church. By Spirit-filled, I am saying that I believe in the baptism in the Holy Spirit, present day manifestations of the Holy Spirit, and the availability of *all* the spiritual gifts that the early church experienced.

The baptism in the Holy Spirit is primarily about experiencing a new and fresh power that infuses and energizes our spirit. Though the Holy Spirit is within every believer, the baptism in the Holy Spirit is an experience that typically takes place *after* ones conversion.

While I was completing my Doctor of Ministry degree, one of my colleagues gave me a book that examined the Greek aorist tense as used in the New Testament. The author of this book gave one example after another of how the predominate use of the Greek aorist tense indicates *completed* action. That is, when the action happened, it was completed. It was a done deal. After the author demonstrated that the aorist tense was completed action, he then used this premise to show how the Bible taught an experience called the baptism in the Holy Spirit that typically occurred after a person's conversion. He also said the use of the aorist tense validates the baptism in the Holy Spirit experience and that every believer should desire and seek it.

One evening when my colleague and I were driving home from a seminar, my friend tried to explain this concept of completed action and the baptism in the Spirit. As I listened to him, I was thinking, "Man, I thought this guy was theologically sound!" After our conversation that evening, I concluded that he had some strange ideas. The book he gave me went back on the shelf and stayed there for five years – until the time I came back from the conference. More on this later!

So, what is the baptism in the Holy Spirit? It is primarily an experience that infuses the believer with a new level of spiritual power to live the victorious Christian life. It is also an experience that builds faith, elevates expectation for believing in the supernatural, and allows you to press in to the supernatural realm in your daily walk with Christ. As I said earlier, Charles Finney, DL Moody, John Wesley, and RA Torrey all believed in and wrote about their experiences of being baptized in the Spirit. These were not men who would be viewed as Pentecostal or Charismatic theologically; yet they taught and believed in the baptism of the Holy Spirit. (I will provide a bibliography of a few of their books that will confirm their belief in this experience.)

THE BIBLICAL FOUNDATION

For the remainder of this chapter and the next, I am going to do my best to lay the biblical foundation to demonstrate from the Scriptures that the Bible *does* teach that the baptism in the Holy Spirit is a real, genuine, and a powerful experience and it is available to *every* believer. Let me stress that we cannot base our theology on an experience or the experiences of others, but we base our theology *only on what the Bible teaches*. There are many people who have a variety of experiences that they build their religious beliefs upon, and it is upon their experiences that they claim authority for their teachings and position or positions.

But experiences can be misleading. This is why God has given us through the inspiration of the Holy Spirit His infallible Word, the Bible. I love how evangelist Billy Graham always backed up his preaching with the phrase, "The Bible says." This is what I will seek to do in the next several pages.

Let's begin by asking, "Where is the first mention of this experience referred to as the baptism in the Holy Spirit"? It was the prophet John the Baptist who first spoke of it. Notice his words in Matthew's gospel:

> I baptize you with water for repentance, but he who is coming after me is mightier than I, whose sandals I am not worthy to carry. *He will baptize you with the Holy Spirit and fire.* His winnowing fork is in his hand, and he will clear his threshing floor and gather his wheat into the barn, but the chaff he will burn with unquenchable fire. (Matt. 3:11-12, emphasis mine)

Who is John the Baptist referring to when he says "*He* will baptize you with the Holy Spirit?" Notice he is referring to *Jesus,* and it is Jesus who is performing the baptizing in the Holy Spirit. It is critical to see that Jesus is doing the baptizing in the Holy Spirit. Jesus baptizes us in the Spirit, and it is the person of the *Holy Spirit* who places us into Christ's body (God's universal family with other believers). Notice how the Amplified Bible makes this clear:

> For by [means of the personal agency of] one [Holy] Spirit we were all, whether Jews or Greeks, slaves or free, baptized [and by baptism united together] into one body, and all made to drink of one [Holy] Spirit. (1 Cor. 12:13, *AMP*)

According to this verse, it is the person of the Holy Spirit, the third person of the Trinity, who places us *into* the body of Christ; but it is *Jesus* Himself who baptizes us *in the Holy Spirit.* These are *two* different baptisms. It is important to keep these two baptisms clear.

Some hold the position that the Bible teaches that there is only one baptism that Christians need to be concerned with. Ephesians 4:5 is the key verse to this position: "one Lord, one faith, one baptism." A look at the context will show that the author Paul is writing about water baptism. He is speaking about being immersed in water. This is the baptism that John the Baptist employed, which symbolized a sinner's genuine repentance.

After Jesus came, water baptism took on another meaning. It showed that the person being baptized was a follower of Jesus and was ready to follow His example. There is also a "baptism of suffering" that Jesus alludes to in Mark 10:38 and Luke 12:50. The writer of Hebrews speaks of a plurality of baptisms:

> Therefore, leaving the discussion of the elementary principles of Christ, let us go on to perfection, not laying again the foundation of repentance from dead works and of faith toward God, of the doctrine of *baptisms*, of laying on of hands, of resurrection of the dead, and of eternal judgment. (Heb. 6:1-2, *NKJV*, emphasis mine)

The Bible clearly expresses that there are various baptisms a believer can and should experience.

Earlier I stated that John the Baptist is the first one who referred to the phrase, "the baptism in the Holy Spirit." He said that Jesus will baptize believers *"with the Holy Spirit and fire"* (see Luke 3:16). What does John mean by "fire?" Fire is a symbol of the Holy Spirit and of God. God appeared to Moses in a burning bush. The Israelites were led through the desert by a pillar of fire. On the day of Pentecost, the Bible says that "divided tongues as of fire appeared to them and rested on each one of them," speaking of the believers gathered in an upper room (Acts 2:3).

Many theologians believe that fire speaks of a refining or cleansing process that takes places when a person is baptized in the Holy Spirit. Others point out that fire is symbolic of the power of God and that being "baptized in fire" is symbolic of an infusion of power.

Spiritual power is definitely the key benefit of the baptism in the Spirit. Regardless of one's interpretation, the fact remains that fire accompanies the baptism in the Holy Spirit.

Waiting for the Power

Before Jesus ascended to heaven, He gave explicit instructions to His disciples to go to Jerusalem and wait until they were *empowered* by the Holy Spirit. We know from other Scriptures that He was referring to receiving the baptism in the Holy Spirit. Notice Jesus' words of instruction:

> And said to them, "Thus it is written, that the Christ should suffer and on the third day rise from the dead, and that repentance and forgiveness of sins should be proclaimed in his name to all nations, beginning from Jerusalem. You are witnesses of these things. And behold, I am sending the promise of my Father upon you. But stay in the city until you are *clothed with power from on high*." (Luke 24:46-49, emphasis mine)

They were to wait in Jerusalem until this power came upon them. Notice the words, *the promise of my Father*. The "promise" refers to the baptism in the Holy Spirit. Notice the same phrase appears in the book of Acts, referring to what Luke had already written in his gospel:

> And while staying with them he ordered them not to depart from Jerusalem, but to wait for *the promise of the Father*, which, he said, "you heard from me; for John baptized with water, but you will be *baptized with the Holy Spirit* not many days from now." (Acts 1:4-5, emphasis mine)

Again, notice that Luke, the author of Acts, identifies "the promise" as "the baptism in the Holy Spirit." When the Holy Spirit fell upon the disciples and baptized them in the Holy Spirit, the apostle Peter referred to the "promise" during his explanation of Pentecost. "This Jesus God raised up, and of that we all are witnesses. Being therefore exalted at the right hand of God, and having received from the Father the *promise of the Holy Spirit*, he has poured out this that you yourselves are seeing and hearing" (Acts 2:32-33, emphasis mine).

Luke then explains this same *promise* of what the disciples had just experienced (the baptism in the Holy Spirit) is available to every believer of all generations.

> Now when they heard this they were cut to the heart, and said
> to Peter and the rest of the apostles, "Brothers, what shall we
> do?" And Peter said to them, "Repent and be baptized every
> one of you in the name of Jesus Christ for the forgiveness of
> your sins, and you will receive the gift of the Holy Spirit. For
> *the promise* is for you and for your children and for all who
> are far off, everyone whom the Lord our God calls to himself."
> (Acts 2:37-39, emphasis mine)

Peter says the promise, the baptism of the Holy Spirit, is available to all believers who have called upon Jesus and experienced salvation. The promise is for us, for our children, and for all people across the planet who know Jesus. Why? Because we need His power!

Using grammar to decipher meaning

Earlier in this chapter, I mentioned that when I was completing my Doctor of Ministry degree, that one of my colleagues gave me a book on the baptism of the Holy Spirit. I don't think the book is in print, but the title is *Christ's Paralyzed Church X-Rayed*. The author, T.M. McCrossan, was a Greek Professor at Manitoba University. The theme of his book is that when you examine (take an x-ray) the Scriptures in the Greek text, particularly the Greek aorist tense, you will find that the Bible clearly teaches that there is an experience called the baptism in the Holy Spirit that is available and subsequent to one's conversion.

The thesis of his book is that the reason why the church lacks power (is paralyzed), is because many within the evangelical community have not accepted this teaching. What is interesting is that even though McCrossan did not equate speaking in tongues with the baptism in the Holy Spirit, he did say that it is a definite experience taught in the Scriptures and is available to every believer.

In his book, he examines the Greek language (which is the language the New Testament was written in), the aorist tense of the Greek, and after a redundancy of examples, conclusively demonstrates that there is a baptism in the

Holy Spirit that can take place after one's conversion for those who will accept it by faith.

Though I don't have time to give multiple examples as McCrossan does, I will give the one key focus of his emphasis. In John 20:21-22, we read the following words of the apostle:

> Jesus said to them again, "Peace be with you. As the Father has sent me, even so I am sending you." And when he had said this, he breathed on them and said to them, "*Receive* the Holy Spirit." (emphasis mine)

Without becoming too technical, let me summarize McCrossan's conclusion. He says the word "receive" is in the aorist tense, which indicates *completed* action. In other words, it is action that is not to take place at some point in the future, but action that has already taken place—thus completed. The word in John 20:22, "receive" is an aorist imperative. And the imperative is a command.

McCrossan writes: "Now the imperative mood, and especially the Aorist imperative, always demands immediate obedience when a positive command is given by the one in supreme authority in the matter specified. This is one of the hard and fast rules of Greek grammar which we have never yet known to fail, and a law of which all these Bible teachers have overlooked."[1]

Okay, I can hear some of you asking, "Why is this Greek grammar such a big issue?" Let me once again quote McCrossan: "If we can prove conclusively—as we most assuredly can—that the Holy Spirit entered each disciple at John 20:22 (fifty days before Pentecost) then all that happened at Pentecost, (their baptism, Acts 1:5) must have been a second definite experience after their conversion."[2]

He is saying that when Jesus breathed on the disciples and gave the command, "Receive the Holy Spirit," the disciples must have received the Holy Spirit because when the aorist tense is used, especially with the imperative mood (command), it always implies *completed* action.

I know that is a mouth full, but thank the Lord for gifted professors who have a love for languages, especially the Hebrew and Greek languages of the Bible.

An interesting conclusion

But how do we know that McCrossan is correct in his conclusion? I had mentioned it wasn't until several years after my conversation with my colleague who gave me this book that I took it off my shelf and began to read it.

Even though I had an incredible and powerful experience at the conference with Cymbala, my theological training taught me that my experience had to be thoroughly biblical, that is, based on the Bible. I studied McCrossan's book and decided to call several seminary professors at three different Southern Baptist institutions.

I shared with them what I had read, and asked them if McCrossan was using sound reasoning of interpretation with the Greek when it came to this passage of Scripture. To my surprise, they all said yes. Though two of them did warn me, "You need to be careful of how you make application," one professor said to me, "I've never seen that before." He did however confirm that it was an aorist imperative, but wanted to call me back after he had time to examine it more closely.

A few days went by and I received his call. He said, "Yes, it is definitely an aorist imperative, and yes, that is a sound conclusion concerning what McCrossan had to say about the aorist tense." He then said this: "Coming out of Chapel today, I asked Dr. McCormick, who had written a book on the gifts of the Holy Spirit, if he had commented on this passage in his book; to which Dr. McCormick replied, 'No, that passage has always been problematic for Baptists.'"

I couldn't believe what I was hearing. This Greek professor told me he had never seen this passage before and that he was going to personally study it! I had confirmation concerning McCrossan's conclusion about the text and I was so excited. This gave biblical validity to my experience. I definitely didn't want to be guilty of what I refer to as *theological gymnastics*, the bending and twisting of Scriptures to fit into one's biblical interpretation. I wanted to be true to the Bible and I became convinced that Professor McCrossan's conclusion was indeed warranted!

In concurring with McCrossan's thesis, let me share a conviction that I have arrived at after many years of preaching, studying the Bible, and reading commentaries. As much as I appreciate scholarship in biblical studies, theologians, and linguistic scholars, I do *not* feel that the average Christian needs to have a doctorate level of expertise in order to draw sound, theological conclusions. All theologians approach the Scriptures with a certain theological bent.

This is not to say that theologians are not immensely valuable. I think we need to be careful in drawing the conclusion that we as individual believers lack the capacity to interpret the Bible correctly without knowing the original languages of the Bible or that it is necessary to read commentaries and perform word studies in order to understand the text correctly. We do have the Holy Spirit as *our Teacher* (see John 14:26; 16:13; 1 Cor. 2:10; 1 John 2:27)!

Is it all Greek?

The New Testament in particular was written in *Koine* Greek, the common language of the people. I don't think Christians in the first century were reading the gospels and letters written by the apostles and thinking, "This is an aorist tense," or "This is a present tense verb." They simply read the content of the books and epistles and drew theological conclusions based on what they were reading in their commonly used language.

This is not to say that the study of Hebrew (the language of the Old Testament) and Greek doesn't have its place in Bible study. It does. The background and the expanded meaning of a word in Greek are quite helpful in shedding additional light on the meaning of the text. But I believe that the basic understanding of the Scriptures, especially major themes and doctrines, are clearly understood by reading the text in our own language.

I do not think the Lord gave us the Scriptures in such a way that we are forced to depend on experts of the languages to understand the meaning of doctrinal truths. He gave us the Bible in common, everyday language so that the common person could read the text in his or her own language and draw his or her conclusions as to what God's Word is teaching. If we had to depend on scholars to interpret a text, then we would always be looking to scholars to explain the meaning of the Scriptures rather than us searching the Scriptures on our own.

That was the problem with Catholicism. Only the priests were able to read the Scriptures and interpret them for the people. And the interpretation they offered was in Latin! When people finally began reading copies of the Scriptures in their language, they realized that much of what the church was teaching was not based on the Bible, but on tradition. This resulted in the Protestant Reformation. People studied the Scriptures on their own and stopped relying on the priests to interpret the Bible for them.

Now, you may be asking, "Why is this important?" I believe it is vital that every believer is able to interpret the Bible individually with proper hermeneutics, or principles of interpretation, in order to find the meaning of the text.

For example, when looking at a verse or a passage of Scriptures, it is important to know the historical context and the cultural background of the recipients of the text. Were there any theological problems the writer addressed? Were there any cultural problems being addressed? What is the textual context of the writing? What is said before and after the verse being examined? These are the kinds of principles used and questions asked when interpreting the Scriptures.

PRINCIPLES OF INTERPRETATION

One principle of hermeneutics that I often use is called looking at the *natural* meaning of the text without bringing in my personal theological presuppositions. In other words, when you read a passage of Scripture, what is the immediate and *natural* interpretation that the text seems to convey and imply? Author Jack Deere in his book, *Surprised by the Power of the Spirit*, has a chapter entitled, "The Myth of Biblical Objectivity." The chapter's thesis is that when every person reads the Bible, he or she brings a different perspective that is shaped by various teachings from a church, a denomination, a pastor, parents, and so forth. That is, we approach the Bible with our minds bent or somewhat biased toward a particular interpretation about a subject related to the Scriptures.

For example, I was saved in a Baptist church and graduated from three Southern Baptist institutions. Both the church and the institutions taught and interpreted the baptism in the Holy Spirit exactly the same. Each institution taught and practiced that certain gifts of the Holy Spirit, such as tongues and prophecy had ceased to function.

People who believe that certain gifts of the Holy Spirit, especially supernatural gifts such as tongues, prophecy, and healing have ceased and are no longer available are called *cessationists*. Therefore, whenever I read the Scriptures about the baptism in the Holy Spirit, tongues, healing, and prophecy, I immediately read the text with certain theological presuppositions that I had concluded were correct, based on what I learned from my church and education.

My Baptist theology had become kind of a theological default that I entered when reading about these subjects. It was like reading the Scriptures through the lens of my Baptist theology instead of looking for the natural meaning of the Scripture. Most of the time, my theology was correct, and I am thankful for the education I received in Southern Baptist institutions. But just as any other person does when hearing any teaching, I listened to many teachings with a particular theological bent, which leaves some room for incorrect interpretation.

This doesn't mean that people lack integrity. It simply means that we are all human and we have the potential to make mistakes in the way we interpret the Bible.

How can we be sure?

Some may say in frustration, "How then can we be sure of anything and know what we believe is correct?" To this question I would point out that nearly all Bible believing evangelicals agree on the major and most significant doctrines of our Christian faith.

For instance, we agree that we are saved by faith and not by our good works. We believe in the deity of Christ, in the substitutionary atonement of Christ, in the literal Second Coming of Christ, in the literal reality of heaven and hell, in the resurrection of the dead, and in the Trinity. We have agreement in these main areas of doctrine. It is just in what I call *peripheral* teachings that we have some level of disagreement.

This is not to say that these differences are not important; but it is to say that there are some levels of disagreement on minor teachings that do not affect our beliefs about Jesus and salvation. These disagreements should not divide us or keep us from loving and respecting each other.

Fundamentally, I concur with Jack Deere's thesis that each person approaches the Scriptures with a certain lens. I am appealing to you to read the Scriptures and believe the text for what it says unless there is a good reason not to. What I mean by "a good reason" is that there is symbolism in the Scriptures where some phrases should be interpreted symbolically instead of literally. Consider the historical, cultural, and theological context and also look for consistency with other passages of Scripture. Taking these approaches will help reveal how the passage should be interpreted. This approach is what I refer to as holistic interpretation.

This is systematic theology: finding the common teachings that are systematically taught in the Bible. For instance, the Bible clearly teaches that we are saved by faith and not by works. If a verse seems to teach the opposite of the rest of Scriptures, we need to look at the verse in its context and determine what the writer is seeking to say. We can look at the rest of Scripture and see other verses that support the truth that we are saved by faith. The Bible will not contradict itself. A theological system or doctrine is not built on one verse or passage in the Bible. Our conclusion must be consistent with the rest of Scriptures.

Putting it into practice

Let's try looking at a passage and finding its *natural* meaning.

> Jesus said to them again, "Peace be with you. As the Father has sent me, even so I am sending you." And when he had said this, he breathed on them and said to them, "Receive the Holy Spirit." (John 20:21-22)

Without examining the Greek tenses of these words, what is the natural understanding of this passage?

It seems evident to me that what the author means to say is that when Jesus breathed on the disciples, they immediately received the Holy Spirit within them. There is no evidence that they received later, but once Jesus breathed, they received the Spirit simultaneously. Without going into the Greek text, I can *naturally* conclude that as Jesus breathed on them, they received the Holy Spirit.

Professor McCrossan points out that if the correct meaning of the words of the apostle John in this passage is that the disciples received the Holy Spirit within them the very moment Jesus breathed upon them, his question - and mine - is: what happened at Pentecost? Why did Jesus tell them to go to Jerusalem and "wait for the promise of the Father" (Acts 1:4)? If they received the Holy Spirit when Jesus breathed upon them, what is the difference in them receiving the Holy Spirit at that time when compared to their receiving the Spirit on the day of Pentecost? I am glad you asked!

I am convinced that when Jesus breathed on the disciples and said, "Receive the Holy Spirit," their spirits within them were made alive. Remember – every person has a body, a soul, and a spirit. Before we come to Christ our spirits are dead and indifferent to the things of God. When we come to Christ, our spirits are made alive.

When Jesus breathed on the disciples, the Holy Spirit came into them, regenerated their spirits that were spiritually dead, and they were born again (the New Birth process). From this point forward the Holy Spirit took up

84

residence in their bodies and lived within them. The same process occurs today when a person surrenders his or her life to Christ; but that's just the beginning.

There is more. There is an additional experience called the baptism in the Holy Spirit that empowers the believer. This baptism is what the disciples experienced on the day of Pentecost.

What was the purpose of Jesus breathing on them? Breath is symbolic of life. The Bible says in Genesis 2:7, "Then the LORD God formed the man of dust from the ground and breathed into his nostrils the breath of life, and the man became a living creature."

Just as God breathed life into Adam causing him to live physically, so Jesus breathed His Spirit into the disciples causing them to live spiritually and causing His Spirit to inhabit them. Notice how breathing is used to symbolize life being imparted in this passage:

Then he said to me, "Prophesy to the breath; prophesy, son of man, and say to the breath, Thus says the Lord GOD: Come from the four winds, O breath, and breathe on these slain, that they may live." (Ezek. 37:9)

When Jesus breathed on the disciples, the Holy Spirit entered them and their bodies became the "temples" of the Holy Spirit (see 1 Cor. 6:19-20). This is the experience of every person who gives his or her life to Christ and is born again by the Spirit of God.

Remember that in the Old Testament era, the Holy Spirit did not dwell in or permanently remain in believers, but came *upon* them for a brief season in order to accomplish a particular task or assignment. Once the task was finished, this special presence of the Spirit lifted. *But since Pentecost*, whenever a person becomes a Christian, the Holy Spirit not only regenerates that person's spirit, but He takes up permanent residence in the life of that believer.

When Jesus breathed upon His disciples, He was imparting His Spirit into them, which was a prelude of what all believers would come to experience *after* Pentecost. As miraculous as the impartation was for the disciples, that was just the beginning! Just a few days later, they would experience *the promise of the Father*, the baptism in the Holy Spirit with fire. This experience would give birth to the first Church and give these early disciples the power they needed to take the gospel to the ends of the planet!

Wouldn't you like to have this power? The next chapter will look more closely at how you can position yourself to receive the baptism in the Holy Spirit.

Discussion Questions

1. Does every Christian have the Holy Spirit? If so, based on what?

2. What is the baptism in the Holy Spirit?

3. Who can be baptized in the Holy Spirit? Do you have to be a Christian for a certain period of time before you can be baptized in the Holy Spirit?

4. Why can't we base our theology on an experience?

5. Where do the Scriptures first mention the baptism in the Holy Spirit?

6. Who is it that performs the baptism in the Holy Spirit?

7. When John the Baptist said Jesus will baptize us "with the Holy Spirit and fire," what is meant by *fire*?

8. Why did Jesus tell the disciples to wait in Jerusalem after He ascended? What were they to wait for?

9. What took place when Jesus breathed on the disciples *prior* to His ascension? Why is this significant?

10. When you became a Christian, how did you know that you were born again? How did the Holy Spirit bring confirmation of your conversion?

11. Why do some Christians fear the Holy Spirit?

12. How should we respond to others who disagree with the Baptism in the Holy Spirit?

Chapter Six

The Baptism in the Holy Spirit
Part 2

In the previous chapter, I established that every believer is baptized by the Spirit, that is, immersed into the body of Christ upon the person's new birth experience when he or she accepts Christ (see 1 Cor. 12:13). There are those within the evangelical community who teach that this is the *only* experience with the Holy Spirit that is available to believers. Some believe the Scriptures teach that when the Holy Spirit baptizes a person into the body of Christ upon conversion, the person has *all* of the Holy Spirit that can ever be received. There is no other experience available.

This is where a major theological divide exists among Pentecostal and Charismatic believers and non-Pentecostal, non-Charismatic believers. That the Holy Spirit is fully realized upon salvation was my theological position for 20 years as a pastor. It wasn't until my encounter with the Holy Spirit at the Fresh Wind Fresh Fire conference with Jim Cymbala that I had a theological shift.

In this chapter, I want to further explain and demonstrate from the Scriptures that there is an *additional* experience available called the baptism in the Holy Spirit that typically takes place *after* one's conversion. I do believe it is possible for this to happen simultaneously at one's conversion experience; but this is not the norm.

The focus of my emphasis in this chapter comes from the book of Acts. The book of Acts is a historical account of the early church written by Luke, the same writer of the gospel of Luke. I find it interesting that some cessationists write that one should not base doctrine on the book of Acts since it is primarily a historical book. Why would anyone make this statement? Acts was written under the inspiration of the Holy Spirit, just as the rest of the Bible was written.

I believe that the reason why anyone would state that doctrine cannot be derived from Acts is because Acts' teachings do not fit into a certain theological structure and by saying that doctrine cannot come from Acts, one is negating the present day activity of the Holy Spirit, specifically the baptism in the Holy Spirit. Would those who hold this position say that you shouldn't base doctrine on the gospels since those are *historical* accounts of the life of Jesus? Of course not! This is an example of people trying to fit their theological conclusions into the Scriptures instead of the Scriptures providing the conclusion.

BIBLICAL HOLY SPIRIT BAPTISM ENCOUNTERS

The book of Acts was written under the inspiration of the Holy Spirit. It not only records the historical events and life of the early church, but in my opinion, it is also the paradigm that we should follow until He comes!

The Day of Pentecost

The experience called the baptism in the Holy Spirit began on the day of Pentecost when the Spirit, who was promised by Jesus, descended upon the disciples. Remember, I have already demonstrated that the Holy Spirit came into them when Jesus breathed on them prior to His ascension (see John 20:22). It is on the day of Pentecost that the promise of the infilling of the Holy Spirit was fulfilled, bringing a special enduement of power in the lives of all who received the Spirit. Notice what Luke records:

> When the day of Pentecost arrived, they were all together in one place. And suddenly there came from heaven a sound like a mighty rushing wind, and it filled the entire house where they were sitting. And divided tongues as of fire appeared to them and rested on each one of them. And they were all filled with the Holy Spirit and began to speak in other tongues as the Spirit gave them utterance. (Acts 2:1-4)

When people heard and saw what was happening, they began questioning the meaning of what they were experiencing. The apostle Peter proceeds to explain to them that what they were witnessing was the fulfillment of the prophet Joel's prophecy (see Acts 2:16-21). After the people heard a further explanation of the Scriptures, they asked Peter what they should do in response to what they heard and experienced. Notice his instructions:

> And Peter said to them, "Repent and be baptized every one of you in the name of Jesus Christ for the forgiveness of your sins, and you will receive the *gift* of the Holy Spirit. For the *promise* is for you and for your children and for all who are far off, everyone whom the Lord our God calls to himself." (Acts 2:38-39, emphasis mine)

Peter first tells them to repent and follow the Lord in water baptism, and then to receive the "*gift* of the Holy Spirit." The "gift" is that which the Father had *promised*, the baptism in the Holy Spirit. Notice Luke's words: "And while staying with them he ordered them not to depart from Jerusalem, but to wait for the promise of the Father, which, he said, 'you heard from me; for John baptized with water, but you will be baptized with the Holy Spirit not many days from now.'" (Acts 1:4-5, emphasis mine)

Remember that the apostles had *already* received the Holy Spirit when Jesus breathed upon them prior to His ascension; but now they were experiencing the baptism in the Holy Spirit that was promised. As you read through the book of Acts, you will discover a consistent *pattern* begins to develop. That pattern is the baptism in the Holy Spirit taking place subsequent to (occurring after) people's conversion experience, except in one occurrence where it happens simultaneously. (We'll take a look at that occurrence below.)

The Samaritans' baptism in the Holy Spirit (Acts 8:4-17)

The next group of people to experience the baptism in the Holy Spirit was the Samaritans. Philip the evangelist went to Samaria and preached the gospel with words and supernatural signs and miracles. Many of the Samaritans believed the gospel, were saved, and followed the Lord in water baptism. When the church in Jerusalem heard that the Samaritans had received the message of Christ they sent Peter and John there to pray for them to receive the Holy Spirit. Notice the text:

> Now when the apostles at Jerusalem heard that Samaria had
> received the word of God, they sent to them Peter and John,
> who came down and prayed for them that they might receive
> the Holy Spirit, for he had not yet fallen on any of them, but
> they had only been baptized in the name of the Lord Jesus.
> Then they laid their hands on them and they received the Holy
> Spirit. (Acts 8:14-17)

Let me point out that they had *already* "received the word of God." They believed in the message of Jesus and were saved, born again Christians. Yet, they had not been baptized in the Holy Spirit. If everyone is automatically baptized in the Holy Spirit upon conversion, why did the apostles send Peter and John down to pray for them to receive the Holy Spirit? It is evident that they had not received this baptism in the Holy Spirit upon their conversion.

One argument against the baptism in the Holy Spirit is that God wanted to show the Jews that the gospel was not for the Jews only, but also for the Samaritans. Historically, Samaritans and Jews did not get along, and Jews could not conceive of Samaritans being favored with God's grace for salvation. So the Spirit was given after conversion so that Peter and John could *see the evidence*. That is, the Spirit was waiting for Peter and John to get there in order to prove that the Samaritans were genuinely saved.

But it seems to me that even if the Samaritans received the Spirit prior to Peter and John's arrival, which I believe happened upon their *conversion* (that is, their spirits being regenerated), the Spirit could have nonetheless fallen fresh upon them, providing verification of their salvation by speaking in tongues. I see no reason for any delay of the reception of the Holy Spirit except that these saved believers had not experienced the baptism in the Holy Spirit.

Peter and John purposefully went to them for special impartation of the baptism in the Holy Spirit through the ministry of laying on of hands. The key thing I want you to see in this text is that the Samaritans were *already* saved, but they had not received the baptism in the Holy Spirit until some time lapsed between their conversion and their Spirit baptism.

Let me point out that even though speaking in tongues is not mentioned in this passage, it is clear that there was some supernatural manifestation that took place when they were baptized in the Holy Spirit. In fact it was so dramatic, that when Simon, a local sorcerer, saw the power imparted by the laying on of hands by the apostles, he wanted to purchase the power.

But Peter rebuked him for thinking that God's anointing could be purchased with money (see Acts 8:18-23). The bottom line is that the Samaritans experienced the baptism in the Holy Spirit *after* they had received the Word following their conversion experience.

Saul's baptism in the Holy Spirit

Saul, whose name was changed to Paul following his conversion, was also baptized in the Holy Spirit *after* his conversion experience. If the baptism of the Holy Spirit was not an additional experience after conversion, Paul should have received *all* of the Holy Spirit when he was converted on the road to Damascus. Why the delay with Paul? He was a Jew.

Those who teach *against* the baptism in the Holy Spirit teach that since the day of Pentecost, when the Holy Spirit was poured out, that every person who receives Christ simultaneously receives all of the Holy Spirit they will ever experience. Remember that every person does receive the Spirit within him or her at conversion, but the baptism in the Holy Spirit experience is for additional power that typically happens post-conversion.

Paul was clearly saved on the road to Damascus where he encountered the risen Lord Jesus and was temporarily blinded (Acts 9:1-9). A disciple named Ananias was sent to Paul to not only heal his blindness, but also to impart the baptism in the Holy Spirit through the laying on of hands. Notice what takes place:

> So Ananias departed and entered the house. And laying his hands on him he said, 'Brother Saul, the Lord Jesus who appeared to you on the road by which you came has sent me so that you may regain your sight *and be filled with the Holy Spirit.*' And immediately something like scales fell from his eyes, and he regained his sight. Then he rose and was baptized; and taking food, he was strengthened. For some days he was with the disciples at Damascus. (Acts 9:17-19, emphasis mine)

I want you to notice several things. First, Ananias calls Saul, "Brother Saul." The word *brother* is a descriptive term of being part of the family of God, a fellow believer. Clearly, Ananias considered Saul as a believer, a follower of Christ.

Second, Ananias laid his hands on Saul. There are times that the Lord uses physical touch to impart the Spirit and spiritual gifts. On the day of Pentecost, the Spirit simply fell upon the disciples. No one laid hands on them. But with the Samaritans, and here with Paul, God chose to use the laying on of hands for the impartation of the Spirit.

Timothy also received an impartation of spiritual gifts through the laying on of hands. Notice what Paul reminds Timothy of in his second epistle to Timothy: "For this reason I remind you to fan into flame the gift of God, which is in you through the *laying on of my hands*" (2 Tim. 1:6, emphasis mine). Often, spiritual gifts and the baptism in the Holy Spirit are imparted to a person through the laying on of hands.

After Paul was baptized in the Spirit, he was baptized in water. But the key thing I want you to once again recognize is that Paul was *already* a believer, but he did not have the fullness of the Holy Spirit upon him. Like the apostles, the Samaritans, and now Paul, experienced the baptism in the Holy Spirit *after* their conversion. A pattern is developing.

Let me point out here that the text does not say that Paul spoke in tongues, but the text doesn't say he didn't. We *do* know from Paul's own words that he did speak in tongues. In writing to the Corinthians he wrote: "I thank God that I speak in tongues more than all of you" (1 Cor. 14:18). It doesn't say when he received his tongues, but it would seem plausible and consistent with the rest of Scripture that his speaking in tongues occurred when he was baptized in the Holy Spirit. More on this later, but it is clear from his writings that Paul spoke in tongues.

The Gentile believers' baptism in the Holy Spirit
The next description of the baptism in the Holy Spirit is with the Gentiles (non-Jews).

There was a man by the name of Cornelius who was a Roman centurion living in Caesarea, who was a God-fearing man. While he was praying he had a vision during which an angel instructed him to send for a man named Peter who was staying in Joppa. Cornelius sent three men to find Peter and bring him back to his house. The next day, prior to the three men arriving, Peter also had a vision in which the Spirit told him that he was to go with the three men.

When Peter arrived at Cornelius' house, Cornelius explained how an angel spoke to him and told him to send for Peter. Peter knew it was a God assignment, and his earlier vision confirmed to him that Gentiles could experience forgiveness and salvation through Christ. Peter proceeds to share the message of Christ, and while he is speaking, the Holy Spirit falls upon them, and Cornelius and his household are baptized in the Holy Spirit and begin to speak in tongues, just as the disciples were baptized and empowered to speak on the day of Pentecost.

> While Peter was still saying these things, the Holy Spirit fell
> on all who heard the word. And the believers from among the
> circumcised who had come with Peter were amazed, because
> the gift of the Holy Spirit was poured out even on the Gentiles.
> For they were hearing them speaking in tongues and extolling
> God. Then Peter declared, "Can anyone withhold water for
> baptizing these people, who have received the Holy Spirit
> just as we have?" And he commanded them to be baptized in
> the name of Jesus Christ. Then they asked him to remain for
> some days. (Acts 10:44-48)

What is unusual about this experience is that Cornelius and his household
were simultaneously converted and baptized in the Holy Spirit. They were
speaking in tongues and praising God. (This is why I said earlier that a person
could be saved and baptized in the Holy Spirit simultaneously, but this isn't
typical.) What is also interesting is that no one laid hands on them. The Spirit
just fell upon them.

In light of this occurrence, I think it is wise not to systematize how the
baptism in the Holy Spirit takes place. We don't want to box God in. He works
as He desires, not according to our plans. But we can still observe patterns from
Scripture of the sequence of events from salvation to baptism in the Holy Spirit.

The disciples of John the Baptist and their baptism in the Holy Spirit

Thus far, the *only* account of the baptism in the Holy Spirit happening simultaneously with salvation is when Peter was sent to the Gentile believers. In every other
case the baptism in the Holy Spirit took place sometime subsequent to conversion.

Let's look at another case. In this instance, Paul was traveling in Ephesus
and came upon a group of disciples connected to the ministry of John the
Baptist. When Paul encounters them, he asks, "Did you receive the Holy
Spirit when you believed" (Acts 19:2)? Why would Paul ask this question if
a person receives all the Holy Spirit he or she will ever receive upon conversion to Christ? The very question itself implies the potential of a *time lapse* of
receiving the Holy Spirit.

We know the Bible teaches that the Holy Spirit comes into people when they
are born again. Why does Paul ask this question if there is not something beyond
a person's conversion experience? The only plausible answer is that there is an
additional experience available after conversion called the baptism in the Holy
Spirit. Some try to explain away the implication of this question by saying that
this was Paul's way of diplomatically inquiring about their salvation. Instead of
directly asking them if they were believers, he chose to ask this question.

But when you read the letters of the apostle Paul, do you ever get the
slightest hint that he was afraid to speak plainly? No! I think Paul was genuinely seeking to ascertain if they had experienced the baptism in the Holy Spirit.
Let's look at the entire account:

> And it happened that while Apollos was at Corinth, Paul passed through the inland country and came to Ephesus. There he found some disciples. And he said to them, "Did you receive the Holy Spirit when you believed?" And they said, "No, we have not even heard that there is a Holy Spirit." And he said, "Into what then were you baptized?" They said, "Into John's baptism." And Paul said, "John baptized with the baptism of repentance, telling the people to believe in the one who was to come after him, that is, Jesus." On hearing this, they were baptized in the name of the Lord Jesus. And when Paul had laid his hands on them, the Holy Spirit came on them, and they began speaking in tongues and prophesying. There were about twelve men in all. (Acts 19:1-7)

There are several things I want to mention about these disciples of John the Baptist. First, they were totally unaware of the Holy Spirit and the message of Christ. They had not heard the gospel of Christ. When Paul discovers this, he explains the message of Jesus and the need to follow Him and be baptized. They gladly received the message of the gospel, became believers in Christ, and followed the Lord in water baptism. *At this point,* they have clearly become *believers*, indicated by the decision to follow Christ in water baptism. Yet, Paul proceeds to lay hands on them for the impartation of the baptism in the Holy Spirit.

Again, according to those who do not believe in the baptism in the Holy Spirit, laying on of hands should not have been necessary because since Pentecost, everyone receives the Holy Spirit immediately upon conversion. As I have indicated, I do agree that everyone receives the Holy Spirit instantaneously upon conversion, but not the experience of the baptism in the Holy Spirit. If infilling and Spirit baptism are simultaneous to conversion, what prompts Paul to lay his hands upon them to receive the Holy Spirit? This shouldn't be required. We must conclude that this is for the second experience we call the baptism in the Holy Spirit.

Notice that when Paul lays his hands upon them, "they began speaking in tongues and prophesying." The significant point is that they are being baptized in the Holy Spirit *after* their conversion experience.

To summarize, out of the five recorded occurrences of people experiencing the baptism in the Holy Spirit, four of them take place after their conversion experience, and one was simultaneous (Cornelius' experience).

- The Day of Pentecost (baptized in the Spirit after conversion)
- The Samaritans (baptized in the Spirit after conversion)
- The Apostle Paul (baptized in the Spirit after conversion)
- The Gentiles (baptized in the Spirit simultaneously with conversion)
- The Disciples of John the Baptist in Ephesus (baptized in the Spirit after conversion)

This is the *biblical pattern* of the early church and should be the expectation of the church in the twenty-first century. To deviate from this sequence places the burden of proof on the person who does not embrace the baptism of the Holy Spirit as being subsequent to conversion rather than the person who does. I do respect the opinions of those within the evangelical community who differ with me, and we will just have to agree to disagree. I do not feel we should allow our differences on when the Holy Spirit baptizes people to divide us or create arguments.

We are brothers and sisters in Christ. We should honor one another's opinions and focus on winning people for the kingdom!

THE EVIDENCE OF THE BAPTISM IN THE HOLY SPIRIT

Among Spirit-filled, Pentecostal/Charismatic believers, there is another area where we find differences of opinions. From my experience and studies of Pentecostal and Charismatic fellowships, the general consensus seems to be that *speaking in tongues* is the evidence that a person has been baptized in the Holy Spirit. This is one of the Fundamental Truths of the Assemblies of God, and the opinion of most who identify themselves as Pentecostal, Charismatic, Spirit-filled believers.

The following statement is number eight of the Assemblies of God Fundamental Truths: "WE BELIEVE. . . The Initial Physical Evidence of the Baptism in the Holy Spirit is 'Speaking in Tongues,' as experienced on the Day of Pentecost and referenced throughout Acts and the Epistles."[1]

Does the Bible teach that speaking in tongues is the physical evidence of the baptism in the Holy Spirit? The key word in their statement is *evidence*. Is there a pattern in the Scriptures? Yes, there is in fact a biblical pattern, and that pattern is speaking in tongues. In the five occurrences of people being baptized in the Holy Spirit, the physical manifestations of their experience is referred to in only three of the experiences. What the Assemblies of God and other Pentecostal fellowships would point out is that in *every case* in which manifestations are mentioned, speaking in tongues is *always* mentioned as a manifestation of the baptism in the Holy Spirit.

In the two experiences where speaking in tongues is not mentioned, there was still something remarkable, powerful, and supernatural, otherwise Simon would not have offered Peter money to buy this power (see Acts 8:18-19). What Simon saw is presumed to be speaking in tongues. The other instance where *no* manifestation is mentioned is when the apostle Paul received the baptism in the Holy Spirit when Ananias laid hands on him. Though the Bible does not mention that Paul spoke in tongues, we do know from his letter to the Corinthians that he did speak in tongues (see 1 Corinthians 14). It would not be inconsistent with the biblical pattern to conclude that Paul spoke in tongues when he was baptized in the Spirit.

Let me affirm that there is ample biblical evidence to conclude that when a person is baptized in the Holy Spirit, the normative evidence is speaking in tongues. What about the possibility of other physical manifestations of being baptized in the Holy Spirit? As I said in the above paragraph, the key word in reading the statement of the Assemblies of God is *evidence*. I have witnessed people falling to the floor under the power of the Holy Spirit, trembling and shaking under the power of the Holy Spirit, experiencing laughter under the power and presence of the Holy Spirit, and other physical manifestations.

These and other physical manifestations have taken place during times of spiritual awakenings and revivals. But from a *biblical* perspective, can we say that these and other manifestations are *evidences* of being baptized in the Holy Spirit? Biblically, the answer is no. The only physical manifestations mentioned in the Bible accompanying the baptism in the Holy Spirit are speaking in tongues and prophesying, and prophesying and tongues were part of the same experience (see Acts 19:6).

"Initial evidence"

This brings me to the phrase *initial evidence*. Does the manifestation of tongues have to be the *first* manifestation that people experience when they are baptized in the Holy Spirit? In other words, could people have a physical manifestation other than speaking in tongues *first* during their baptism in the Holy Spirit and then later begin speaking in tongues?

I don't want to be so systematized in my theology that I box in God, and I don't feel it is necessary to be dogmatic on the issue. But I do want to say that I believe, from a biblical perspective, that speaking in tongues is the first (initial) affirmative *evidence* of the baptism in the Holy Spirit. I believe this because speaking in tongues is the *only* sign mentioned each and every time the Scriptures record a baptism in the Holy Spirit. Again, the only *biblical evidence* I can point to that affirms a person has been baptized in the Holy Spirit is speaking in tongues. I will leave the process and timing up to the Spirit!

Personally, I feel that I *was* baptized in the Holy Spirit when I was prayed for at the Fresh Wind and Fresh Fire conference, though I did not begin praying in tongues until a few months later. When I came home from the conference, I had a new passion for God, His Word, and for worship to an extent that I had never experienced before—so something *definitely* happened! I *do* believe that speaking in tongues can be part of the package you receive when you are baptized with the Holy Spirit. I also believe that if someone would have encouraged me to speak out in faith, perhaps tongues would have flowed from my lips! I am not so much concerned with the process or timing, but I would encourage you to *expect* to speak in tongues and exercise faith for tongues when you are praying for the baptism in the Holy Spirit because it is *scriptural*.

WHY SEEK THE BAPTISM IN THE HOLY SPIRIT?

Simply put—you need it! If the early disciples needed the baptism in the Holy Spirit, why would we want anything less? I can assure you that we need His fullness just as much today in the twenty-first century as they did in the first century. Even though the early church faced different challenges from our challenges, we still face significant difficulties and we too have flesh and blood and a sin nature. With modern technology, temptation has moved to another level.

There are numerous temptations we face today that the early believers could have never imagined. Satan is real, demons are real, and if we are to combat the demonic forces that are active in this world, we need a power source beyond ourselves. We live in a dark and evil day. What was once considered wrong is now considered right, and what was once considered right is now considered wrong.

As Christians, we are constantly being opposed or questioned because of our faith, and in the name of tolerance, every type of deviant behavior is promoted and accommodated. If we as believers disagree with immorality, we are labeled as bigots. We are in a battle, and if we expect to be victorious, we must appropriate the power of the Holy Spirit. The baptism in the Holy Spirit is how we appropriate His power and anointing that enables us to live wise, discerning, and productive lives!

In many churches today the ministry of the Holy Spirit has been neglected, and in many cases abandoned. Tragically, we are reaping the consequences of trying to build churches without the Spirit's presence and power in our midst. We have become dead, lifeless, powerless, and have forgotten that we are engaged in a spiritual battle that can be won only through the Spirit and not by the flesh. For too long we have sought to win battles through fleshly, clever, and innovative methods. I am not opposed to innovation, new ideas, or modern technology, but those are simply tools for ministry.

The late Dr. A.W. Tozer, author and pastor, said, "If the Holy Spirit was withdrawn from the church today, 95 percent of what we do would go on and no one would know the difference. If the Holy Spirit had been withdrawn from the New Testament church, 95 percent of what they did would stop, and everybody would know the difference."[2]

Our power source is and always will be the Holy Spirit. Unfortunately, the church today is wounded, battle scarred, and in a state of spiritual paralysis. It is time for the church at large to recognize that "it is not by might, not by power, but by my Spirit says the Lord" that we live a victorious life (Zech. 4:6). The wonderful and glorious truth is that the Lord Jesus promised us that He would send us His Spirit and that we would not be left to fight the battles alone. He will empower, enable, and anoint us to win that battle as we depend on Him!

HOW TO RECEIVE THE BAPTISM IN THE HOLY SPIRIT

Since my experience of being baptized in the Holy Spirit, I have talked with many people about their experience and exactly how it happened with them. One thing I have learned is that even though there are similarities in experiences, we cannot create a formula and say "this is how it happens." We can't say "If you follow steps one, two, and three and push the presto button, you will be suddenly overcome with the power and anointing of the Spirit." We are all in different places in our spiritual journey, and God deals with us on an individual basis. We also have different levels of faith, belief systems, and faith experiences and we carry various forms of baggage from our past. I am simply saying that we cannot come up with a "one formula fits all" approach.

Yet I do think there are some basic steps along the way that assist in preparation for receiving the baptism in the Holy Spirit. I am not saying that each of these items has to be present before you are baptized in the Holy Spirit, but I do believe the Spirit uses them. Here are a few suggestions.

- **Desire**

   There first must be a deep and passionate desire to experience more of the presence and power of God. I am referring to a hunger and thirst to know God at a more intimate level, to experience Him, and move deeper in your relationship with Him.

   This means there must be *dissatisfaction* with where you are in your spiritual journey. Many people are quite content with knowing they are going to experience eternal life in heaven when they die. They desire no more. We need to have an all-consuming yearning and intense desire to experience more of His presence and power in our lives!

- **Faith**

   We not only begin the Christian life *by faith*, but we advance and move to deeper levels of intimacy with God by *exercising our faith*. Just because we desire to experience more of God's presence and power doesn't mean we have the faith to accomplish it. But the good news is that every person can acquire more faith.

   Faith is available to every person who is willing to read and study His Word and apply its principles. The apostle Paul writing to the Romans said, "So faith comes from hearing, and hearing through the word of Christ" (Rom. 10:17). You don't have to be in full-time ministry to have mountain-moving faith. You just have to feed upon and saturate your mind with the Word of God and your faith will increase, grow, and develop.

It is important for you to come to the place that you not only believe that the experience referred to as the baptism in the Holy Spirit is biblically based, but also that it is available for you.

God desires to empower you and develop a more intimate relationship with you. He doesn't want you to endure the Christian life but to enjoy the Christian life. Notice where Paul says our source of joy is derived from: "For the kingdom of God is not a matter of eating and drinking but of righteousness and peace and joy in the Holy Spirit" (Rom. 14:17). Jesus has come not only to give you eternal life, but also an abundant life here and now (see John 10:10).

The Bible is filled with examples of God honoring those who are willing to exercise their faith. In fact, we must exercise our faith to please God. In the great faith chapter of the Bible, the writer of Hebrews says, "And without faith it is impossible to please him, for whoever would draw near to God must believe that he exists and that he rewards those who seek him" (Heb. 11:6). So start believing that the baptism in the Holy Spirit is real, powerful, and available to you!

- **Seeking**

There is something God loves and enjoys when we choose to seek Him out. He loves for us to seek Him, pursue Him, yearn for Him, and to do so with passion. I think one of the reasons why the Lord doesn't baptize everyone instantly is because He enjoys being sought after. When we are seeking Him, we spend more time in His presence, in worship, in His Word, and in prayer.

He also uses this time of seeking Him to take us to deeper levels and to teach us spiritual principles. He leads us to see if there is anything within our lives that is hindering or obstructing the flow of the Spirit. There could be something from our past that we have never dealt with. We may have unforgiveness or bitterness that we need to repent of. There may be some habitual sin that needs to be forsaken.

There are many things that God reveals to us about ourselves when we begin to seek Him. The key is that He wants and desires that we constantly seek Him through His Word, worship, and prayer. Notice the following Scriptures.

You have said, "Seek my face." My heart says to you, "Your face, LORD, do I seek." (Ps. 27:8)

Seek the LORD and his strength; seek his presence continually! (Ps. 105:4)

The LORD looks down from heaven on the children of man, to see if there are any who understand, who seek after God. (Ps. 14:2)

You will seek me and find me, when you seek me with all your heart. (Jer. 29:13)

One thing have I asked of the LORD, that will I seek after: that I may dwell in the house of the LORD all the days of my life, to gaze upon the beauty of the LORD and to inquire in his temple. (Ps. 27:4)

O God, you are my God; earnestly I seek you; my soul thirsts for you; my flesh faints for you, as in a dry and weary land where there is no water. (Ps. 63:1)

The young lions suffer want and hunger; but those who seek the LORD lack no good thing. (Ps. 34:10)

But may all who seek you rejoice and be glad in you; may those who love your salvation say continually, "Great is the LORD!" (Ps. 40:16)

Blessed are those who keep his testimonies, who seek him with their whole heart. (Ps. 119:2)

I love those who love me, and those who seek me diligently find me. (Prov. 8:17)

Clearly, the Lord loves and desires for us to pursue Him with all our hearts! And when we do, we not only find Him, but we also receive His rewards of going to deeper and deeper levels of intimacy in which rivers of living water constantly spring forth from the river of the Spirit within us!

- **Worship**
For me personally, this was a critical step of experiencing the fullness of the Holy Spirit. When I received my prayer language, I was on my knees in worship to the Lord. I had just completed reading Pastor Jack Hayford's book, *The Beauty of Spiritual Language* (which I highly recommend) and was on my second day of fasting.

I had been worshiping the Lord for about 25 minutes and began speaking out in repeated phrases of hallelujahs, with the expectation that the Spirit would take over my tongue and begin praying through me. Hayford wrote that some people just start speaking in tongues, but he suggested speaking forth words of praise in faith that the Spirit would take over my verbal praise and begin praising and praying through me. I spoke and He took over!

God deserves and expects our worship. In reference to seeking Him, worship is one of the ways that especially pleases Him. Jesus speaking to the woman at the well said, "But the hour is coming, and is now here, when the true worshipers will worship the Father in spirit and truth, for the Father is seeking such people to worship him.

God is spirit, and those who worship him must worship in spirit and truth" (John 4:23-24). Focus on that word *seeking*. He is seeking worshippers, and as we worship Him, His Spirit comes down!

- **Fasting**

   I mentioned I was on my second day of fasting when I received my prayer and praise language. People fast for many reasons, but from what I understand in the Scriptures, we are to fast especially when we need a breakthrough in our lives. We may be seeking a spiritual breakthrough or wisdom in making an important decision or the answer to a significant prayer need.

   The late Bill Bright, founder of Campus Crusade for Christ, said, "Fasting is like a spiritual atomic bomb."[3] He means that fasting releases supernatural power. Fasting unleashes the power of the Spirit in your life. Jesus knew this and so He regularly practiced the discipline of fasting. It is interesting that when the Spirit of God led Him into the wilderness to experience His temptation, He fasted *forty* days. "Then Jesus was led up by the Spirit into the wilderness to be tempted by the devil. And after *fasting* forty days and forty nights, he was hungry" (Matt. 4:1-2, emphasis mine).

   The book of Esther tells us that the Jewish nation was facing a crisis and the Lord had destined a woman by the name of Esther to be a change agent in history. But Esther clearly knew her limitations—and she knew that she going to need divine favor and God's intervention to accomplish her task. Notice what she did to seek the favor and intervention of God:

> Then Esther told them to reply to Mordecai, "Go, gather all the Jews to be found in Susa, and hold a fast on my behalf, and do not eat or drink for three days, night or day. I and my young women will also fast as you do. Then I will go to the king, though it is against the law, and if I perish, I perish. Mordecai then went away and did everything as Esther had ordered him. (Esth. 4:15-17)

Fasting is a discipline that God honors when we are seeking Him and when we need a breakthrough in our lives. Notice that the early disciples practiced fasting.

> While they were worshiping the Lord and *fasting*, the Holy
> Spirit said, "Set apart for me Barnabas and Saul for the work
> to which I have called them." Then after fasting and praying
> they laid their hands on them and sent them off. (Acts 13:2-3,
> emphasis mine)

> And when they had appointed elders for them in every church,
> with prayer and *fasting* they committed them to the Lord in
> whom they had believed. (Acts 14:23, emphasis mine)

In light of these Scriptures, I would definitely recommend combining
fasting with prayer in seeking the baptism in the Holy Spirit. God honors
our fasting because He sees we are willing to deny ourselves something
physical in order to gain something spiritual. Fasting is also a reflection that
we are desperate enough to press in and not settle for spiritual mediocrity.
He blesses us when we fast!

- **Prayer**
  I often say that prayer is our most powerful resource, but tragically one
  of the most neglected. If Jesus, the Son of the living God prayed, why
  do we think that we as mere humans do not need to pray? Prayer is definitely a major key in taking us to the next level in our spiritual journey.
  Prayer is inextricably connected to growing, developing, and advancing
  our faith; and it is the key to releasing the power of the Holy Spirit. Notice
  the words of Jesus:

> And I tell you, ask, and it will be given to you; seek, and you
> will find; knock, and it will be opened to you. For everyone
> who asks receives, and the one who seeks finds, and to the one
> who knocks it will be opened. What father among you, if his
> son asks for a fish, will instead of a fish give him a serpent;
> or if he asks for an egg, will give him a scorpion? If you then,
> who are evil, know how to give good gifts to your children,
> how much more will the heavenly Father give *the Holy Spirit*
> to those who ask him! (Luke 11:9-13, emphasis mine).

The fullness of the Holy Spirit is available to all who are willing to
seek Him in prayer and are bold when they ask! I am convinced the Lord
wants to give us the desires of our hearts, especially when they are things
that will deepen and advance our personal relationship with Him. So pursue
Him, ask Him, and He will reward and give you the desires of your heart!

Conclusion

As I close this chapter, let me encourage you not to give up if you do not receive the baptism in the Holy Spirit immediately after the first time you ask. Most people I talk with experience the baptism in the Holy Spirit after a season of pressing in. As I said earlier, I think one of the reasons for the delay is that God simply loves and enjoys our presence when we are seeking, praying, worshiping, and spending time with Him. He is not in a hurry. I also think there are times in which God is doing a refining work deep within us, or that there is a need to expose an area of resistance within our lives. His ways are not our ways and His timing is not ours. But I can assure you, if you will press in and not give up, you will be gloriously rewarded with the fullness of the Holy Spirit!

Discussion Questions

1. What is the significance of the day of Pentecost?

2. What was the response of the people when the disciples were baptized in the Holy Spirit?

3. What was the apostle Peter's explanation of what the people were witnessing?

4. After the disciples, which people group next experienced the baptism in the Holy Spirit?

5. How do we know they were already believers when Peter and John came to them?

6. Even though the Scriptures do not say that the Samaritans spoke in tongues, what does the text say that would cause some people to draw that conclusion?

7. When was Saul the apostle Paul converted? What is the significance of his visit from Ananias? How do we know that he was already a believer when Ananias came to him?

8. When Peter was led by the Holy Spirit to the house of Cornelius, what took place when they were baptized in the Holy Spirit?

9. When the apostle Paul came across some of John the Baptist's disciples, what is the significance of Paul's question, "Did you receive the Holy Spirit when you believed?"

10. What is meant by the phrase, "the initial physical evidence of the baptism in the Holy Spirit?" Why would some conclude that speaking in tongues is the biblical evidence that a person has been baptized in the Holy Spirit?

11. Why should a Christian seek the baptism in the Holy Spirit?

12. What are some practical steps that a believer can take in pursuing the baptism in the Holy Spirit?

13. If you have been baptized in the Holy Spirit, what did you personally experience that confirmed that you had received Spirit baptism?

14. What difference has Spirit baptism made in your spiritual journey with Christ?

Chapter Seven

The Church:
The Body of Christ

I love the church! My entire adult life has been devoted to serving the church. As a senior pastor, this has been my life calling. The first church I served as senior pastor was a small country church in Dadeville, Missouri, while completing my bachelor's in religious studies. This small town had a population of 219, and we averaged about 70 people in our congregation. The church viewed their ministry as a place to provide opportunities for students to fulfill their calling and to gain ministerial experience while completing their education.

I thoroughly enjoyed serving this church and I have fond memories of my first pastorate. I was the ripe age of 23! Now at age 56, I have been serving as a pastor for 33 years and I still love and appreciate the church of the Lord Jesus. At times, I still feel quite inadequate and undeserving. Yet, I have never doubted my calling and I am thankful for His graciousness for appointing me to serve as one of His undershepherds.

In the New Testament, there are several metaphors that are used to describe the church. Some of the most well know metaphors are *the bride of Christ, the body of Christ, a building, God's house, living stones and holy priesthood, pillar and the bulwark of truth*, and *a flock* (see 1 Cor. 3:9; 2 Cor. 11:2; Eph. 5:32; 1 Tim. 3:15; Heb. 3:3,6; 1 Pet. 2:4-8). The Church is *God's* Church. He purchased it. It is special, unique, precious, significant, holy, and dearly loved and prized by Jesus who bought it with His own blood. Paul admonishes the Ephesians' elders with these words: "Pay careful attention to yourselves and to all the flock, in which the Holy Spirit has made you overseers, to care for the church of God, which he obtained with his own blood" (Acts 20:28). We need to love His church, protect His church, serve His church, honor His church, and advance His church.

What comes to mind?

When you mention the word "church," you will discover that people have various ideas, opinions, and feelings about what a church is. Because churches are made of people, people have been hurt and offended at a church and consequently, have left congregations disillusioned. Churches occasionally experience conflict that has caused some people to give up attending a church. Even though it is wrong and it grieves the Holy Spirit when people leave the church, it is understandable why some people have given up on being part of the church.

People can hurt and offend others. Throughout our years of ministry, Pam and I have both been hurt, disappointed, and even disillusioned with people. But let me hasten to say that this has not been the norm of our ministry, but rather the exception. Instead of giving up on the church, we are to practice forgiveness, extend grace, and learn to worship and minister together as a family. Even in loving and caring families, there are disagreements, harsh words, and inappropriate behavior. If this happens in a family unit that cares for and loves one other, why would we think that a church, with multiple members and families, should be any different?

There are those who refuse to go to church because they say churches are filled with hypocrites. After 33 years of serving as a pastor and currently serving my seventh church, I can assure you that churches are *not* filled with hypocrites. This is not to say that there may be a small number of people in any congregation that are living hypocritical lives, but for the most part, the congregations the Lord has allowed me to serve are sincere, loving, and compassionate people doing their best to be faithful to the Lord in all that they do. This doesn't mean that they are perfect or without their short comings.

None of us will reach perfection until we experience our complete transformation in Christ. As a result, there will be times that a person's behavior, attitudes, and actions are less than perfect and prove to be quite disappointing. But generally, Bible-believing churches are filled with godly, faithful, sincere, compassionate, giving, and loving people who are seeking to fulfill the mission of Christ and extend His kingdom to the ends of the world!

WHAT IS THE CHURCH?

Let me begin by saying what the church is *not*. It is not a building. I know we often point to a church structure and say, "That's my church." Even though most of us know what people mean when they say "That's my church," the correct wording would be, "That's where my church meets for worship." The church is not made of brick and mortar, but people. *People* comprise the church and a building is simply the place where a particular local fellowship of believers meets for worship and ministry. Jesus didn't die for a building but for people!

The church is not a denomination. Denominations are organizations that are made of many churches that hold to a set of doctrinal truths that are distinctive. These fellowships of churches have selected to organize and structure themselves around those distinctives in ways they feel can more effectively advance the kingdom. They establish goals and priorities to help them accomplish their mission. Though there are many wonderful denominations advancing the cause of Christ, a denomination is *not* synonymous with a church.

The Greek word for *church* is ἐκκλησία (ekklesia), which literally means an *assembly*. It is a called out assembly of people who have come together for a specific purpose. The Enhanced Strong's Lexicon defines *ekklesia* as "a gathering of citizens called out from their homes into some public place, an assembly."[1] In the New Testament, the church represents those who have been called out by the Holy Spirit; who have entered a personal relationship with Jesus Christ through repentance and faith; and who meet together for worship, prayer, spiritual development, and to spread the message of Christ regionally and globally to advance His kingdom.

The word *church* in the New Testament is used in two ways. First, it refers to the universal Church, that is, the extended body of Christ throughout the world. The Church represents literally thousands of congregations. Every born again believer is part of the Church universal. Second, "church" refers to local congregations of believers, that gather in specific locations for the purpose of worship, teaching, fellowship, edification, and sharing the good news of the gospel.

An example of the word *church* used in a universal sense can be found in Jesus' words to Peter when Peter professed Jesus to be the Christ, the Son of the living God:

> And I tell you, you are Peter, and on this rock I will build *my church*, and the gates of hell shall not prevail against it. (Matt. 16:18, emphasis mine)

The *church* in this passage refers to all the redeemed throughout all the ages up until Christ returns. It refers to all believers who have been placed in the universal family of God because of their faith in Him. It doesn't refer to a particular religious institution or denomination, but to the people of God living in all ages.

Another example of *church* being used in a universal way is found in Paul's letter to the Ephesians:

> Husbands, love your wives, as Christ loved *the church* and gave himself up for her, that he might sanctify her, having cleansed her by the washing of water with the word, so that he might present the church to himself in splendor, without spot or wrinkle or any such thing, that she might be holy and without blemish. (Eph. 5:25-27, emphasis mine)

Another example is Paul writing to Timothy:

> If I delay, you may know how one ought to behave in the household of God, which is *the church* of the living God, a pillar and buttress of the truth. (1 Tim. 3:15, emphasis mine)

Again, Paul is not speaking of a particular congregation, but the church universal, all congregations of Christ. The universal church represents every person who has accepted Christ as personal Lord and Savior. Every person who has been spiritually birthed into the kingdom belongs to the universal church.

But then there are local churches, individual congregations, made of individual believers, who have joined together to do the work of the kingdom. As you read the New Testament, you will discover that there are multiple local congregations in various cities and regions carrying forth the mission of Christ.

For instance, Paul writes "To the church of God that is in Corinth" (1 Cor. 1:2), "To the church of the Thessalonians" (1 Thess. 1:1). The apostle John writing the revelation he received from Christ (the Book of Revelation) refers to seven specific congregations in seven specific cities (see Rev. 2:1,8,12,18; 3:1,7,14). Each of these congregations had its own spiritual leaders who gave oversight to their respective congregations. They met on a regular basis with the mission of impacting their region with the message of the gospel.

THE PURPOSE OF THE CHURCH

Why did Christ establish the church? Why do local congregations exist? What is the mission of the thousands of congregations throughout the planet? There are several reasons why local churches are not only necessary, but also why every born again believer should be part of a local congregation.

Purpose #1: To advance the message of the gospel and His kingdom

Jesus commands His followers to share and spread the message of the good news of Christ. Prior to His ascension, Jesus gave the following command to His disciples:

> And Jesus came and said to them, "All authority in heaven
> and on earth has been given to me. Go therefore and make
> disciples of all nations, baptizing them in the name of the
> Father and of the Son and of the Holy Spirit, teaching them
> to observe all that I have commanded you. And behold, I am
> with you always, to the end of the age." (Matt. 28:18-20)

We are commissioned by Christ to make disciples, that is, lead people to Christ and teach them what it means to be a follower of Christ, and helping them to practice their faith until the end of the age. Again, this is not a suggestion but a command from the Lord Jesus. If we profess to be followers of Christ, there is no option of disobeying this command. It is our heavenly assignment from our Commander and Chief. Luke in the book of Acts quotes Jesus' words to the disciples: "But you will receive power when the Holy Spirit has come upon you, and you will be my witnesses in Jerusalem and in all Judea and Samaria, and to the end of the earth (Acts 1:8).

A witness is one who gives an account of the truth. As believers and followers of Christ, we have been given the task of sharing the good news of the gospel, His message, His teaching, and the teachings of the apostles as inspired by the Holy Spirit. We are to begin in our own vicinity and region and then branch out to the very ends of the earth. This is an impossible task to accomplish as individual believers. But when we work together with other believers in a local congregation, we will see amazing things begin to take place!

Because we have been given a global mandate, it is imperative that each local congregation establishes a mission strategy to reach the world. If a local congregation is part of a denomination, they should financially support the missional arm of the denomination. If a church is independent and non-denominational, then the church should adopt and send individual missionaries to reach the nations with the gospel.

Missions should be a priority of *every* body of believers. To fulfill the commission given to us by the Lord, we cannot take the missions mandate as optional. We must develop and be committed to a global mission strategy of reaching and impacting the nations of the world with the message of the kingdom!

Purpose #2: Establish, teach, and preserve biblical truth

A second key focus of a local congregation is to ensure that the truth of the gospel and the teachings of Christ are continually taught, preserved, and handed down to succeeding generations. A local body of believers not only has the responsibility to ensure sound, biblical teaching, but also ensure that heretical teachings and practices are exposed and rejected.

This is one reason why I have written this material. As shepherds of a local congregation, the leaders of our congregation and I have the responsibility to guard and protect our flock from doctrinal and theological error. Satan would love to distort the truth of the gospel. This is one of his specialties. A congregation must stand up for biblical truth and guard it.

One of the Scriptures I referenced above was Paul's letter to Timothy where he said: "If I delay, you may know how one ought to behave in the household of God, which is the church of the living God, *a pillar and buttress of the truth*" (1 Tim. 3:15, emphasis mine).

Paul refers to the church as a "pillar and buttress of the truth." The church has the responsibility to teach, strengthen, and defend the truth of the Scriptures. When we join as believers in Christ under the leadership of the Holy Spirit, one of our functions is to become protectors of the truth, ensuring that sound doctrine and teaching is proclaimed. We need to realize that there are those who will seek to come into the church in an effort to deceive people and teach false doctrine.

To Timothy, the apostle Paul wrote:

> I charge you in the presence of God and of Christ Jesus, who
> is to judge the living and the dead, and by his appearing and

108

his kingdom: preach the word; be ready in season and out of season; reprove, rebuke, and exhort, with complete patience and teaching. For the time is coming when people will not endure sound teaching, but having itching ears they will accumulate for themselves teachers to suit their own passions, and will turn away from listening to the truth and wander off into myths. (2 Tim. 4:1-4)

The apostle Paul writing to the leadership of the churches in Ephesus wrote these moving words:

Pay careful attention to yourselves and to all the flock, in which the Holy Spirit has made you overseers, to care for the church of God, which he obtained with his own blood. I know that after my departure fierce wolves will come in among you, not sparing the flock; and from among your own selves will arise men speaking twisted things, to draw away the disciples after them. Therefore be alert, remembering that for three years I did not cease night or day to admonish every one with tears. (Acts 20:28-31)

Paul was so concerned with the potential of deception by false leaders that he was brought to tears. It is critical for the leadership of a church to be theologically grounded and have the discernment and boldness to see and expose false teachings. A believer who is not part of a local body is in serious risk of being misled. This is especially true with the various forms of media and the Internet that make it easy for people to encounter false teachings. A local church is designed for personal protection and accountability.

The instruction and teaching environment in the local church is not only to ensure sound teaching, but also to be a place that provides opportunity for continued spiritual growth and development in our walk with Christ. I have three degrees in theological studies and I am amazed at how much *more* there is to learn from the Scriptures in developing my walk with Christ.

Coming together with other believers in a class or small group study will enrich your knowledge and understanding of the Scriptures and provide the needed wisdom of applying biblical principle in your daily life. The Scriptures give us instruction and direction in life to equip us to be effective in our spiritual journey.

All Scripture is breathed out by God and profitable for teaching, for reproof, for correction, and for training in righteousness, that the man of God may be complete, equipped for every good work. (2 Tim. 3:16-17)

Purpose #3: Edify and strengthen one another in the faith

Living in the world is challenging and difficult. We are bombarded with temptation from multiple sources including a materialistic culture, humanist philosophical systems, various ideologies, people, and from the demonic realm. Life itself has its disappointments, heartaches, failures, and experiences that have the potential to wear down and undermine our faith.

Because there is an onslaught of attacks on our faith, values, and principles, it is imperative that we have a place to be encouraged, strengthened, and reenergized in our souls, body, and spirits. The place that God has designed for this is the church. The church is not an organization (though it should be organized). Rather, it is an organism of living beings who have entered an eternal realm called the kingdom of God, and who have been equipped and empowered by the person of the Holy Spirit. Individually we are weak and vulnerable but collectively we are strong and a mighty force to advance the kingdom of God and its message.

In Paul's first letter to the Corinthians, he gives considerable attention to the church and the need for every member to be a part and a contributor to the edification of the body. The word *body* is a word Paul often uses to refer to the church. We are the body of Christ, having His Spirit living within us. Notice how he emphasizes that every member is critical to the proper functioning of the body:

> For just as the body is one and has many members, and all the members of the body, though many, are one body, so it is with Christ. For in one Spirit we were all baptized into one body—Jews or Greeks, slaves or free—and all were made to drink of one Spirit. For the body does not consist of one member but of many. If the foot should say, "Because I am not a hand, I do not belong to the body," that would not make it any less a part of the body. And if the ear should say, "Because I am not an eye, I do not belong to the body," that would not make it any less a part of the body. If the whole body were an eye, where would be the sense of hearing? If the whole body were an ear, where would be the sense of smell? But as it is, God arranged the members in the body, each one of them, as he chose. If all were a single member, where would the body be? As it is, there are many parts, yet one body. The eye cannot say to the hand, "I have no need of you," nor again the head to the feet, "I have no need of you." On the contrary, the parts of the body that seem to be weaker are indispensable, and on those parts of the body that we think less honorable we bestow the greater honor, and our unpresentable parts are treated with greater modesty, which our more presentable parts do not require. But God has so composed the body, giving greater honor to the

part that lacked it, that there may be no division in the body, but that the members may have the same care for one another. If one member suffers, all suffer together; if one member is honored, all rejoice together. (1 Cor. 12:12-26)

This is a large passage of Scripture, but it is necessary for us to see the emphasis Paul places on *each* member being part of the body and the significant part *each* is required to fulfill. Again, you can't perform this assignment in isolation, sitting at home watching a church service on television. As wonderful and inspiring as the service may be, that is not God's design for you, unless you are viewing the program at a separate time from your local church's worship service.

It is transparently clear from the above passage that every member is important, that every member has his or her place, and that every member is to be providing edification to other members within the body. It is not a matter of the gifts or lack of gifts, for every person has been uniquely gifted to contribute to the overall health and edification of the body, His church.

Paul in his epistle to the Ephesians concerning the church says the following:

And he gave the apostles, the prophets, the evangelists, the shepherds and teachers, to equip the saints for the work of ministry, for building up the body of Christ, until we all attain to the unity of the faith and of the knowledge of the Son of God, to mature manhood, to the measure of the stature of the fullness of Christ, so that we may no longer be children, tossed to and fro by the waves and carried about by every wind of doctrine, by human cunning, by craftiness in deceitful schemes. Rather, speaking the truth in love, we are to grow up in every way into him who is the head, into Christ, from whom the whole body, joined and held together by every joint with which it is equipped, when each part is working properly, makes the body grow so that it builds itself up in love. (Eph. 4:11-16)

In this passage, Paul explains that God calls and assigns different people to different positions for the purpose of equipping the saints for the work of the ministry. As a pastor, shepherd, and teacher, I have been called to this task. But every believer also has his or her individual assignment in His body. The reason is *"for building up the body of Christ, until we all attain to the unity of the faith and of the knowledge of the Son of God, to mature manhood, to the measure of the stature of the fullness of Christ, so that we may no longer be children, tossed to and fro by the waves and carried about by every wind of doctrine, by human cunning, by craftiness in deceitful schemes."*

It is my responsibility along with yours to build, strengthen, and bring edification to His church. The purpose for strengthening and edifying the church is to prevent people from being led astray into false and heretical teachings. Not everyone within the church has the same calling or gifting or assignment; but all believers and members of the body have the responsibility of doing their part to ensure the stability and health of their church. Notice again these words from the above passage: *"From whom the whole body, joined and held together by every joint with which it is equipped, when each part is working properly, makes the body grow so that it builds itself up in love."*

The whole body, all inclusive, every person - has the responsibility of adding to the body and strengthening of the body. It's everyone's assignment, not just a select few. How can believers contribute if they are not part of a local body? They can't! This is a critical point. By not being part of a local church, believers are not only being disobedient, but they are also not fulfilling the purpose for which they were saved in the first place. Every member is significant and needed—period!

By the way, in the last passage, Paul refers to Christ as *the head*, that is, the head of His body. Let me ask you a question. How effective is a head without a body? What can a head accomplish without a body? Nothing! Christ needs His body, the church, every believer, you and me—to carry forth His mission of advancing the kingdom of God. If all believers refused to be connected to His body, His church would be in deplorable shape. His mission would never be accomplished.

Let's work together, contribute, and do our part to strengthen, edify, and build His body and His kingdom around the world. It is an awesome assignment. And the exciting thing is that regardless of your gifts or abilities, you can make a profound contribution to accomplish His assignment that is significant, eternal, and will be spoken of throughout the ages!

Purpose #4: Fellowship and encouragement
Notice this description of the activities of the early church when they met together:

> And they devoted themselves to the apostles' teaching and the fellowship, to the breaking of bread and the prayers. And awe came upon every soul, and many wonders and signs were being done through the apostles. And all who believed were together and had all things in common. And they were selling their possessions and belongings and distributing the proceeds to all, as any had need. And day by day, attending the temple together and breaking bread in their homes, they received their food with glad and generous hearts, praising God and having favor with all the people. And the Lord added to their number day by day those who were being saved. (Acts 2:42-47)

This early church was a tight-knit group of believers who loved and cared for each other, prayed together, shared meals together, and worshipped together. They were truly part of a universal family, bound together with the Spirit of Christ living within them and empowering them as they shared the gospel, which He confirmed with signs and wonders. They knew they were part of something that was huge; but they never could have imagined that their impact would have global significance. Nor could they have imaged that you and I in the twenty-first century would be reading about their activities!

Just as the early believers needed one another, we too need each other. It is not God's will for believers to live in isolation from other believers. There is a spiritual synergy released when we meet as brothers and sisters in Christ. Jesus said, "For where two or three are gathered in my name, there am I among them" (Matt. 18:20). Though God is always present wherever we go, there is a special anointing and power that is released when we gather together in His name.

This is why the writer of Hebrews says, "not neglecting to meet together, as is the habit of some, but encouraging one another, and all the more as you see the Day drawing near" (Heb. 10:25). Notice the phrase "encouraging one another." We all have times in our lives when we need encouragement.

There is a bond that believers share with one another that is strong and powerful. Sometimes our bond can even be stronger than the bond between members of our own family. The church is a spiritual family. And it is the presence of the Holy Spirit in our lives that builds our intimacy and love between family members. An intimate fellowship coexists between believers that draws us together in our relationship with Christ. We can gather with believers from other nations and although we may not understand one another's language, we sense our spiritual bond. We call this fellowship, which is a word used in Acts 2:42 (above). The New American Commentary says the following about the word *fellowship*:

> The Greek word used here (*koinōnia*) is one Paul often employed, but it appears only here in all of Luke-Acts. Its basic meaning is "association, communion, fellowship, close relationship." In secular Greek it could involve the sharing of goods, and Paul seems to have used it this way in 2 Cor. 9:13. It was also used of communion with a god, especially in the context of a sacred meal; and Paul used it in that sense in 1 Cor. 10:16. Since it appears in a list in Acts 2:42, it is not easy to determine its exact nuance in this context. The key may be to see the terms "breaking of bread" and "prayer" in apposition to "fellowship." The meaning would then be that they devoted themselves to a fellowship that was expressed in their mutual meals and in their prayer life together.[2]

How can you experience fellowship if you are not part of a local body of believers? How can you give or receive encouragement? How can you edify others and be edified if you are not part of a local body of believers? God's design is for every believer to be part of a local congregation. The church is not only for your good and spiritual health, but for the health and benefit of others as well. You not only have something to gain but you also have something to impart and contribute to the edification of the body.

Not only do we need to strengthen others, we also don't want to battle the world, the flesh, and our enemy Satan alone. We need each other. There really is strength in numbers. The Bible says, "And though a man might prevail against one who is alone, two will withstand him—a threefold cord is not quickly broken" (Eccl. 4:12). This establishes that there is strength when we remain together. We all have gifts of the Holy Spirit that differ, yet, all are needed to bring completion to the entire body (see 1 Cor. 12).

Another key reason why we need to be part of a local congregation is accountability. No matter who we are, we all need accountability. Apostles, prophets, pastors, teachers, evangelists, missionaries, and every believer needs someone to hold them accountable. We are not an island to ourselves. When we refuse accountability we open the door that can lead us to spiritual drift. Read this verse carefully:

> Take care, brothers, lest there be in any of you an evil, unbe-
> lieving heart, leading you to fall away from the living God.
> But *exhort one another every day*, as long as it is called 'today,'
> that none of you may be hardened by the deceitfulness of sin.
> (Heb. 3:12-13, emphasis mine)

Notice that the writer of Hebrews uses the word *brothers*, which implies he is writing to believers, telling us that we all have a responsibility to "exhort one another every day." How can this happen if we are not part of a fellowship of believers? Obviously it can't. We need to be joined with other believers, and when we do, we will not only find the needed strength to live in obedience to Christ, but we also will be part of assisting and advancing the greatest movement on the planet—the kingdom of the living God!

There are many other things I can say about the purpose of church, but this is not a book *on the church*. I want to stress that you are a vital part of the local body. The body needs you and you need the body. Now let's look at a few other aspects about the church of which we are part.

THE ORDINANCES OF THE CHURCH

An ordinance is simply a command given by Christ to His church that we are to practice until His return. Most evangelical churches recognize two ordinances: water baptism and the Lord's Supper, also called *communion*. There are different traditions concerning the mode and frequency of administering them, but for the most part, evangelical churches are in agreement.

The Ordinance of Water Baptism

Water baptism is *symbolic* of one's personal faith and commitment to Christ. It doesn't wash away one's sins, but acts as a symbol that indicates someone has turned from a life of sin to a life in Christ. Jesus Himself was baptized in water, not for the purpose of attaining righteousness because He was righteous in every way. He submitted to water baptism to provide an example for us to follow in identifying with Him.

When we follow the Lord in water baptism, we are demonstrating that we are Christians, proclaiming to others that we have made a decision to follow Christ. Water baptism is also symbolic of the death and resurrection of Christ, and of our own spiritual death and resurrection in Christ.

The word *baptize*, (Greek, *baptizo*), literally means to submerge or plunge under. This is why most evangelical churches administer this ordinance by immersing the person totally under the water rather than by sprinkling. It represents a *burial* and *resurrection*. When we placed our faith in Christ, it was as if we died on the cross with Him, were placed in the tomb with Him, and raised to new life with Him. When a person receives Christ, and is baptized in water, he or she is placed *under* the water, symbolizing a burial, a picture of the death of Christ and His burial in the tomb.

Water baptism also represents our dying with Him by faith in His sacrificial death for us on the cross. Our ascension from the water pictures the resurrection of Christ and our spiritual resurrection with Him. It is a glorious symbol of the gospel and it proclaims the heart of the His message—the death, burial, and resurrection of the Christ. Notice the following Scriptures:

> Do you not know that all of us who have been baptized into Christ Jesus were baptized into his death? We were buried therefore with him by baptism into death, in order that, just as Christ was raised from the dead by the glory of the Father, we too might walk in newness of life. For if we have been united with him in a death like his, we shall certainly be united with him in a resurrection like his. (Rom. 6:3-5)

> Having been buried with him in baptism, in which you were also raised with him through faith in the powerful working of God, who raised him from the dead. And you, who were dead in your trespasses and the uncircumcision of your flesh, God made alive together with him, having forgiven us all our trespasses, by canceling the record of debt that stood against

us with its legal demands. This he set aside, nailing it to the cross. (Col. 2:12-14)

Jesus was baptized by immersion by John the Baptist in the Jordan River.

> Then Jesus came from Galilee to the Jordan to John, to be baptized by him. John would have prevented him, saying, "I need to be baptized by you, and do you come to me?" But Jesus answered him, "Let it be so now, for thus it is fitting for us to fulfill all righteousness." Then he consented. And when Jesus was baptized, *immediately he went up from the water*, and behold, the heavens were opened to him, and he saw the Spirit of God descending like a dove and coming to rest on him; and behold, a voice from heaven said, "This is my beloved Son, with whom I am well pleased." (Matt. 3:13-17)

Notice Mathew says that Jesus *"went up from the water."* If Jesus simply had water poured over his head, there would have been no need for Him to be in the water and coming up out of the water. Jesus was immersed in the water and then came up.

When Philip the Evangelist baptized the Ethiopian eunuch, he immersed the Ethiopian:

> And as they were going along the road they came to some water, and the eunuch said, "See, here is water! What prevents me from being baptized?" And he commanded the chariot to stop, and they both went *down into the water*, Philip and the eunuch, and he baptized him. And when they came up out of the water, the Spirit of the Lord carried Philip away, and the eunuch saw him no more, and went on his way rejoicing. (Acts 8:38-39, emphasis mine)

Notice they both went "down into the water." There would be no reason to enter the water if water baptism was simply a sprinkling or pouring of water upon the head. Baptism is an act where a person is submerged under the water, which necessitates going into the body of water. They were not baptized "by," "beside," or "near" the water, but *"in the water."*

The Bible teaches *believer's baptism*. This is why we do not baptize infants. A person must first come to understand that Christ died for his or her sins, exercise faith in His sacrifice on the cross, and then identify with Christ by being baptized in water. You must be a believer *before* you are baptized. If you are not a believer when you are baptized, you are just getting wet!

Even though water baptism doesn't save or wash away your sins, it is the first step of obedience in following Christ. It demonstrates that you are serious about your faith. When people say they are Christians, they are stating that they have made a decision to *follow* Christ. Christ Himself was baptized and He commands us to be baptized. For the Christian to refuse to be baptized is an act of disobedience to the command of Christ. When people in the Bible came to Christ, believing and receiving the message of Christ, they followed the Lord in water baptism. Luke writes, "So those who *received his word* were baptized, and there were added that day about three thousand souls." (Acts 2:41, emphasis mine).

In Samaria, when Philip preached the gospel many came to faith in Christ. Once it was evident they believed and were saved, they were then baptized in water. "But when *they believed* Philip as he preached good news about the kingdom of God and the name of Jesus Christ, they were baptized, both men and women." (Acts 8:12, emphasis mine)

In Acts chapter ten, Luke records Peter preaching to the Gentiles. When they believed in the message of Christ, they were filled with the Holy Spirit, began speaking in tongues and praising God. It was evident to Peter that they were believers, so he commanded them to be baptized in water.

> While Peter was still saying these things, the Holy Spirit fell on all who heard the word. And the believers from among the circumcised who had come with Peter were amazed, because the gift of the Holy Spirit was poured out even on the Gentiles. For they were hearing them speaking in tongues and extolling God. Then Peter declared, "Can anyone withhold water for baptizing these people, who have received the Holy Spirit just as we have?" *And he commanded them to be baptized in the name of Jesus Christ.* Then they asked him to remain for some days. (Acts 10:44-48)

Let me give one last example from the Scriptures. One of the most amazing conversions is that of the Philippian jailer:

> And the jailer called for lights and rushed in, and trembling with fear he fell down before Paul and Silas. Then he brought them out and said, "Sirs, what must I do to be saved?" And they said, *"Believe in the Lord Jesus,* and you will be saved, you and your household." And they spoke the word of the Lord to him and to all who were in his house. And he took them the same hour of the night and washed their wounds; and he was *baptized at once,* he and all his family. (Acts 16:29-33, emphasis mine)

This should suffice to demonstrate from the Scriptures that water baptism is for those who have *believed,* having received the message of forgiveness through Christ. Faith in Christ requires knowledge of your sins and understanding that Christ died for your sins on the cross. It also involves repentance of sins.

Please understand that one does not need an extensive theological understanding of the atonement in order to be saved. But coming to Christ does require having a basic understanding of the meaning of salvation, experiencing the conviction of sin, and making a decision to follow Christ. Children can come to faith in Christ, but an infant has no comprehension of sin, redemption, and repentance. This is why we wait for children to come to an understanding of salvation and make a decision to receive Christ before we baptize them in water. Until then, they are covered under the blood of Christ until they reach an age of accountability.

There is one last thing I would like to say about water baptism. Jesus said that when we receive Him and make a decision to follow Him, we are to confess our commitment to Christ before others. In my experience with the Baptist tradition, this confession was called a *public profession of faith*. Notice the words of Jesus:

> So everyone who *acknowledges me before men*, I also will acknowledge before my Father who is in heaven, but whoever denies me before men, I also will deny before my Father who is in heaven. (Matt. 10:32-33, emphasis mine)

Water baptism is a great way to publically acknowledge your decision to follow Christ. It is a celebration of the new life that you have in Him. Something special takes place within your spirit when, as an act of your obedience, you are baptized in water. I encourage people to invite their family and friends to witness the transforming message that is found in the good news of Jesus Christ.

If you have never followed the Lord in water baptism, there is no reason to delay. I would encourage you to arrange for it as soon as possible. The early believers were baptized the very *same* day they came to Christ. "So those who received his word were baptized, and there were added *that day* about three thousand souls." (Acts 2:41, emphasis mine) There is no reason to postpone being baptized!

The Ordinance of Communion

As with the ordinance of baptism, there are different traditions and names for Communion. Among Evangelicals, the most common name is *Communion* or the *Lord's Supper*. The first time this ordinance was administered was by Jesus following the Passover meal with His disciples.

> Now as they were eating, Jesus took bread, and after blessing it broke it and gave it to the disciples, and said, "Take, eat; this is my body." And he took a cup, and when he had given

thanks he gave it to them, saying, "Drink of it, all of you, for this is my blood of the covenant, which is poured out for many for the forgiveness of sins. I tell you I will not drink again of this fruit of the vine until that day when I drink it new with you in my Father's kingdom." (Matt. 26:26-29)

In 1 Corinthians, the apostle Paul writes:

"For I received from the Lord what I also delivered to you, that the Lord Jesus on the night when he was betrayed took bread, and when he had given thanks, he broke it, and said, "This is my body which is for you. Do this in remembrance of me." In the same way also he took the cup, after supper, saying, "This cup is the new covenant in my blood. Do this, as often as you drink it, in remembrance of me." For as often as you eat this bread and drink the cup, you proclaim the Lord's death until he comes. (1 Cor. 11:23-26)

First and foremost, the Lord's Supper is a time for the body of Christ to remember *the dear and sacrificial price that was required for our salvation.* Notice the words of Jesus from the passage above: *"Do this in remembrance of me."* Though our salvation is a *free* gift offered to all who are willing to believe, the Father paid a dear price—the death of His only Son. Jesus, in instituting this ordinance, was telling us that He wants us to never forget that He paid the ultimate price for our salvation.

Each time we share in the Lord's Supper, we are reminded that we have been forgiven and justified by His death on the cross. He personally came to this planet and paid our sin debt. The price involved the Son of God being humiliated, shamed, beaten, spit upon, and nailed to a cross. We must never forget the sacrifice. It is the greatest expression of love and it demonstrates the extreme extent that a loving God will pay in order to provide forgiveness and reconciliation.

Second, when we share in Communion, we are doing just that: communing with one another and the Lord Jesus through the presence of the Holy Spirit in a very intimate act. We *are* the body of Christ, the Holy Spirit living within us, and we are connected to Christ and to one another through the sacrifice He made. When we share in Communion, we are remembering together as a redeemed community of believers the sacrifice of Christ on the cross.

The act of sharing Communion is a reminder of our oneness and unity as the Body of Christ. The Lord's Supper is exclusively for those who *know* Him. It is a family meal between God's children that binds His church together as they remember His sacrifice and forgiveness extended to all who will believe. Communion is such a special time for God's people to express thanksgiving and praise for all the benefits released to us through His death.

Third, the sharing of the Lord's Supper is not an elaborate formality - it is simple. Jesus following the Passover meal, in a very simple way, passed out the bread, and then the cup as He shared with His disciples the meaning of each item. I am not against church traditions that have a formal presentation of the Lord's Supper, but when Jesus shared Communion, it was in a simple manner.

Fourth, Communion is a time of personal reflection and examination. Our participation in the Lord's Supper is to be taken seriously, never approached in a frivolous or light-hearted way. We are remembering the most sacred act in the history of mankind: Christ taking on human flesh and offering up His body as a sacrifice to God for the sins of the world.

When examining ourselves in light of the holy sacrifice He made, we should look inwardly and ask, "Is there anything in my life that is unacceptable or sinful?" "Are there any sins I need to repent of?" "Have I backslidden from my love and passion for the Lord and the things of God?" "Are there any behaviors in my life that are unacceptable or out of sync with the teachings of Scripture?" "Do I have unforgiveness or is there a root of bitterness in my heart?"

When we share in the Lord's Supper, this is an excellent time for us to take a spiritual inventory and recommit ourselves anew and afresh to Christ and His church. Notice what Paul writes about Communion:

> Let a person examine himself, then, and so eat of the bread
> and drink of the cup. For anyone who eats and drinks without
> discerning the body eats and drinks judgment on himself. That
> is why many of you are weak and ill, and some have died.
> But if we judged ourselves truly, we would not be judged.
> (1 Cor. 11:28-31)

One thing is clear from this passage of Scripture: the Lord takes the observance of His Supper very seriously. We are to approach it in a spirit of reverence. We must ensure that hearts are right with Him. If we come to the Lord's Supper knowing we have unconfessed sins in our lives, this can potentially lead to sickness and even physical death. This heightens our responsibility to reflect deeply prior to participating in this ordinance as we approach the Lord's Table.

Fifth, each time we come together for the Lord's Supper we are declaring the heart of the gospel. Several years ago I heard a pastor preach on the subject, "Three Looks Concerning the Lord's Supper." He said there is a *backward* look, remembering the cross; an *inward* look, self-examination; and a *future* look, anticipating His coming.

Jesus said, "For as often as you eat this bread and drink the cup, you proclaim the Lord's death *until he comes*" (1 Cor. 11:26, emphasis mine). Each time we share in the Lord's Supper we are to remember (look backward);

examine ourselves (look inward); and we are also proclaiming His death until His glorious return (a future look).

Lastly concerning the Lord's Supper, let me point out that the frequency of a church participating in the Lord's Supper varies considerably. Some churches observe the Lord's Supper every Sunday, some once a month, others once a quarter. Jesus never commanded how often we are to observe the Lord's Supper. He simply said, "For as often as you eat this bread and drink the cup..." (1 Cor. 11:26). There is no certain requirement as to *how often* we are to share in the Lord's Supper. He leaves that up to each local congregation.

THE LEADERSHIP OF THE CHURCH

According to the Scriptures, the church is to have structure and leadership. The Bible clearly outlines and gives the qualifications of those who are to become leaders in a local congregation. There are two key offices mentioned: the bishop (overseer) and the deacon. Paul writing to Timothy delineates the spiritual qualifications of these two offices, which for the most part are identical.

It is clear that no one should be placed in leadership quickly, as he or she should first be proven concerning the leader's spiritual development and maturity in the Lord. This is what Paul says concerning these two leadership positions:

> The saying is trustworthy: If anyone aspires to the office of *overseer*, he desires a noble task. Therefore an overseer must be above reproach, the husband of one wife, sober-minded, self-controlled, respectable, hospitable, able to teach, not a drunkard, not violent but gentle, not quarrelsome, not a lover of money. He must manage his own household well, with all dignity keeping his children submissive, for if someone does not know how to manage his own household, how will he care for God's church? He must not be a recent convert, or he may become puffed up with conceit and fall into the condemnation of the devil. Moreover, he must be well thought of by outsiders, so that he may not fall into disgrace, into a snare of the devil. Deacons likewise must be dignified, not double-tongued, not addicted to much wine, not greedy for dishonest gain. They must hold the mystery of the faith with a clear conscience. And let them also be tested first; then let them serve as deacons if they prove themselves blameless. Their wives likewise must be dignified, not slanderers, but sober-minded, faithful in all things. Let deacons each be the husband of one wife, managing their children and their own households well. For those who serve well as deacons gain a

good standing for themselves and also great confidence in the
faith that is in Christ Jesus. (1 Tim. 3:1-13, emphasis mine)

The office of overseer

First, we have the office of the "overseer." Some translations use the word,
bishop. This is the person who has been called, appointed, and is ultimately
responsible for overseeing the congregation. He or she is to provide spiritual
oversight, to preach and teach the Scriptures, teach sound doctrine to protect
the flock from heretical teaching, develop and train others to become spiritual leaders, provide vision for the congregation and leadership of the church,
exercise spiritual discipline when necessary, and seek to maintain the unity of
the church.

The New American Commentary says this about the word *overseer*: "The
word 'overseer' receives such translations as 'bishop' (KJV, ASV), 'Presiding-
Officer' (TCNT), 'superintendent' (Goodspeed), or 'pastor' (Williams). In
such passages as Acts 20:17, 28 and Titus 1:5, 7 the terms 'elders' and 'overseers' appear together to suggest that the positions are partially, if not fully,
interchangeable."[3]

Today, we would typically refer to this person as the *senior pastor* or *lead
pastor*. Among the leadership of elders, he or she would be the *lead* elder. It
is not my intention to discuss the various forms of church government, as they
vary in churches and denominations. But suffice to say there is a designated
leader who is to provide the necessary direction for the church as they seek to
impact their region and the world for Christ.

Even though there appears to be a plurality of elders in local congregations,
there seems to be one key elder who was appointed as *overseer*, or *lead elder*.
With any organization, it is necessary to have a leader. Whether it is in the home
or a corporation, someone has to assume the role of leader. Two or more heads
is not normal and leads to division and dysfunction. The lead overseer is not
to be dictatorial, but is to confer with others who have been appointed to assist
in overseeing the congregation. It is team leadership with the lead elder having
the respect of the others.

The office of deacon

The second office is that of *deacon*. Deacons assist in ministering to the various
needs of the congregation. The Greek word for deacon is *diakoneo*, which literally means *servant*. The New American Commentary says the following about
the office of deacon:

> The term "deacon" refers literally to someone who serves.
> Some modern versions have used the term "church helper"
> (GNB) or "Assistant-Officer" (TCNT) in verse 8. Bible
> scholars view the overseer as providing administrative

leadership for the church. They see the deacon as helping the overseer in the ministries or work of the church.[4]

Deacons are servants of the church who assist the elders of the congregation in ministering to the needs of the flock effectively. They too must meet the spiritual qualifications set forth by Paul, which are no less significant than the qualifications for the overseer. They are responsible to the elders and will be of significant value in serving the congregation.

The most important thing I want you to see is that God has designed structure for His church. Some people are against structure and organization, but the Bible is clear that God desires His church to have structure, to be well ordered, and to manage the affairs of the congregation efficiently.

I have occasionally heard people say, "I'm against organized religion." When I hear this I have to wonder, "Are you for *disorganized* religion?" The entire planet is meticulously designed with structure and order. The Bible even tells us He has established governments for the purpose of establishing order (see Rom. 13:1-7; 1 Pet. 2:13-17). If He has designed His planet and established governments to facilitate order, then certainly He desires to have some level of structure and order in His church.

Other passages for further study in dealing with church leadership are 1 Corinthians 12:28-32; Ephesians 4:11-14; Titus 1:5-9; and 1 Peter 5:1-5.

Conclusion

Those who serve in leadership with His church have a tremendous responsibility. They will stand and give an account to God for how they have taken care of His flock. The congregation should pray for them, honor them, and encourage them. For those who lead well and are faithful to their assignment, God will reward them when He establishes His kingdom (1 Peter 5:4).

This has been a brief summation of the church and its significance. I can't imagine a world without churches. The influence of the church worldwide is enormous and eternal. It has been the most persecuted and maligned institution on earth, but it is still marching onward and advancing the kingdom of God. Let me close this chapter with the words of our Lord to the apostle Peter:

> "And I tell you, you are Peter, and on this rock I will build my church, and the gates of hell *shall not prevail against it*."
> (Matthew 16:18, emphasis mine)

Discussion Questions

1. What are some the metaphors used in the Bible to describe the church?

2. Describe what the word *church* means?

3. Why is it that some people have negative feelings about the church?

4. Why would it be incorrect to point to a building and say, "That's my church?"

5. The word church is used two ways in the Bible? What are those two ways?

6. What is the purpose of the church?

7. What is a church ordinance? How many are there?

8. What is the meaning of the ordinance of water baptism? When you were baptized in water what did it mean to you?

9. What is the meaning of the ordinance of communion, the Lord's Supper? What does the Lord's Supper mean to you?

10. According to the Scriptures, who are assigned the responsibilities of leading the church, and what are their titles? What do you feel are the responsibilities of the church body to leadership?

Chapter Eight

Spiritual Disciplines

*D*iscipline. The very word can cause us to recoil and feel tired. It implies effort. But reaching any level of excellence requires discipline. In the field of athletics, no athlete will reach the pinnacle of his sport without rigorous, consistent, daily discipline. The same is true of musicians, doctors, engineers, tradesmen, technicians, professors, or executives of a successful company.

There are no short-cuts. Even when one has raw talent or intellectual prowess, uncompromising and tenacious discipline is needed in order to advance to the highest level of one's pursuits in life. Achieving excellence in any field *always* has a price. It is one of those non-negotiable truths in every sphere of life.

As I am writing this chapter, I am occasionally looking up at my television screen. The 2012 US Tennis Open is taking place between two exceptional tennis players. Novak Djokovic and his opponent, Andy Murray are young 25 year olds. As I watch them hit the ball back and forth, making amazing shots, I can't help but wonder how many times have they done this throughout their young lives? How many times do you think they have spent hitting tennis balls over that net? How many hours have they practiced hitting their serve, back-hand, slice, overhead, or topspin? From the time they first picked up a tennis racket until standing on the court of the 2012 US Open, how many games have they played? We will never know the answer to these questions, but one thing I do know is this: neither of these athletes achieved this level of play without strenuous, tiring, determined, and daily discipline.

What is true in every other pursuit in life is true of our spiritual development. Growing and advancing spiritually does not happen automatically. It is not a process of osmosis. It too takes daily discipline. The apostle Paul knew this.

In the Greco-Roman world in which he lived, Paul was surrounded by athletes and may have attended the Isthmian Games, athletic contests much like our modern day Olympics. The games were named after the Isthmus of Corinth, where the games were held. Athletes participated in running, boxing, wrestling, and other sports. It is evident that Paul was familiar with them by his writings. He definitely knew that discipline was a requirement for an athlete. In challenging Christians toward spiritual maturity and advancement in their spiritual pilgrimage, he would often use the analogy of the athlete. Notice his words to the Corinthians where these games were held:

> Do you not know that in a race all the runners run, but only one receives the prize? So run that you may obtain it. Every athlete exercises self-control in all things. They do it to receive a perishable wreath, but we an imperishable. So I do not run aimlessly; I do not box as one beating the air. But I discipline my body and keep it under control, lest after preaching to others I myself should be disqualified. (1 Cor. 9:24-27)

Did you notice the words Paul uses in this passage of Scripture? They are quite graphic and pulsating with passion, fervency, and determination. To appreciate the meaning of these words, I have provided the definition of a few choice words in this text from the Enhanced Strong's Lexicon:

"Run" (v. 24)

trecho **1** to run. 1A of persons in haste. 1B of those who run in a race course. **2** metaphor. 2A of doctrine rapidly propagated. 2B by a metaphor taken from runners in a race, to exert one's self, strive hard. 2C to spend one's strength in performing or attaining something. 2D word occurs in Greek writings denoting to incur extreme peril, which it requires the exertion of all one's effort to overcome.[1]

"That you may obtain it" (v. 24)

Katalambano **1** to lay hold of. 1A to lay hold of so as to make one's own, to obtain, attain to, to make one's own, to take into one's self, appropriate. 1B to seize upon, take possession of. *1B1* of evils overtaking one, of the last day overtaking the wicked with destruction, of a demon about to torment one. *1B2* in a good sense, of Christ by his holy power and influence laying hold of the human mind and will, in order to prompt and govern it. 1C to detect, catch. 1D to lay hold of with the mind. *1D1* to understand, perceive, learn, comprehend.[2]

"Athlete" (v. 25)

agonizomai **1** to enter a contest: contend in the gymnastic games. **2** to contend with adversaries, fight. **3** metaph. to contend, struggle, with difficulties and dangers. **4** to endeavour with strenuous zeal, strive: to obtain something.[3]

"Exercises self-control" (v. 25)

egkrateuomai **1** to be self-controlled, continent. 1A to exhibit self-government, conduct, one's self temperately. 1B in a figure drawn from athletes, who in preparing themselves for the games abstained from unwholesome food, wine, and sexual indulgence.[4]

"Discipline" (v. 27)

hupopiazo **1** to beat black and blue, to smite so as to cause bruises and livid spots. **1A** like a boxer one buffets his body, handle it roughly, discipline by hardships. **2** metaph. **2A** to give one intolerable annoyance. **2A1** beat one out, wear one out. **2B** by entreaties. **3** that part of the face that is under the eyes.[5]

"Keep it under control" (v. 27)

doulagogeo **1** to lead away into slavery, claim as one's slave. **2** to make a slave and to treat as a slave i.e. with severity, subject to stern and rigid discipline.[6]

There is no possible way you can read the full expression of these words from their Greek origins without realizing that Paul's path to spiritual growth, maturity, and development required strenuous and uncompromising discipline. Along with the word *discipline*, he uses the words *self-control* and *under control*.

It is obvious that Paul is determined, focused, and has made a clear and resolute decision that involves his will. It is also evident that his path to spiritual maturity is not a simple "name it and claim it" proposition. It required gut-wrenching effort on his part as he daily yielded and surrendered his will to the empowering presence of the Holy Spirit.

Paul would never settle for mediocrity in his life of faith. There was no question as to his plans, and hesitation or retreat was not in his vocabulary. His determination and commitment for spiritual advancement is seen in his epistle to the Philippians. He is in a never ceasing pursuit of advancement, knowing that his spiritual development would lead him to a deeper level of intimacy with Christ his Lord.

> Not that I have already obtained this or am already perfect, but I press on to make it my own, because Christ Jesus has made me his own. Brothers, I do not consider that I have made it my own. But one thing I do: forgetting what lies behind and straining forward to what lies ahead, I press on toward the goal for the prize of the upward call of God in Christ Jesus. Let those of us who are mature think this way, and if in anything you think otherwise, God will reveal that also to you. Only let us hold true to what we have attained. (Phil. 3:12-16)

Let me again expand on a few words in their Greek meaning:

"I press on" (v. 12)

dioko **1** to make to run or flee, put to flight, drive away. **2** to run swiftly in order to catch a person or thing, to run after. **2A** to press on: figuratively of one who in a race runs swiftly to reach the goal. **2B** to pursue (in a hostile manner). **3** in any way whatever to harass, trouble, molest one. **3A** to persecute. **3B** to be mistreated, suffer persecution on account of something. **4** without the idea of hostility, to run after, follow after: someone. **5** metaph., to pursue. **5A** to seek after eagerly, earnestly endeavour to acquire.[7]

"Straining forward" (v. 13)
epekteinomai **1** to stretch out to or towards. **2** to stretch (one's self) forward to.[8]

Notice that Paul uses the word *strain* once and *press* twice. Again, reading the definitions of these words tells us that Paul is exerting a tremendous amount of personal discipline as he seeks conformity to Christ. His one passion in life is to please and exalt Christ with every fiber of his being. His desire is that Christ may be magnified through his life or through his death (see Phil. 1:20-23).

Let me clarify that Paul's efforts in seeking conformity to Christ through spiritual discipline are not for the purpose of achieving or earning his salvation. Paul makes it absolutely clear throughout his writings that a person is not saved or justified in the sight of God by any degree of personal effort or achievement. In these verses, Paul is speaking about progressive sanctification, growing in the Lord, ever advancing, by practicing spiritual discipline and yielding to the influence of the Holy Spirit. When we yield to the Spirit, we are empowered by the Spirit, transformed by the Spirit, and conformed by the Spirit to the person of Christ.

We cannot achieve any level of spiritual advancement through our own efforts. It is only as we cooperate with the Holy Spirit, yielding and surrendering to Him that we receive the ability to have Christ formed progressively in our lives (see Gal. 5:16-26).

Training for Godliness
Before I delve into what I consider to be three of the most critical spiritual disciplines, let me share one other verse Paul writes to Timothy: "Have nothing to do with irreverent, silly myths. Rather *train* yourself for godliness" (1 Tim. 4:7, emphasis mine).

The word "train" is the word from which we get our English word "gymnasium." Notice the definition in the Enhanced Strong's Lexicon:
gumnazo **1** to exercise naked (in a palaestra or school of athletics). **2** to exercise vigorously, in any way, either the body or the mind.[9]

A school of "palaestra" is a school for wrestling. Wrestling is a sport that requires incredible strength and stamina. Notice in the second definition the word "vigorously." There is no way to get around the fact that we are expected to put forth maximum effort as we pursue growth and development in our faith.

When I was in high school, I wrestled competitively for 3 years. Because I had taken Judo lessons for several years as a child, I had an advantage. But even though I had an advantage in skills, I had to have a high level of endurance in order to win each contest. And there was only one way to get endurance—rigorous training. During the wrestling season, we exercised, practiced techniques, ran wind sprints, ran up and down the bleachers, and wrestled until we could barely crawl off the mats. The apostle Paul is saying that if we expect to spiritually advance in our faith and become warriors for Christ, discipline must be a daily routine in our lives. No exceptions.

WHAT ARE SPIRITUAL DISCIPLINES?

Now, what exactly are spiritual disciplines? They are simply tools to assist us in reaching our goal of godliness and conformity to Christ. They are exercises that will serve as catalysts to propel us to a higher spiritual dimension. They are like fuel to our spirit that releases the anointing and power of the Holy Spirit within us to take over and control our lives. Donald Whitney in his book *Spiritual Disciplines for the Christian Life* writes:

> Think of the Spiritual Disciplines as ways we can place ourselves in the path of God's grace and seek Him much as Bartimaeus and Zacchaeus placed themselves in Jesus' path and sought Him. As with these two seekers, we will find Him willing to have mercy on us and to have communion with us. And in the course of time we will be transformed by Him from one level of Christlikeness to another (2 Cor. 3:18).[10]

When it comes to spiritual disciplines, there are many that can be incorporated in our lives. A list may include Bible reading, prayer, worship, evangelism, serving, stewardship, fasting, study, meditation, simplicity, and solitude. There are several disciplines I could address, but I will be focusing on the daily intake of the Word, daily prayer, and daily worship.

Daily Intake of the Word

Notice I said "daily." Just as we need food for physical nourishment, we need spiritual food (the Word) to nourish and sustain our spirit. Jesus said, "Man shall not live by bread alone, but by every word that comes from the mouth of God" (Matt. 4:4). Try skipping meals for a few days and you will feel the effects of physical weakness. When we skip and neglect a steady intake of the Word, we become weak and spiritually drained.

The Word reminds us of who God is, what He has done for us, and what He is going to do for us. It also reminds us of the uniqueness of our relationship, how to develop and build intimacy in our relationship, how to think correctly, how to face trials and challenges, and a multiplicity of other topics. The Word spells out clearly what our responsibilities are as believers, to one another, to our neighbors, and to our world.

In the twenty-first century, it is critical that we become immersed in the Word. We are faced with numerous challenges and philosophical ideas that contradict our values and beliefs as Christians. We need to know what the Word says about the various issues, values, and beliefs that are being propagated through educational institutions and the media. With the advancement of technology, the media has become a powerful source of information, often promoting ideas and values that are diametrically opposed to Christian beliefs.

Unfortunately, it is unlikely that the values promoted in the media will change, which means we need to have a solid biblical and theological mindset in order to counteract the barrage of influences that are trying to shape our minds and our generation. If we have clear answers from the Scriptures, we can thwart the lies of the enemy that are shaping people's values and worldview. This means we must be knowledgeable of the Scriptures and know with precision what the Bible teaches so that we can give a proper defense of our faith.

A steady intake of the Word of God builds our faith, renews our minds, gives us direction and guidance, provides encouragement and hope, corrects false premises and improper thinking, brings conviction and correction when needed, and provides stability to navigate through life. Consider the following Scriptures:

> Consequently, faith comes from hearing the message, and the message is heard through the word about Christ. (Rom. 10:17, *NIV*)

> But as for you, continue in what you have learned and have firmly believed, knowing from whom you learned it and how from childhood you have been acquainted with the sacred writings, which are able to make you wise for salvation through faith in Christ Jesus. All Scripture is breathed out by God and profitable for teaching, for reproof, for correction, and for training in righteousness, that the man of God may be complete, equipped for every good work. (2 Tim. 3:14-17)

> I have stored up your word in my heart, that I might not sin against you. (Ps. 119:11)

No spiritual discipline is more important than the regular intake of God's Word. Nothing can substitute for it. There is simply no way a person can experience spiritual health and be productive in his or her spiritual life apart from a steady, consistent, daily intake of the inspired Scriptures. It is in the Scriptures that we discover how to live in a way that is pleasing to God, how to live in spiritual victory, and how to develop spiritual intimacy with the Lord Jesus Christ. We also learn how to live a fulfilled, joyful, and meaningful life.

There is simply no other source of the essential information we need for the ongoing development of our spiritual lives than that which is found between the covers of the book we affectionately refer to as the Bible. Regardless of how busy we become, we must remember that the most transforming practice available to us is disciplining ourselves to have a consistent intake of the Word of God.

A consistent intake of the Word of God builds up and brings edification to our faith. If there has ever been a day when we need our faith developed and strengthened, it is the day in which we live. It may be a word of encouragement, an insight for our family, wisdom concerning our finances, guidance concerning certain relationships, comfort in the midst of a crisis, or a word concerning personal decisions made throughout the day.

The Scriptures speak to a variety of issues that we may face in life and God can give us a specific word from the Scriptures to help us in that season. But if we have not disciplined ourselves to feed upon the Word, we cannot expect to receive a word.

There is no excuse for not reading or hearing the Word. Technology and the Internet have made it easy for almost anyone to access a vast number of resources that help us assimilate the Word.

There are multiple ministries on television that are preaching the Word. Numerous websites not only provide multiple translations of the Bible, but also commentaries and other biblical resources to enhance our study. The good news is that most of these resources are absolutely free! And with a simple click of the mouse, we can now listen to and watch some of the most gifted expositors of the Word without ever leaving our homes. The bottom line is that our ability to hear and have a steady intake of the Word of God has never been easier and more accessible. Let's take advantage of every opportunity afforded to us in an effort to saturate our hearts and minds with the truths of the Word and become students of the Scriptures!

Daily Prayer

Prayer is one of the keys in releasing the infilling of the Holy Spirit in our lives. It releases the fountain of the Spirit and allows the river of the Spirit to flow. But like a water faucet, unless the valve is turned in the right position, the water will remain contained in the pipe. It doesn't flow until the valve is opened. The same is true of the Holy Spirit. The way to open the valve of the Spirit is through prayer and seeking the face of God. Prayer releases the flow of the Spirit and allows us to drink, to be filled, to be led, to be controlled, and to experience deep satisfaction that comes from living the life of the Spirit.

The discipline of prayer is more challenging than the intake of the Word because prayer involves a deeper level of faith. Disciplining yourself to pray requires that you believe prayer will make a difference in your life, your circumstances, your spiritual development, and that it has an effect on whatever it is you are praying about. This requires a level of faith. It requires believing the promises in the Scriptures concerning prayer. It requires faith to believe that when you pray, your Heavenly Father not only takes notice, but He is also listening. It takes faith to believe that when you pray He will intervene and begin working out the requests and petitions that you are bringing to Him.

One reason why this discipline is more difficult to practice is because our faith level fluctuates. There are some days that we have faith to move mountains, and other days when we wonder if God is listening or is even aware of our situation. Added to the challenge is that we have an enemy, Satan, who does everything within his power to undermine our faith and bring discouragement in our lives. If he can weaken our faith, he knows it will affect our prayer life. It is in times of discouragement that we have to be especially disciplined and push through, believing that prayer does have the power to change whatever we are dealing with or facing in life.

We must never stop praying; rather we need to intensify our prayers, believing that prayer will change our circumstances and have an impact in any given situation.

In reading the Gospels, it becomes evident that Jesus was a man of prayer and that prayer was a priority in His life. If Jesus, the holy, sinless, anointed, Spirit-filled Son of the living God deemed it necessary to pray and communicate with His Heavenly Father, why would we ever feel that we can function in life without it? Jesus prayed because He knew that prayer makes a difference. He knew that prayer and communion with His Father provided strength, wisdom, encouragement, and supernatural enablement. Notice the following verses that reference some of the occasions in the life of Jesus that He prayed:

- Before choosing the twelve disciples
  "In these days he went out to the mountain to pray, and all night he *continued in prayer* to God." (Luke 6:12, emphasis mine)
- After feeding the 5,000
  "And after he had dismissed the crowds, he went up on the mountain by himself *to pray*. When evening came, he was there alone." (Matt. 14:23, emphasis mine)
- After healing the leper
  "But now even more the report about him went abroad, and great crowds gathered to hear him and to be healed of their infirmities. *But he would withdraw to desolate places and pray*." (Luke 5:15-16, emphasis mine)
- The transfiguration
  "Now about eight days after these sayings he took with him Peter and John and James and went up on the mountain *to pray*." (Luke 9:28, emphasis mine)
- The disciples saw power in His prayer life
  "*Now Jesus was praying in a certain place*, and when he finished, one of his disciples said to him, 'Lord, teach us to pray, as John taught his disciples.'" (Luke 11:1, emphasis mine)
- Gethsemane
  "Then Jesus went with them to a place called Gethsemane, and he said to his disciples, 'Sit here, *while I go over there and pray*.'" (Matt. 26:36, emphasis mine)

It is clear that in the life of Jesus, prayer was a priority. He was setting the example. He was demonstrating that prayer is not just a religious exercise, but prayer is a vital component in our relationship with God. It was in prayer that He found the wisdom and strength needed to live in a world that was hostile toward Him, and the power to fulfill the mission assigned to Him by His Heavenly Father.

The essence of being a Christian is making a decision and commitment to become followers of Christ and seeking to emulate His example. He expects His followers to pray, and tells us that when we pray, things will begin to take place and doors will begin to open. Read His words concerning prayer:

> *Ask*, and it will be given to you; seek, and you will find; knock, and it will be opened to you. For everyone who asks receives, and the one who seeks finds, and to the one who knocks it will be opened. (Matt. 7:7-8, emphasis mine)

> And he told them a parable to the effect that they ought *always to pray* and not lose heart. (Luke 18:1, emphasis mine)

> And he said to them, "This kind cannot be driven out by anything *but prayer*." (Mark 9:29, emphasis mine)

Let me ask a question. When we look at the life of Jesus and see what He said about prayer, what could possibly be our rationale for not devoting ourselves to prayer? Shouldn't prayer be one of those spiritual disciplines that we automatically engage in, knowing that everything we do has the potential to be affected? When we pray, we are inviting the presence and the power of God to come down and invade every aspect of our lives.

I don't know about you, but I need His presence, His wisdom, His guidance, His anointing, and His power in every single facet of my life on a daily basis. There are no exceptions. We never know what a day is going to bring, and I want to be prayed up and asking for God's presence to rest upon me and abide in my life.

Jesus prayed, He tells us to pray, and He expects us to pray. A prayerless life makes a statement. When we choose not to pray, we are expressing an attitude of self-sufficiency and self-dependency. We are in essence saying to God that we really don't need His presence, His power, or His influence in our lives. Even though we may not be thinking this outright, this is what a prayerless life implies to God. I cannot imagine living life without praying and seeking God's favor upon my life.

Prayer should be daily, throughout the day, and unceasing to the extent that we develop a mindset of talking and communicating with our Heavenly Father on a consistent basis. It should be as natural as breathing. It should *never* be neglected. Let me share a few additional thoughts concerning prayer.

- **Prayer demonstrates that we believe the <u>Scriptures</u>**
The Scriptures are filled with admonitions to pray. They assume that prayer is part of our spiritual DNA. We are told to continue to pray and not to give up.

> "Rejoice in hope, be patient in tribulation, be constant in prayer." (Rom. 12:12)

> "Continue steadfastly in prayer, being watchful in it with thanksgiving." (Col. 4:2).

> "Pray without ceasing." (1 Thess. 5:17)

Remember, the Scriptures are written for our instruction and edification under the inspiration of the Holy Spirit. The Holy Spirit was not just filling pages with words to complete the Bible. These words are the very words of God and they tell us that we are to be steadfast in praying and refuse to give up. Why? Because prayer has the power to change things, bring about transformation, affect the lives of people, and even has an impact on nations across the planet.

So, the Spirit in the Scriptures tells us to pray. When we pray, we are following the instructions of the inspired Scriptures. When we fail to pray, we are living in disobedience to the Word. Prayer is not a suggestion in the Bible but a command. If we desire to be obedient to the Word of God we have no option but to pray!

- **Prayer acknowledges that God is our <u>source</u>**
When we pray, we are looking to God as our source. By disciplining ourselves to pray, we are saying to God that we need His presence and power in our lives. We are acknowledging that He is good, gracious, and our provider. Daily prayer engages the Spirit of God in the activities of our day. Whether it is for direction in life, facing a challenge, or making a difficult decision, seeking God's direction reinforces that we acknowledge Him as our source.

When we are discouraged and feel overwhelmed with fear or anxiety, we need to pray. He is well able to meet our every need!

Tragically, many people look in every other direction in life to have their needs met instead of looking to God. Even as believers, we must be careful not to look to others before we look to the Lord. After their miraculous deliverance from Egyptian bondage, the Israelites did not want to wait for God's instruction and they refused to seek His counsel. As a result, they paid a dear price.

But they soon forgot his works; *they did not wait for his counsel.* But they had a wanton craving in the wilderness, and put God to the test in the desert; he gave them what they asked, but sent a wasting disease among them. (Ps. 106:13-15, emphasis mine)

When the Israelites crossed the Jordan into the Promised Land, the Gibeonites came to make a treaty with them. The Lord had already instructed the Israelites not to make treaties with anyone. The Gibeonites purposely deceived them and Joshua made a treaty. The Scriptures tell us the reason why the Israelites were deceived: "So the men took some of their provisions, *but did not ask counsel from the LORD.*" (Josh. 9:14, emphasis mine).

Saul, the first king of Israel, made blunder after blunder as the leader of the nation. His poor decision making was directly related to his not seeking the counsel of the Lord. "So Saul died for his breach of faith. He broke faith with the LORD in that he did not keep the command of the LORD, and also consulted a medium, seeking guidance. He did not seek guidance from the LORD. Therefore the LORD put him to death and turned the kingdom over to David the son of Jesse" (1 Chron. 10:13-14, emphasis mine).

Many of the kings of Israel and Judah made this same mistake. King Asa was afflicted by disease but never bothered to seek help from the Lord. "In the thirty-ninth year of his reign Asa was diseased in his feet, and his disease became severe. *Yet even in his disease he did not seek the LORD,* but sought help from physicians. And Asa slept with his fathers, dying in the forty-first year of his reign." (2 Chron. 16:12-13)

One last example I want to give is King Ahaziah. He had an accident and fell through the lattice in his upper chamber and became sick. But instead of seeking God, amazingly he sought the help of a pagan god.

> Then the angel of the LORD said to Elijah, "Go down with him; do not be afraid of him." So he arose and went down with him to the king and said to him, "Thus says the LORD, 'Because you have sent messengers to inquire of Baal-zebub, the god of Ekron—*is it because there is no God in Israel to inquire of his word?*—therefore you shall not come down from the bed to which you have gone up, but you shall surely die.'" (2 Kings 1:15-16, emphasis mine)

God is our source! Practicing and incorporating the discipline of daily prayer pleases the Lord because we are acknowledging that He is our source and the answer to our every need. He takes pleasure in being our provider. He is pleased when we come to Him.

How often have we made mistakes and poor decisions that we regret because we did not take the time to pray and seek the guidance and direction of the Spirit? I am sure that all of us would have to confess guilt in this area. Let's pray daily, declaring that God is our help, our guide, our comfort, our strength, our refuge, our strong tower, our shield — yes our source for every need and situation we will ever experience or face in life!

- **Prayer captures God's attention**
The God of this universe invites us to come into His presence and pray. He implores us to seek His face. He extends a call and challenge for us to come before Him, petition Him, ask of Him, and seek from Him. When we do, He promises not only to listen to our prayers, but also to answer them in remarkable and amazing ways!

> *Call to me* and I will answer you, and will tell you great and hidden things that you have not known. (Jer. 33:3, emphasis mine)

> But when you pray, go into your room and shut the door and pray to your Father who is in secret. And your Father *who sees* in secret will reward you. (Matt. 6:6, emphasis mine)

> *For the eyes of the Lord are on the righteous*, and his ears are open to their prayer. But the face of the Lord is against those who do evil. (1 Pet. 3:12, emphasis mine)

> I waited patiently for the LORD; *he inclined to me* and heard my cry. (Ps. 40:1, emphasis mine)

> Because he *inclined his ear to me*, therefore I will call on him as long as I live. (Ps. 116:2, emphasis mine)

Can you see the awesome God who created the universe bending down and inclining His ear to you as you pray? It happens! Prayer gets His attention. When you and I come before Him in prayer, He is pleased and enjoys hearing from us. Every father loves the presence of his children and yearns for communication with his kids. It is amazing that the planet has over seven billion people, yet every time you and I pray, we capture His attention. It seems unbelievable, but this is exactly what God's Word says.

If you knew for sure that God was going to meet you at a certain time, in a designated place, on a particular day of the week, wouldn't you do everything within your ability to make that appointment? You wouldn't dare miss it! The fact of the matter is that God has promised that when we come before Him in prayer, without exception, He will not only meet with us, but He will also listen to our prayers.

Why would we ever go a single day in our lives without seeking the face of God and communing with Him in prayer? Think about this question for awhile before you go to the next thought.

• **Prayer expresses our <u>faith</u>**

Let me be so bold to say that if we are prayerless, we are faithless. It's true. There is no other way to say it. If we really had faith that God hears and answers our prayers, why wouldn't we pray and pray often? We have promise after promise from the Scriptures that God hears and answers prayer.

The only reasonable explanation as to why we don't pray consistently is because we don't believe His promises are true. Prayerlessness is even more significant than failing to believe the Scriptures because it goes directly to the heart of the issue: do we really believe and trust God? Are we questioning the character of God by not placing our faith in Him to answer prayer? Are we not to some degree questioning the integrity of God when we don't pray, knowing that He says He will hear and answer our prayers?

I think prayerlessness is a faith issue and it is no small matter. Prayer really is an expression of our faith, and when we don't pray, we are expressing a lack of faith. Prayer and faith go together. They are inseparable. "And this is the confidence that we have toward him, that if we ask anything according to his will he hears us" (1 John 5:14).

Faith is how we begin our spiritual journey with the Lord, how we advance in our journey, and how we see the supernatural released in our lives during our journey. Willingness to exercise faith is not optional for the believer. As a matter of fact, we cannot please God unless we are people of faith, as the writer of the book of Hebrews explains. "And without faith it is *impossible* to please him, for whoever would draw near to God must believe that he exists and that he rewards those who seek him" (Heb. 11:6, emphasis mine).

Prayer requires that we exercise a certain level of faith. When we pray, our faith is being released in the presence of God. This is pleasing to Him. He takes notice. I have to wonder how many things we have forfeited or what could have been different in our lives had we simply prayed. How many breakthroughs have we missed out on because of a lack of prayer? How many miraculous and supernatural interventions of the Spirit could we have experienced had we been more committed to prayer? Again, faith when combined with prayer releases a spiritual synergy.

In Matthew's gospel, the disciples attempted to cast a demon out of a boy but they failed. They brought the boy to Jesus, who rebuked and cast out the demon. When the disciples saw this, they did not understand why they were not able to cast out the demon. Look at Jesus' explanation:

> And Jesus answered, "O faithless and twisted generation, how long am I to be with you? How long am I to bear with you? Bring him here to me." And Jesus rebuked the demon, and it came out of him, and the boy was healed instantly. Then the disciples came to Jesus privately and said, "Why could we not cast it out?" He said to them, "*Because of your little faith. For truly, I say to you, if you have faith like a grain of mus-tard seed, you will say to this mountain, 'Move from here to there,' and it will move, and nothing will be impossible for you.*" (Matt. 17:17-21, emphasis mine)

The disciples' failure was due to a lack of faith. Throughout the Scriptures, faith is a key component to answered prayer and moving in the supernatural. Matthew chapter 21 gives an account of Jesus cursing a fig tree for not producing its fruit. The disciples were amazed that the tree withered instantly after Jesus cursed it. Notice what Jesus says about the withering of the fig tree:

> When the disciples saw it, they marveled, saying, "How did the fig tree wither at once?" And Jesus answered them, "Truly, I say to you, if you have faith and do not doubt, you will not only do what has been done to the fig tree, but even if you say to this mountain, 'Be taken up and thrown into the sea,' it will happen. And whatever you ask in prayer, you will receive, if *you have faith.*" (Matt. 21:20-22, emphasis mine)

Clearly, faith combined with prayer unleashes a special anointing of the power of the Spirit. As was stated earlier, I am not a proponent of the "name it and claim it" theology, but I do believe that faith is integral to answered prayer.

This brings me back to my point that prayer is an expression of our faith. When we have faith, we will normally incorporate prayer in our daily lives. Faith is that which elicits prayer. When we pray, we are exercising our faith and God always honors and rewards our faith!

- **Prayer assures us of God's <u>blessings</u>**

    Who doesn't want to experience the blessings and favor of the Lord in their lives? God *promises* to bless those who pray. Again, this comes back to having faith in the Scriptures, and ultimately in God.

Here are a couple verses to consider. "You also must help us by prayer, so that many will give thanks on our behalf for the *blessing granted us through the prayers* of many" (2 Cor. 1:11, emphasis mine).

"If you then, who are evil, know how to give good gifts to your children, how much more will your Father who is in heaven give *good things to those who ask him*" (Matt. 7:11, emphasis mine)!

One of my favorite Scriptures and promises in the Bible is found in the book of Ephesians: "Now to him who is able to do *far more abundantly* than all that we ask or think, according to the power at work within us" (Eph. 3:20, emphasis mine).

These are promises of the Lord for those who pray! I want the blessings of the Lord in every aspect of my life, from my ministry, my family, my church, and my relationships, to my decisions and finances. When my wife and I pray, we pray for God's blessings upon our children and grandchildren. We pray for God's protection in their lives from sickness, disease, accidents, and demonic attacks. We pray for blessings upon our church family, for our church staff and leadership, for missionaries, for the extended body of Christ, for our nation, and the list goes on. We believe that God blesses our prayers and sends out blessings as a direct result of our prayers.

I also pray that the Lord will station warring angels in our midst and surround our family and church. I pray for the supernatural to be released among us and that our church will be so blessed that it will impact our city, our region, and beyond. I need the blessings of the Lord in my life. I take serious Jesus' words in John chapter 15 when He says, "apart from me you can do nothing" (John 15:5). If we desire to be blessed of the Lord, be a blessing to others, and make an impact for the kingdom of God, then it is absolutely imperative that we pray!

- **Prayer releases God's power**
  One of the most amazing prayer meetings in the early church is found in Acts chapter 4. After they prayed, the Spirit came down and God's power was unmistakably displayed in their midst. Notice the following verse:

  > And when they had *prayed*, the place in which they were gathered together was shaken, and they were all filled with the Holy Spirit and continued to speak the word of God with boldness. (Acts 4:31, emphasis mine)

There is a direct correlation between their prayers and the power of the Spirit falling in their midst. Every significant move of the Spirit was birthed in a prayer meeting. From the early church in Acts to the Moravians in the 1720s to the church today, prayer is the key to opening the door of the supernatural. If we expect to live under the anointing and power of the Holy Spirit, we definitely need this key called prayer in order to unlock and release God's power. We need God's power for Spirit-filled living, for exercising spiritual gifts, for resisting the temptations of the flesh, for taking authority over the enemy, and for thwarting the attacks of the enemy that will inevitably come our way. This brings us to the next point.

- **Prayer restricts demonic <u>activity</u>**
  One of the dangers of living in our postmodern world that is so highly technologically advanced is to underestimate the power of the unseen world. Paul writing to the Ephesians says:

  > For we do not wrestle against flesh and blood, but against the rulers, against the authorities, against the cosmic powers over this present darkness, against the spiritual forces of evil in the heavenly places. Therefore take up the whole armor of God, that you may be able to withstand in the evil day, and having done all, to stand firm. (Eph. 6:12-13)

  Paul says our enemy is in the unseen world. The enemy can't be physically seen but is nonetheless present. An unseen enemy is much more dangerous because we can forget that he is there, and we assume that we are safe. But Paul states in this passage that we have enemies and they will attack.

  One of the best weapons against our enemies is prayer. Paul describes several ways to battle the enemy, but notice what he says in verse 18 of this section on spiritual warfare: "Praying at all times in the Spirit, with all prayer and supplication. To that end keep alert with all perseverance, making supplication for all the saints" (Eph. 6:18).

  A few years ago, I experienced the most intensive spiritual battle in my ministry. I have no doubt that it was a spiritual attack. It was aggressive and nothing like I had ever experienced before. A few weeks before this attack, my worship leader, Pastor Derek Whitehouse, asked if I would be willing to get together on Thursday mornings to worship and pray. I love to worship, so I agreed and we began to meet.

  What took place surprised both of us. When we began worshipping and praying, the intensity of praying in our spiritual language went into a different realm than we had ever experienced. As we began praying "in the Spirit," we noticed we both began praying in tongues that we knew were *new,* that we had never prayed in before. In addition to the new tongues, our praying in the Spirit was clearly aggressive, combative, and even militant.

Though I did not understand everything at the time, it wasn't long before we both realized we were engaged in what I would describe as warfare praying. The Spirit was praying through us with such intensity, that even my hands were making motions as though I was making declarations in the Spirit. I felt the Spirit take over my hands and make forceful gestures in conjunction with my prayers. I definitely sensed my physical motions were in alignment with my praying. This continued for several weeks until the battle was won.

As I write this chapter, we are still meeting every Thursday morning and our prayer and worship time is still at a level that surprises both of us. We love it! It is awesome! We know the Lord has birthed an anointing in our prayer and worship time that has taken us to a new level. We are definitely seeing things change in a powerful and amazing way!

I share this to say that there is power in prayer. The supernatural is released. Battles are fought and won in prayer. Never underestimate the power of prayer and always press in deeper when you know you are under attack. You will be victorious.

Samuel Chadwick, a Wesleyan Methodist minister, said, "Satan dreads nothing but prayer. [The devil] fears nothing from prayerless studies, prayerless work, prayerless religion. He laughs at our toil, he mocks at our wisdom, but he trembles when we pray."

In the Lord's Prayer, Jesus said, "And lead us not into temptation, but deliver us from evil" (Matt. 6:13). Literally, the phrase says, "deliver us from the evil one." That's why the NIV translates this last phrase, "evil one." His Word tells us to pray specifically for deliverance from the evil one. Notice the next few verses:

> And when he came to the place, he said to them, "Pray that you may not enter into temptation." (Luke 22:40)

> Do not be anxious about anything, but in everything by prayer and supplication with thanksgiving let your requests be made known to God. And the peace of God, which surpasses all understanding, will *guard your hearts and your minds* in Christ Jesus. (Phil. 4:6-7, emphasis mine)

We are not to fear the enemy, but to resist him through prayer and the Word of God. There is incredible power in prayer.

- **Prayer intensifies God's <u>presence</u>**
  The Bible teaches that "Jesus Christ is the same yesterday and today and forever" (Heb. 13:8). I never want to box God in and limit what

He can do. I never want to relegate the supernatural to the first century. What He did in the past, He can do in the present. He never ceases to be the God of the supernatural. I want to live with the expectancy that the supernatural can always be experienced in our midst.

In 2 Chronicles, we read the account of Solomon dedicating the temple that he constructed to the Lord. He prayed and consecrated the temple and asked for God's blessing upon it and the people. As soon as he finished praying, the presence and the glory of the Lord filled the temple. "As soon as Solomon *finished his prayer*, fire came down from heaven and consumed the burnt offering and the sacrifices, *and the glory of the LORD filled the temple*." (2 Chron. 7:1, emphasis mine)

Prayer ushers in the presence of the Lord. When we pray, He comes down in our midst and makes His presence known. God's presence opens the door to the supernatural and the gifts of the Spirit being released and manifested to a greater degree.

There is an interesting Scripture in Luke's gospel: "On one of those days, as he was teaching, Pharisees and teachers of the law were sitting there, who had come from every village of Galilee and Judea and from Jerusalem. *And the power of the Lord was with him to heal*" (Luke 5:17, emphasis mine).

What does "and the power of the Lord was with him to heal" exactly mean? Although Jesus was God in the flesh, He did self-impose limitations upon Himself while ministering in this world. Even though the full implication of these words is probably not fully realized by us, it appears that there were certain times when there was a deeper level of anointing and power available. I think it would be correct to assume that a heightened level of power would imply a heightened level of the presence and anointing of the Spirit. If this is the case, we need to pray for a deeper level of God's presence moving in our midst so that there will be a greater intensity of God's power.

Earlier, I referenced Acts 4:31. We are told in that passage that when the disciples prayed, "the place in which they were gathered together was shaken, and they were all filled with the Holy Spirit and continued to speak the word of God with boldness." Even though they had already been baptized in the Holy Spirit, they were "filled with the Spirit." This tells me that the level of fullness of the Spirit varies in our lives. The Spirit filled them to a deeper level of capacity than they had before they prayed.

There are times when we need a greater level of fullness and anointing than others. It is available, but notice that it came *after* they spent time in prayer. Let's pray believing for more. Let's ask the Lord to so saturate us with His presence that people we encounter on a daily basis will sense the presence and the power of His Spirit upon our lives!

Daily Worship

The last discipline I want to challenge you with is daily worship. When I experienced the baptism in the Holy Spirit, worship took on an entirely new dimension in my life. The first night I came home from the Fresh Wind Fresh Fire Conference, Pam and I pressed into a time of worship that was beyond anything we had ever experienced. I lit candles, turned off the lights, we laid on the floor, and had a time of worship. I was soaking in the Spirit before I even knew there was such a thing! But I can say without any hesitation that making worship a priority in my life has proven to be one of those disciplines that has definitely maintained the freshness and fullness of the Spirit.

Worship is something God not only *desires* from us, but He also *seeks* from us. God is worthy of our worship and adoration! Jesus, speaking to the woman at the well said: "But the hour is coming, and is now here, when the true worshipers will worship the Father in spirit and truth, *for the Father is seeking* such people to worship him. God is spirit, and those who worship him must worship in spirit and truth" (John 4:23-24, emphasis mine).

Seldom do we read that the "Father is seeking." Here, Jesus says the Father is seeking worshippers who will worship Him in spirit and truth. God loves and desires our worship, not simply because He is worthy of our worship, but because He desires to engage His Spirit with our spirits. He enjoys spending time with us. He is Creator and we are His creation. He yearns for us to experience His presence, to build relationship and commune with Him.

Worship is the door that serves as a catalyst. When we worship, His Spirit comes down in our midst and a special intimacy takes place between Father and child. The Bible teaches us that He dwells in the presence of those who worship. The Psalmist wrote, "But You are holy, O You Who dwell in [the holy place where] the praises of Israel [are offered] (Ps. 22:3; *AMP*). I don't know about you, but if praise and worship is where God loves to dwell, then I am going to worship Him often!

What actually is worship? How is it defined? William Temple, Archbishop of Canterbury, wrote, "To worship is to quicken the conscience by the holiness of God, to feed the mind with the truth of God, to purge the imagination with the beauty of God, to open the heart to the love of God, and to devote the will to the purpose of God."[11] The well-known first question of the Westminster Shorter Catechism is "What is the chief end of man?" and the equally well-known answer is, "Man's chief end is to glorify God and to worship Him forever."[12]

A.W. Tozer wrote, "Man was made to worship God. God gave to man a harp and said, 'Here above all the creatures that I have made and created I have given you the largest harp. I put more strings on your instrument and I have given you a wider range than I have given to any other creature. You can worship Me in a manner that no other creature can.' ...Worship is the missing jewel in modern evangelicalism. We're organized; we work; we have our agendas. We have almost everything, but there's one thing that the churches, even the gospel churches, do not have: that is the ability to worship. We are not cultivating the art of worship. It's the one shining gem that is lost to the modern church, and I believe that we ought to search for this until we find it."[13]

The late Oswald Chambers said, "Worshipping God is the great essential of fitness. If you have not been worshipping. . . when you get to work you will not only be useless yourself, but a tremendous hindrance to those who are associated with you."[14]

Warren Wiersbe has this to say about personal interaction with God: "You and I may disagree on some aspects of Christian doctrine, but I am sure there is one thing we definitely agree on: You and I personally, and the church collectively, are desperately in need of transformation. We are weary of 'business as usual.' We need and want a transforming experience from the Lord, the kind of spiritual visitation that will help to heal our broken homes and our split churches; that will strip away our religious veneer and get us back to reality; that will restore true spiritual values and replace the cheap and counterfeits we've been foisting on ourselves and the lost world; that will, most of all, bring such glory to God that the world will sit up and take notice and confess that 'God is truly among you'" (1 Cor. 14:25).[15]

Charles Stanley states, "Now one of the reasons probably is because so many of us have been so strong in evangelism, church growth, and our programs that somewhere along the way praise got left out. There's nothing wrong with programs and there's nothing wrong with evangelism and church growth because all of that is part of a living, growing and vital church; but whatever happened to praise? It may not be quite so evident to some people as it is to others, because first of all, they never missed it, they never experienced it, they know little about it, and so praise appeared to be something new. But let me tell you, friend, that it is not new. It is not man-made, it is not new, it is not some theological strain, it is not some new avenue or fad, it is not some new denominational hand-me-down, it doesn't belong to a certain group: It is a command in the Word of God. And what's happening is, the Holy Spirit is invading this generation and enabling the church of the Lord Jesus Christ to fulfill its goal to exalt and praise Almighty God."[16]

All these are excellent definitions and thoughts of the meaning and importance of worship. Worship to me is simply me honoring Him as creator and redeemer, adoring Him for His love and grace, expressing my thanksgiving to Him for His forgiveness and the gift of eternal life, acknowledging His lordship over my life, acknowledging Him as my provider and shepherd, and expressing my love for Him as my God. I worship Him because He is worthy of my praise!

There is so much more that could be said on this subject but let me share a few additional thoughts about worship.

- **Worship involves joyful praise**
  When you read the Psalms, you discover that worship and joyful praise are often linked together. The Lord takes pleasure when worship is filled with joyful praise. Whether in private or corporate worship, we can worship with

a joyful spirit unto the Lord. When we reflect on the goodness of God, what He has provided, what is yet to be provided because of our personal relationship with Him, we burst forth in joyful and celebrative praise!

My soul will be satisfied as with fat and rich food, and my mouth will praise you with joyful lips. (Ps. 63:5)

Oh come, let us sing to the LORD; let us make a joyful noise to the rock of our salvation! Let us come into his presence with thanksgiving; let us make a joyful noise to him with songs of praise! (Ps. 95:1-2)

Make a joyful noise to the LORD, all the earth! (Ps. 100:1)

- **Worship involves unconditional surrender**

God wants all of us - second to none. When our hearts are surrendered to Him, to His plans, and to His purpose for our lives, we are demonstrating worship. When we unconditionally surrender to Him, we are acknowledging that He is the priority of our life, the love of our life, and is infinitely worthy of our praise.

The reverend doctor G. Campbell Morgan, a British evangelist and Bible scholar, said: "Religion is that which binds a man. Every man is bound somewhere, somehow, to a throne, to a government, to an authority, to something that is supreme, to something to which he offers sacrifice, and burns incense, and bends the knee."[17]

Jesus stated that we are to worship in spirit and in truth (see John 4:24). Before we can worship in spirit and truth we must have the Spirit within us. The Holy Spirit takes up residence in every person who repents of his or her sin and places faith and trust in the Lord Jesus. Yet, having the Holy Spirit living within us does not guarantee that we will always worship in spirit and truth. To worship God in spirit is to worship from the inside out. It means to be sincere in our acts of worship.

No matter how wonderful our worship service and music may be, if we are not living in sincerity and walking in the spirit of truth, we are living in hypocrisy and our worship is just a religious exercise. The balance of worshipping in spirit is worshipping in truth.

Our worship should reflect that we are bound to no one other than our Lord and Savior Jesus Christ. It is difficult to worship when we are still clinging to other things and have not relinquished everything to God. Jesus states that it is impossible to serve more than one master. Notice His words: "No one can serve two masters, for either he will hate the one and love the other, or he will be devoted to the one and despise the other. You cannot serve God and money"

(Matt. 6:24). How can we offer pure and unadulterated worship if we have hearts that are not totally surrendered to the Lord? That's duplicity.

Jesus deserves our undivided loyalty and allegiance. Let's make sure we come into His presence with hearts that are true and faithful to Him.

- **Worship focuses on and responds to God**

The more we focus on God, the more we understand and appreciate how worthy He is. As we come to understand and appreciate His worthiness, we can't help but respond to Him. Just as an indescribable sunset or breathtaking mountaintop evokes a spontaneous response within our spirits, so does an encounter with the worthiness of God evoke the response of worship.

Living in Sarasota, Florida, Pam and I will often walk on the beach in the evening. As the sun begins to go down, it is interesting to watch the people on the beach. Without exception, almost everybody stops and watches the sun as it slowly fades into the horizon. The sun sets every day, but watching it take place is so spectacular that people can't help but stop and watch as the sun appears to descend into the ocean. People have their cameras and camcorders in hand capturing this magnificent scene. It is breathtaking each time it happens!

Can you imagine what it will be like to bow in the presence of Almighty God, creator and sustainer of the universe? Worship will be instant and spontaneous. I want to encourage you to focus on God's majesty, His beauty, His love, His grace, and His promises. Try to picture Him on the cross dying for your sins. Then ask the Spirit to impress upon you the vision of the resurrected Lord Jesus in all of His majesty and glory. He will usher you into worship as you bask in His presence.

- **Worship is expected both publicly and privately**

> "Let us not give up meeting together, as some are in the habit
> of doing, but let us encourage one another—and all the more
> as you see the Day approaching" (Heb. 10:25, *NIV*).

The early believers were expected to practice both corporate and private worship. One of the first things every new believer should develop is the habit of faithfully assembling with other believers in meetings where the primary purpose is to worship the Lord Jesus in the presence of the Spirit.

Christianity is not an isolationist religion. The New Testament describes the church with such metaphors as body, building, and household—each of which speaks of a relationship between individual units and a larger whole. It is not an option for the believer to choose not to worship with other believers. Worship is a biblical mandate. Your private devotional life doesn't exempt you from worshipping with other believers.

On the other hand, regardless of how fulfilling, exciting, and glorious our corporate worship may be, it doesn't take away our responsibility to worship privately. There are experiences in our private worship that we will never have in corporate worship. Jesus participated in both public worship (in the synagogues) and in private worship, alone in the wilderness or elsewhere. Our corporate worship should be an overflow of our private worship.

- **Worship is cultivated throughout one's life**
Worshipping God throughout a lifetime requires discipline. Worship is all about our heart's passion and love for the Lord Jesus. It is a response of the heart that loves and desires more intimacy with God. And though it is a response of the heart, it does require some level of discipline.

For instance, there will be times when we do not feel spiritual or close to the Lord; nevertheless, we cannot put our worship on hold. As a matter of fact, it is during these times that we need to press in. And when we do, the Spirit will gently meet and lovingly encourage us in the Lord.

Earlier, I mentioned that worship is focusing on and responding to God. The more we worship God, the more we become like Him. People are transformed by what they focus on. We emulate what we think about. If one is constantly thinking about being successful in business, then one will study those things that make one successful and emulate people who are successful in that particular field. If our focus is pleasure, then our life and priorities will reflect that. If our focus is materialism, then our lifestyle and surroundings will reflect that.

What I am saying is this: when our focus is on the Lord and on worshipping Him, our lifestyle will reflect that aim. Worshipping God must be our focus. Worship can be cultivated, developed, and intensified as we practice worship and grow and mature in our relationship with Him.

Any discipline, from hitting a golf ball to playing an instrument, requires outside help from those more experienced. When it comes to worship, I have found that worshipping with others can accelerate and advance our spiritual development in this discipline. I want to encourage you to plan worship times with friends in your home. This can significantly broaden your worship experience and intimacy with the Lord. It can also be a time when you learn to practice your spiritual gifts and develop them. Praying in the Spirit, words of knowledge, prophecy, the laying on of hands for healing, and the exercise of other spiritual gifts can all be done in worshipping and praying with others. Worship is not confined to a building because His presence is not confined to buildings. Learn to practice and cultivate worship!

Conclusion

As I bring this chapter to a close, I want to mention two books that have blessed and given me direction in the area of spiritual disciplines. I am sure there are others, but the two that have impacted my life are *The Celebration of Discipline*, by Richard Foster, and *Spiritual Disciplines for the Christian Life*, by Donald Whitney. I have dealt with only three spiritual disciplines in this chapter: daily intake of the Word, daily prayer, and daily worship. In these books just mentioned, the authors expound on all the disciplines that will be extremely beneficial in your spiritual journey of growth. I strongly recommend them.

Spiritual disciplines are not easy to maintain. This is why they are called *disciplines*. But for those who learn, practice, and excel in them, great is their reward! I am reminded of the words of Tom Landry, coach of the Dallas Cowboys for almost three decades: "The job of a football coach is to make men do what they don't want to do in order to achieve what they've always wanted to be."[18] To illustrate what Coach Landry means, let me leave you with a moving illustration that begins chapter one in Donald Whitney's book, *Spiritual Disciplines for the Christian Life:*

> Imagine six-year-old Kevin, whose parents have enrolled him in music lessons. After school every afternoon, he sits in the living room and reluctantly strums "Home on the Range" while watching his buddies play baseball in the park across the street. That's discipline without direction. It's drudgery.
>
> Now suppose Kevin is visited by an angel one afternoon during guitar practice. In a vision he's taken to Carnegie Hall. He's shown a guitar virtuoso giving a concert. Usually bored by classical music, Kevin is astonished by what he sees and hears. The musician's fingers dance excitedly on the strings with fluidity and grace. Kevin thinks of how stupid and klunky his hands feel when they halt and stumble over the chords. The virtuoso blends clean, soaring notes into a musical aroma that wafts from his guitar. Kevin remembers the toneless, irritating discord that comes stumbling out of his.
>
> But Kevin is enchanted. His head tilts slightly to one side as he listens. He drinks in everything. He never imagined that anyone could play the guitar like this.
>
> "What do you think, Kevin?" asks the angel.
>
> The answer is a soft, slow, six-year-old's "W-o-w!"

The vision vanishes, and the angel is again standing in front of Kevin in his living room. "Kevin," says the angel, "the wonderful musician you saw is you in a few years." Then pointing at the guitar, the angel declares, "But you must practice!"

Suddenly the angel disappears and Kevin finds himself alone with his guitar. Do you think his attitude toward practice will be different now? As long as he remembers what he's going to become, Kevin's discipline will have a direction, a goal that will pull him into the future. Yes, effort will be involved, but you could hardly call it drudgery.[19]

Discussion Questions

1. What comes to your mind when you hear the word *discipline*?

2. What are spiritual disciplines?

3. Why is the discipline of having daily intake of the Word important? What advantages have you personally experienced?

4. How important are the Scriptures to Jesus? Why is this significant?

5. Why is daily prayer important?

6. How important was prayer to Jesus? What are the implications of the prayer life of Jesus?

7. What are the advantages of having a daily prayer life?

8. How would you describe the word *worship*?

9. Why should we worship?

10. What are some of the elements of worship?

11. Of the spiritual disciplines, which ones do you feel are most difficult to maintain? Why?

12. How often and why should a local church focus on prayer?

Chapter Nine

Spiritual Gifts

T he Bible teaches that the Holy Spirit gives spiritual gifts to those in the body of Christ for the purpose of building and edifying His church. Christ desires that His church is vibrant, strong, and healthy. To accomplish this, the Holy Spirit gives to each member of His body various gifts that will enhance the growth of His church both spiritually and numerically. A key passage in the Bible that describes and explains spiritual gifts is found in the apostle Paul's first epistle to the Corinthians. It is a rather extensive passage and I want to point out several significant statements it makes about spiritual gifts. Please read it carefully.

> Now there are varieties of gifts, but the same Spirit; and there are varieties of service, but the same Lord; and there are varieties of activities, but it is the same God who empowers them all in everyone. To each is given the manifestation of the Spirit for the common good. For to one is given through the Spirit the utterance of wisdom, and to another the utterance of knowledge according to the same Spirit, to another faith by the same Spirit, to another gifts of healing by the one Spirit, to another the working of miracles, to another prophecy, to another the ability to distinguish between spirits, to another various kinds of tongues, to another the interpretation of tongues. All these are empowered by one and the same Spirit, who apportions to each one individually as he wills. For just as the body is one and has many members, and all the members of the body, though many, are one body, so it is with Christ. For in one Spirit we were all baptized into one body—Jews or Greeks, slaves or free—and all were made to drink of one Spirit. For the body does not consist of one member but of many. If the foot should say, "Because I am not a hand, I do not belong to the body," that would not make it any less a part of the body. And if the ear should say, "Because I am not an eye, I do not belong to the body," that would not make it any less a part of

the body. If the whole body were an eye, where would be the sense of hearing? If the whole body were an ear, where would be the sense of smell? But as it is, God arranged the members in the body, each one of them, as he chose. If all were a single member, where would the body be? As it is, there are many parts, yet one body. The eye cannot say to the hand, "I have no need of you," nor again the head to the feet, "I have no need of you." On the contrary, the parts of the body that seem to be weaker are indispensable, and on those parts of the body that we think less honorable we bestow the greater honor, and our unpresentable parts are treated with greater modesty, which our more presentable parts do not require. But God has so composed the body, giving greater honor to the part that lacked it, that there may be no division in the body, but that the members may have the same care for one another. If one member suffers, all suffer together; if one member is honored, all rejoice together. (1 Cor. 12:4-26)

In this passage, Paul says several things about spiritual gifts and the need for them within a church. *First*, he says that there are a variety of gifts. The gifts are numerous because the needs within the church are diverse. He illustrates this by comparing Christ's church with our physical bodies. Just as our physical bodies have many different members that allow it to function and operate properly, so does the church have various spiritual gifts given by the Spirit that make it possible for the church body to function as an effective unit. God has created our bodies with many parts. Some are visible while others are hidden and unnoticed. The same is true of His church. The church is His body, and for it to operate correctly, it too must have a diversity of parts that use a variety of gifts.

Second, it is the Holy Spirit who imparts the various gifts. The Spirit is the one who makes the selection of which gifts are given to individual members so that the body will be fully equipped, effective, and have the ability to reach maximum potential for ministry. The differing gifts add to and complement one another for the strengthening of the body.

Third, it is the Holy Spirit who empowers and enables these gifts. This is why we need to be living and walking in the realm of the Spirit. He provides us the power and ability to exercise the gifts He gives us for the purpose of bringing edification in the church. He knows exactly how the gifts need to function within His body. In any given worship service, the Spirit is aware of the individual needs of each person present and is able to empower those gifts to function when needed.

Fourth, every gift is significant and necessary. Our body functions best when all of our body parts are working correctly. I have had two surgeries in my lifetime. In both situations, my body gave me notice that there was a

152

problem—pain in my abdomen. My first surgery was at the age of 19 when my appendix came close to rupturing. The physician removed it the old fashion way, by making an incision instead of laparoscopic surgery, as is the standard procedure now. The second surgery took place when I was 49 years of age. I was experiencing significant pain in my abdomen once again. After spending several hours in the emergency room and going through a battery of tests, the doctors discovered I had a benign tumor in my colon. The only answer was surgery, and once again, a fairly significant incision had to be made.

Neither of these surgeries were pleasant situations. Parts of my body were malfunctioning. And even though these areas of my body were unseen, it was critical that they were functioning correctly, because they affected my *entire* body. Paul says the same thing about the diversity of gifts the Spirit gives to His body, the church.

There are many different spiritual gifts within the body and they are all needed. Each gift and gift-bearer has a significant role to play in order for the body to function correctly and maintain its overall health. Every gift has been specifically and individually given to each of the members and none should be marginalized. Each gift has its function and responsibility within the body and each is needed. No exceptions. Without these individual gifts operating correctly within the body, the body will not function to its maximum potential. Every gift must be valued and appreciated. This includes those gifts that often work behind the scenes and receive little if any recognition. All have significance and are critical to the entire body.

The Gifts

How many spiritual gifts are there? Are all the gifts given to the church in the first century available today? Have some of the gifts ceased to be given because they are no longer needed? As I read and study my Bible, I cannot find one Scripture that says any of the spiritual gifts will be eliminated. Why would we need any less spiritual gifts than the early church needed for them to operate and advance the kingdom?

There are some who teach that certain gifts of the Spirit have passed away or ceased to exist, but I cannot find any biblical justification for this position. Every spiritual gift the Holy Spirit gave to the early church is available for believers today. Even though we live in the twenty-first century, we are no different from the early church in terms of our needs and challenges to building the church. We too need all the gifts of the Holy Spirit to be imparted and empowered within us in order to reach our highest level of ministry and impact our world for Christ.

Why then would some teach that certain gifts have ceased to operate or pass away? The primary reason centers on certain gifts that are more controversial than others, namely speaking in tongues, prophecy, healing, words of wisdom, and words of knowledge. These gifts are more susceptible to abuse than the other gifts, a reason why some prefer to ignore them or teach that they are no longer available. Many churches and denominations take the position that some gifts are not available today, often allowing one's theological traditions and biases to overrule the clear teaching of the Scriptures. But what does *the Bible* say about these more controversial gifts?

In Paul's letter to the Corinthians, chapters 12-14 deal extensively with the gifts of the Holy Spirit. The church in Corinth had all of the gifts of the Holy Spirit operating in their midst with power. But the exercising of the gifts in any church can be abused. This church was no exception. Thus, it becomes necessary for Paul to devote three chapters of this epistle to teaching and correcting their understanding of spiritual gifts.

As Paul begins his letter, in the very first chapter, he writes the following:

> I give thanks to my God always for you because of the grace of
> God that was given you in Christ Jesus, that in every way you
> were enriched in him in all speech and all knowledge—even as
> the testimony about Christ was confirmed among you—so that
> you are not lacking in any gift, *as you wait for the revealing of
> our Lord Jesus Christ.* (1 Cor. 1:4-7, emphasis mine)

I want to point out two significant things in this passage. First, Paul says this church does not lack in "any gift." Every gift of the Spirit was imparted to the members of this church. All the gifts were in operation. Second, notice the phrase I italicized: "*as you wait for the revealing of our Lord Jesus Christ.*" Paul certainly doesn't imply that any of the gifts will cease. The clear implication of Paul's statement is that he expects all of the gifts of the Spirit to be in operation until the Second Coming of Christ, until "*the revealing of our Lord Jesus Christ.*" The Second Coming of Christ has definitely not taken place. Paul fully expects all of the gifts to be in operation until He comes!

So what biblical justification is given to limit the operation of certain gifts? As I said earlier, it is chiefly a case of theological bias, the misinterpretation of the Scriptures, and traditional teaching. When I was in college and seminary, the only passage of Scripture cited in an effort to prove that certain gifts of the Spirit have ceased is the following:

> Love never ends. As for prophecies, they will pass away; as
> for tongues, they will cease; as for knowledge, it will pass
> away. For we know in part and we prophesy in part, but when
> the perfect comes, the partial will pass away. When I was a
> child, I spoke like a child, I thought like a child, I reasoned
> like a child. When I became a man, I gave up childish ways.
> For now we see in a mirror dimly, but then face to face. Now
> I know in part; then I shall know fully, even as I have been
> fully known. So now faith, hope, and love abide, these three;
> but the greatest of these is love. (1 Cor. 13:8-13)

154

The key phrase that is cited to "prove" that certain gifts, particularly "the gift of tongues," have ceased is the phrase, "but when the perfect comes, the partial will pass away." A pastor that I dearly admired used this phrase to say that the gift of tongues has passed away. He was a phenomenal preacher, but his theological bias circumvented the clear interpretation of the text. He and other cessationists held that "the perfect" is the Bible, believing that because the Bible has been completed and is available, we no longer need tongues or supernatural signs or gifts. The Scripture often used to argue this view comes from the book of James: "But the one who looks into the perfect law, the law of liberty, and perseveres, being no hearer who forgets but a doer who acts, he will be blessed in his doing" (Jas. 1:25).

I will be the first to admit and preach that the Bible is perfect, in every way. It is God's inspired and infallible Word without any error. But the context of the passage in 1 Corinthians is not referring to the Bible. The "perfect" in the Corinthian passage refers to the Second Coming of Christ. There are no reputable evangelical scholars of commentaries who would say that this use of "perfect" refers to the Bible. According to Paul, when the "perfect comes" (1 Cor. 13:10), "knowledge will pass away." Has this happened since the completion of the Bible? If anything, knowledge is increasing. When Jesus returns, it is then that we will all have perfect knowledge as we will have the mind of Christ. We will not need to learn as we will understand and know everything when we receive our new bodies and minds in Christ.

The second significant statement Paul makes is that in relationship to "the perfect coming," we will no longer "see in a mirror dimly, but then face to face." Do we really have total clarity about things in the Spirit? Are there still not things that we understand partially but not fully? Do not things happen in this life that at times leave us confused, but we by faith trust the Lord has a reason? I don't think any of us has perfect vision and clarity concerning many things in life.

Third, Paul says that when "the perfect" comes, "then I shall know fully, even as I have been fully known" (1 Cor. 13:12). Paul was not around at the completion of the Scriptures. The interpretation of "the perfect" as the completion of the Scriptures does not make sense in this context. However, if "the perfect" refers to the Second Coming of Christ, this passage makes complete sense. In fact, theological scholars say that "the perfect" does refer to Christ's Second Coming.

This passage in 1 Corinthians is the chief passage in the entire Bible that is used to argue that certain spiritual gifts have ceased. As we have seen, this passage does not support that position. When one is desperate to prove one's point, one runs the risk of twisting Scripture into what one wants it to mean. As I mentioned in an earlier chapter, this is what I refer to as theological gymnastics. We must allow the Scriptures to speak for themselves as we seek to interpret their meaning. We cannot force a meaning into the Scriptures in order to fit into our theological biases. We have to consider the entire context of a passage if we are to interpret it correctly.

Based on the Scriptures, we must conclude that all of the gifts of the Holy Spirit provided to the early church are available to His church today. Praise be unto the Lord!

The Various Gifts of the Spirit

There are three main passages in the Bible that list the various gifts: Romans 12:3-8, Ephesians 4:8-12, and 1 Corinthians 12:4-11, 28. How many gifts are there? This depends on how a person views and defines the nature of spiritual gifts. In his book, *Your Spiritual Gifts Can Help Your Church Grow*, Dr. Peter Wagner lists 28 spiritual gifts. In Hayford's *Bible Handbook*, the writer points out a distinction within the Godhead of distribution of the gifts: God the Father (see Rom. 12:3-8); God the Son (see Eph. 4:11); and God the Holy Spirit (see 1 Cor. 12:4-11, 28).

I am not sure that it is necessary to be concerned with this distinction as much as simply recognizing that there are a variety of gifts that God imparts to His body. Some of the gifts imparted are actually *people*, who have been called and provided as *gifts* to His church for edification—apostles, prophets, evangelists, pastors, and teachers. These are people with a special calling upon their lives to the body of Christ. They are uniquely equipped to minister and build the body of Christ and to equip God's people for the work of the ministry (see Eph. 4:11; 1 Cor. 12:28-29).

Other gifts appear to be permanent gifts in people's lives for serving and ministering within the body (practical service). These gifts are teaching, serving, giving, mercy, and hospitality (see Rom. 12:3-8; 1 Pet. 4:10-11). Then there are the nine gifts of the Holy Spirit which can function within any member of the body as the Holy Spirit sees fit. The basic gifts of the Spirit are *prophecy, tongues, interpretation of tongues, word of knowledge, word of wisdom, discerning of spirits, working of miracles, gifts of healing,* and *faith*. A person may have one or more of these gifts in which they function on a regular basis, or the Spirit may come upon any person to exercise one of these gifts at any time or on any occasion. Many of the gifts are self explanatory (teaching, serving, giving, mercy, hospitality), but let me define the gifts of the Spirit as described in 1 Corinthians 12.

- "The word of wisdom" is a supernatural utterance that reveals God's purpose or perspective to a specific circumstance (12:8).
- "The word of knowledge" is supernatural revelation of information concerning a specific situation, event, or person (12:8).
- "Faith" goes beyond saving faith, but is specifically related to God's activity in a particular matter (v.9).

- "Healings" refers to the miraculous manifestation of healings of diseases beyond the scope of natural or human intervention (v.9).
- "Working of miracles" is the superseding of natural law and process for the accomplishing of God's purpose in a situation (v.10).
- "Prophecy" is the work of the Spirit that discloses truth, bringing edification, exhortation, and comfort to God's people (v.10).
- "Distinguish between spirits" means the supernatural recognition of demonic activity in a situation or in the motives of people (v.10).
- "Various kinds of tongues" is the supernatural utterance of a language not known to the speaker. This is used both for witness (see Acts 2:8-13) and for personal communication with God for the purpose of edification in prayer and worship (see 1 Cor. 12:10; 14:2).
- "Interpretation of tongues" is the public interpretation of a message in tongues for the benefit of the congregation (v.10).

Paul does not suggest that the gifts are the possession of the individual or to be ranked in terms of their importance. The function of the gifts is like the individual placement of people in the body of Christ. Each person has a place, and each person is resourced with the Holy Spirit in such a way as to benefit the whole body (see 1 Cor. 12:11).[1]

CAUTION AND THE PROPER USE OF THE GIFTS

Though the gifts of the Spirit are necessary and vital to empower, edify, and build a healthy church, they can be abused. Within the Corinthian church, members were abusing certain spiritual gifts and causing problems. In chapters 12-14, Paul addresses the gifts and how they are to be used properly. The gifts of prophecy and tongues were two particular gifts being abused. Therefore the apostle gives specific instructions on how these gifts should function and operate within the congregation.

I think it is important to make a clarification concerning tongues. A distinction needs to be made between the *gift* of tongues (a message in tongues given to the congregation, which requires an interpretation) and one's *praying and praising in tongues*. As I have mentioned earlier, the biblical pattern that takes place when a person is baptized in the Holy Spirit is the impartation of speaking in tongues, which is a *prayer and praise language. Prayer and praise* tongues are a different expression of tongues from when someone gives a *message in tongues* in the church. On the day of Pentecost, the Scriptures say that the people were proclaiming "the mighty works of God" (Acts 2:11); and when the Gentiles were baptized in the Spirit they were "extolling God" in tongues (Acts 10:46). Pastor Jack Hayford refers to these kinds of tongues as "spiritual language" for the purpose of prayer and praise.[2]

As Spirit-filled believers, we have the ability to not only pray and praise God in our native tongue, but also in our spiritual language given to us by the Holy Spirit. The Bible teaches that we are edified when we utilize our spiritual language in prayer and praise. Notice Paul's words:

> For one who speaks in a tongue speaks *not to men but to God*; for no one understands him, but he utters mysteries in the Spirit. On the other hand, the one who prophesies speaks to people for their upbuilding and encouragement and consolation. The one who speaks in a tongue *builds up himself*, but the one who prophesies builds up the church. (1 Cor. 14:2-4, emphasis mine)

When we use tongues for prayer and praise, the only one who understands is God. The Spirit is praying through us or praising God through us as we cooperate with the Holy Spirit. Again, look at Paul's words:

> For if I pray in a tongue, my spirit prays but *my mind is unfruitful*. What am I to do? I will pray with my spirit, but I will pray with my mind also; I will sing praise with my spirit, but I will sing with my mind also. (1 Cor. 14:14-15)

In this passage, Paul is saying there are times when he prays in the Spirit (in tongues) in which he is not aware of the substance of his prayers; but then he also prays with his "mind" (his own language) in which he knows and understands what he is praying. When he refers to his mind as "unfruitful," he is saying that he does not understand what he is praying in his spiritual language-language that he doesn't understand. He even says that he sings praise songs in the Spirit (in tongues) by which the Spirit is giving praise to God in a language he doesn't understand.

But then he sings with his "mind" (his own language) that he does understand. He employs both spiritual language and his own language in his worship and prayer time. So praying and praising in the Spirit in this context is *different* from giving a message in tongues in the congregation.

A *message in tongues* is an inspired utterance of the Holy Spirit that is given in the context of a worship service *for the congregation*. When someone gives a message in tongues to the congregation, an interpretation is *necessary*; and there can only be three messages in tongues in any one worship service. Notice Paul's instructions:

> If any speak in a tongue, let there be only two or at most three, and each in turn, and let someone interpret. But if there is no one to interpret, let each of them keep silent in church and speak to himself and to God. (1 Cor. 14:27-28)

158

In the above passage, these tongues refer to *messages* in tongues given to the congregation which require an interpretation. These are the tongues spoken of in 1 Corinthians 12:30. Within this context, not everyone in the congregation functions in this gift. The Spirit could come upon any person within the congregation and a message in tongues could be given, but not everyone in the congregation will operate in this gift. This is why the answer to the questions in 1 Corinthians 12 requires a *no* answer.

> Are all apostles? Are all prophets? Are all teachers? Do all
> work miracles? Do all possess gifts of healing? Do all speak
> with tongues? Do all interpret? But earnestly desire the
> higher gifts. And I will show you a still more excellent way.
> (1 Cor. 12:29-31)

Occasionally in our worship services, when we are either praying or giving praise to God in tongues, someone will ask me if this is biblical since there are more than three people speaking in tongues at the same time without an interpretation being given. My response to them is that when people are praying or praising in tongues, an interpretation is not required. It is only when someone gives *a message* in tongues that an interpretation is required. When a person gives a message in tongues to the congregation, the congregation always becomes quiet and waits for the interpretation.

I have noticed that typically, people give a message in tongues while there is an interlude between worship songs. Following the message in tongues, the interpretation is given. The Bible supports this orderly occurrence of a message being delivered in tongues, followed by an interpretation of that message.

The other gift of the Spirit that has the potential to be abused is the gift of prophecy. Prophecy is a message given in a language the congregation understands. It is designed for edification, exhortation, and bringing comfort to God's people.

> On the other hand, the one who prophesies speaks to people
> for their upbuilding and encouragement and consolation.
> (1 Cor. 14:3)

A prophecy can be a word of exhortation, encouragement, or comfort to the congregation. It is not designed to bring condemnation or to tear down, but rather to edify and build up. Prophecy takes place when the Spirit comes upon a person and gives him or her special anointing to speak a word or message that will bring edification to an individual or the church as a whole.

A prophetic word may be intended for a specific person in the congregation or for the entire congregation. It may be a particular Scripture that the Spirit places on the heart of someone to share. It can be a word that brings confirmation to the congregation about the Spirit's leading. It may be a word for leadership. A congregation can be blessed, encouraged, affirmed, and confirmed through various prophecies as the Spirit moves upon His people.

Yet, the gift of prophecy can be abused. In my brief experience serving in a Spirit-filled environment, I would say this gift is more likely to be abused than others. This is why the Bible tells us that all prophecies are to be evaluated and tested.

> Let two or three prophets speak, and let the others weigh what is said. If a revelation is made to another sitting there, let the first be silent. For you can all prophesy one by one, so that all may learn and all be encouraged, and the spirits of prophets are subject to prophets. For God is not a God of confusion but of peace. (1 Cor. 14:29-33)

The reason why prophecies are to be weighed or tested by others is because people "prophesy in part" (1 Cor. 13:9). The Spirit typically provides only a partial word or message. When a prophetic word is given to us, we need to make sure we do not add to what we *think* it means. This is where prophets can quickly lead people or a congregation astray. The prophet must share only the words the Spirit reveals. If prophets choose to offer their opinion concerning an interpretation, they must be careful to distinguish between the two.

Let me share a word about personal prophecies or directive prophecies. By personal or directive, I am referring to when a person says he or she has a prophetic word specifically for an individual. Extreme caution needs to be used when it comes to personal prophecy, especially when people are told they should take certain directives or actions.

The Holy Spirit does give prophetic words that are intended for particular people, but I feel it is critical for other prophets or church leadership, such as the elders, to be present when the prophetic word is given. As they listen to the prophecy, they should seek to affirm within their spirits if they too have confirmation concerning the prophetic word, that is, if they agree with what is being prophesied. The person who is the recipient of the prophetic word should also have confirmation within his or her spirit. There should be peace, not confusion or tension.

I have heard of people sharing prophetic words concerning who others are to marry, or that the person should change jobs, move to another state, or that God is calling them into full-time ministry. These are life-altering decisions and should always have confirmation from the Bible and from others. The Bible says there is safety in a multitude of counselors (see Prov. 11:14). I wholeheartedly agree!

I have experienced well-intentioned people who genuinely felt they have a prophetic word for others, but in the end their feeling proved to be just that—*a feeling*. They thought they were hearing from God, but they were incorrect. Unfortunately, many people have been hurt and confused because someone *thought* he or she heard a word of prophecy for someone else, and that "word" ended up being false. This is why prophetic words are to be tested by the Bible and by others. People may have the best intentions and truly believe they have a word from the Lord, but can be totally off base. As a result, many people want nothing to do with the prophetic ministry. This is why "weighing" the prophetic word is necessary.

On the other hand, when the gift of prophecy is exercised correctly as the Scriptures outline, prophecy can be effective, encouraging, affirming, and powerful in the life of a congregation or individuals. Pam and I are part of a fellowship called Ministers Fellowship International (MFI). They are not a denomination, nor do they provide ministerial credentials. They are a Spirit-filled fellowship of non-denominational churches for ministers to network, build relationships, and receive help and assistance to sharpen their skills and build their churches.

In 2011, Pam and I were quite discouraged and uncertain about our future. Personally, I had never been so discouraged in my entire ministry. I was actually considering leaving the pastorate and becoming a hospital chaplain. In October of 2011, the MFI annual conference convened in Portland, Oregon. In deep discouragement, I had decided not to attend. On Monday, the first day of the conference, the chairman of MFI, Pastor Frank Damazio, called me and told me that I needed to get on a plane and come to the conference. He assured me that I would get clarification for my ministry. I thought it was a crazy idea, but I talked it over with Pam and we made quick arrangements to get flights to Portland and attend the conference.

We arrived late Monday night and were there in time for the main sessions that began on Tuesday morning. I had attended three other MFI conferences, but this was the first time that they had prophetic teams for those who wanted to receive personal prophetic ministry. The MFI leadership encouraged us to sign up to meet with a team, which we did, despite my skepticism about "hearing a word from the Lord." There were three people on this team, and as they began to share, I couldn't believe what I was hearing. They knew nothing about us, but their prophetic utterances were right on target. We were blessed, encouraged, and renewed in the calling God placed upon our lives and ministry. Thank the Lord for the gift of prophecy!

GIFTS VERSUS SPIRITUAL MATURITY

When it comes to the gifts of the Spirit, there is a danger of developing spiritual pride. This is especially true when you start thinking that the gift comes from you instead of the Holy Spirit. People can become so enamored with the gift and the person who has the gift that they forget that it is the Holy Spirit that enables and empowers the gift. Some people feel as if they are inferior Christians because they do not have certain gifts. They feel inadequate and less than spiritual. But let me make it clear that having spiritual giftings does *not* make a person spiritual.

As a matter of fact, you can be filled with spiritual gifts and still be a carnal and immature believer. A case and point is the Corinthian church. I mentioned earlier that this church appeared to function in all of the gifts of the Holy Spirit. They came behind in no gift-they had them all (see 1 Cor. 1:7). Yet, though they possessed an abundance of gifts, spiritually they were immature in their faith. They were like newborn babies. Notice the words of Paul:

> But I, brothers, could not address you *as spiritual people*, but as people of the flesh, as infants in Christ. I fed you with milk, not solid food, for you were not ready for it. And even now you are not yet ready, for you are still of the flesh. For while there is jealousy and strife among you, are you not of the flesh and behaving only in a human way? (1 Cor. 3:1-3, emphasis mine)

Here is a church filled with gifts of the Holy Spirit but the apostle could not address them as "spiritual people." They had to be fed with "milk" and not with "meat" because they were so immature, like little babies. What an indictment! But that was the case. So don't ever be intimidated by those who operate in spiritual gifts, thinking they are more spiritual than you. Spiritual gifts are not to be equated with spiritual maturity.

If you want a measurement of spiritual maturity, look to the fruit of the Spirit, not the gifts of the Spirit. "But the fruit of the Spirit is love, joy, peace, patience, kindness, goodness, faithfulness, gentleness, self-control; against such things there is no law." (Gal. 5:22)

It is the fruit of the Spirit in the lives of people that really distinguishes those who are mature in their faith. The "fruit of the Spirit" operating in a person's life is the true measurement of spiritual maturity, not the gifts of the Spirit. So don't feel less than spiritual because you don't have certain gifts that others have. The Spirit gives the gifts individually to those in the body where needed. Focus on yielding your life to the Holy Spirit. He will form within you the fruit of the Spirit, and in time, the gifts you need will be imparted unto you!

Seeking Spiritual Gifts

I want to correct a fallacy that I have heard often: "You are not to seek spiritual gifts." The common phrase is, "Don't seek the gift, seek the Giver." I know what people mean by this statement, but it isn't biblical. As a matter of fact, the apostle Paul tells us just the opposite—seek spiritual gifts! "Pursue love, and *earnestly desire* the spiritual gifts, especially that you may prophesy" (1 Cor. 14:1, my emphasis).

Notice Paul says, "earnestly desire the spiritual gifts." The phrase "earnestly desire" comes from the Greek word ζηλόω (zeloo). The Enhanced Strongs

Lexicon gives the following meanings: to burn with zeal, to be zealous in the pursuit of good, to desire earnestly, pursue, to strive after, to exert one's self.[3]

This is the word from which we get our English words "zeal" and "zealous." Paul is saying that when it comes to spiritual gifts, be zealous to go after them, pursue them, strive to have them. There is no hint in the Scriptures that we shouldn't desire or seek spiritual gifts. Paul actually says the opposite!

Another exciting thing about this verse (1 Cor. 14:1) is that Paul is speaking to *Christians*. I was taught that when you are born again and experience the New Birth, the Holy Spirit deposits certain gifts within you and whatever gifts you receive at conversion are the only ones you will ever possess. But in this passage the apostle is saying "earnestly desire spiritual gifts," which tells me that I don't have to settle for what I have, but I can seek to add to my present giftings. I can pursue the Spirit and ask for additional gifts to be imparted in my life.

In saying this, let me provide balance by saying that we need to be careful concerning our motivation for additional gifts. If our motivation is self-centered, it is wrong. Our motivation for additional gifts must never be to impress others or feed our personal egos. But if our motivation for additional gifts is for the purpose of imparting blessing to others, bringing edification to the Body of Christ, and extending the kingdom, then the Holy Spirit is pleased by our desire and I am confident that He will increase our giftings!

DISCOVERING YOUR SPIRITUAL GIFTS

How do you know which spiritual gifts you have? There are several *Spiritual Gift Inventories* available that can be accessed online that provide some guidance, but I don't think you should limit your giftings by taking a test. To me, this is too mechanical. First, I think you should consider the passions the Lord has placed within you. I believe that God will give you a passion for the area or areas in which He has gifted you.

I also think it is helpful to experiment by serving in several areas. I have known people who didn't think they had a gifting in a particular area, but when they tried it, they loved it and realized their gifting. Try serving in several areas within the church and ask the Holy Spirit to show you where He has gifted you. For instance, if you enjoy working with children, you may be gifted to serve in the Children's Ministry. The same thing can be said about youth or adult ministries.

If you have a gift to communicate and relate to others, you may want to consider volunteering as a substitute teacher in a small group or class. If you feel you have the gift of hospitality, why not volunteer to assist in serving meals in your church or when there are fellowships in your class or small group. If you love and enjoy talking with people, you may be gifted to serve as a greeter, welcoming people as they arrive to the services. If you have a passion for prayer, the Lord may be leading you to serve on a prayer team.

There are many areas within the church that need volunteers, and by serving in multiple areas of interest, the Lord can bring confirmation concerning your giftings. Discovering your gifts isn't something to get worried or stressed out about. Simply pray, seek the direction of the Lord, and be open to serving in various positions. He will lead you to discover your gifts and place you exactly where you need to be in order to advance His kingdom!

Exercising Spiritual Gifts
It is clear in Paul's letter to the Corinthians that spiritual gifts were being misused. Much of what he writes concerning the gifts is designed for correction and instruction. Though he encouraged freedom in the exercising of spiritual gifts, he also called for order in the expression of gifts. He provides guidelines to ensure that they will not cause division or lead to confusion in a worship service, especially when unbelievers are present. This is especially true concerning giving a message in tongues and prophecy. These appear to be the two areas that became problematic in the Corinthian church. Paul addresses this problem and gives specific direction about these gifts and their use.

> What then, brothers? When you come together, each one has a hymn, a lesson, a revelation, a tongue, or an interpretation. Let all things be done for building up. If any speak in a tongue, let there be only two or at most three, and each in turn, and let someone interpret. But if there is no one to interpret, let each of them keep silent in church and speak to himself and to God. Let two or three prophets speak, and let the others weigh what is said. If a revelation is made to another sitting there, let the first be silent. For you can all prophesy one by one, so that all may learn and all be encouraged, and the spirits of prophets are subject to prophets. For God is not a God of confusion but of peace. (1 Cor. 14:26-33)

Let me share several things concerning exercising spiritual gifts. First, those desiring to exercise their gifts are to come under the authority of the leadership of the church. In our church, we ask that unless one is a member of our church, please refrain from exercising one's gifts, particularly a message in tongues in prophecy. This is simply to protect the flock and maintain integrity within the church. If an unknown person comes to worship with us, why should we let him or her minister without knowing the person's theological background, lifestyle, character, or level of integrity? The pastors and elders are given the responsibility of guarding the flock and ensuring that they are protected (see Acts 20:28-31).

In our church, to teach in a leadership position, we require that one is a member in good standing and is theologically in agreement with our doctrinal statement. This is expected of every leader. Why should we allow someone to come into our congregation and prophesy or give a message in tongues to our entire congregation without knowing who they are? As the shepherd of my flock, I have the responsibility to protect the flock, so I think this is a good policy to establish in the exercising of gifts.

Second, Scripture teaches that if someone has a prophetic word, then that word is to be "weighed," that is, evaluated to see if others confirm the authenticity of the word. This also provides safety for the congregation. It ensures that the gifts are not being misused, but are practiced with integrity.

Third, if a person feels he or she has a spiritual gift, then others within the body should be able to confirm the presence of that gift. Look for others to provide encouragement and affirmation. If you feel you have a gift of teaching and your class starts off with 25 people and dwindles to five, I think it would be safe to assume that teaching is not your gifting! Don't be afraid to ask others to help you discover your giftings. Having affirmation from others within the body is a great way to discover the gifts the Spirit has imparted into you for His service. He knows the need of each local congregation, and the Spirit distributes gifts as needed within His body (see 1 Cor. 12:7).

Conclusion

In concluding this chapter, remember that the purpose of spiritual gifts is to build, strengthen, and edify the body of Christ. Gifts should never become a source of strife or division. The Holy Spirit who gave gifts to the early church is the same Spirit who dispenses gifts today. We should never be jealous of each other's gifts or feel inferior if we don't have a particular gift. If you really desire a certain gift, ask the Holy Spirit for it. He may well see fit to impart it to you. But if that gift is not imparted, remember that He has given you the gifts you need to complement and edify the local body where He has placed you to serve. As we remain faithful and obedient to Him, His Spirit will fill and use us to advance His kingdom—and He will be glorified in His church!

Discussion Questions

1. What is the purpose and function of spiritual gifts?

2. Who dispenses spiritual gifts to those members within the body, the church? What does this imply?

3. Who empowers the gifts to operate within the church? What does this imply?

4. Which gifts are necessary for the proper function of the body?

5. Why would some people teach that certain gifts of the Spirit have ceased, for instance tongues, miracles, and prophecy?

6. Is there any biblical justification for those who would claim that certain gifts are no longer in operation within the church? If not, why do some feel certain gifts are no longer available?

7. What Scriptures imply the continuation of all of the gifts?

8. Are spiritual gifts a sign of spiritual maturity? If not, how do we measure spiritual maturity?

9. What are some of the cautions concerning the use and operation of spiritual gifts? Which gifts can potentially cause harm in the church?

10. What measures should we take to ensure the proper function of spiritual gifts? Whose responsibility is it?

11. Is it appropriate to desire or seek spiritual gifts?

12. What are some ways in which we can discover our spiritual gifts?

Chapter Ten

Spiritual Warfare

W hen I became a Christian at the age of 18, spiritual warfare was not just
an unfamiliar term, but the concept itself had never even entered my
mind. Little did I realize that by surrendering my life to Christ and being born
again, I was simultaneously being delivered from one kingdom and transferred
to another one. Yet this is exactly what took place. In Colossians Paul writes, "He
has delivered us from the domain of darkness and transferred us to the kingdom
of his beloved Son". (Col. 1:13)

Not only did I *not* think in terms of kingdoms, but I was also totally oblivious
to having been held captive in another kingdom and under the subjugation of
another prince who had control and dominion in my life! But make no mistake
about it, prior to coming to Christ, every person belonged to another kingdom.
Without knowing it, we were being led by another prince who was leading us to
the final destination of an eternity in hell. Notice this passage of Scripture:

> And you were dead in the trespasses and sins in which you
> once walked, following the course of this world, following the
> prince of the power of the air, the spirit that is now at work in
> the sons of disobedience. (Eph. 2:1-2)

This Scripture tells us several things. First, prior to coming to Christ, we were
"dead." By dead, Paul means that we were spiritually dead, totally unresponsive to
the life of God and destined to spend eternity in a sinner's hell. Second, our direction in life was "following the course of this world, following the prince of the
power of the air." Our priorities, ambitions, and focus in life were on this world
and its system of thought; and we were unknowingly being led by "the prince of
the power of the air" whom the Bible calls the devil, or Satan.

Third, we were "sons of disobedience." This means that there were spiritual laws that God had introduced to mankind, and instead of following and
obeying the laws of God, we chose to ignore them and live for self. Instead of
being obedient, we lived a life of disobedience. This made us rebels and sinners
in the sight of a holy, righteous God. This is why Christ died on the cross: to
offer us the forgiveness of sin and the gift of eternal life.

The Bible teaches that there exist two kingdoms: one called the kingdom of darkness and the other the kingdom of light. The kingdom of darkness is led and controlled by Satan and his followers, known as demons. Both Satan and demons appear to have been angels who served God at one time in eternity past. Satan appears to have had a higher ranking, referred to as an archangel, who was known by the name of Lucifer, also called Satan. Though there are many things that we do not know about Satan and demons, we do know that the Bible indicates that Satan led an unsuccessful revolt against God, resulting in a significant number of angels to follow him in the rebellion.

As a result, God threw Satan and his followers out of heaven. They and the sin they promote are the reason for the chaos, rebellion, deception, destruction, and death that plagues our world. Many Bible scholars point to two passages of prophecy which seem to have a dual interpretation of what caused the kingdom of darkness to be formed—one in Isaiah and the other in Ezekiel. Isaiah's prophetic words are directed to the Babylonian King Sennacherib (705-681 B.C.). Behind the words of this prophecy concerning Sennacherib's fall are words that depict Satan's rebellion and his fall from heaven:

> How you are fallen from heaven, O Lucifer, son of the morning! How you are cut down to the ground, you who weakened the nations! For you have said in your heart: "I will ascend into heaven, I will exalt my throne above the stars of God; I will also sit on the mount of the congregation on the farthest sides of the north; I will ascend above the heights of the clouds, I will be like the Most High." Yet you shall be brought down to Sheol, to the lowest depths of the Pit. (Isa. 14:12-15, *NKJV*)

Ezekiel's prophecy is given about the king of Tyre, but clearly has a double meaning pointing back to Satan's deception in the Garden of Eden:

> Moreover, the word of the Lord came to me: "Son of man, raise a lamentation over the king of Tyre, and say to him, Thus says the Lord God: 'You were the signet of perfection, full of wisdom and perfect in beauty. You were in Eden, the garden of God; every precious stone was your covering, sardius, topaz, and diamond, beryl, onyx, and jasper, sapphire, emerald, and carbuncle; and crafted in gold were your settings and your engravings. On the day that you were created they were prepared. You were an anointed guardian cherub. I placed you; you were on the holy mountain of God; in the midst of the stones of fire you walked. You were blameless in your ways from the day you were created, till unrighteousness was found

in you. In the abundance of your trade you were filled with violence in your midst, and you sinned; so I cast you as a profane thing from the mountain of God, and I destroyed you, O guardian cherub, from the midst of the stones of fire. Your heart was proud because of your beauty; you corrupted your wisdom for the sake of your splendor. I cast you to the ground; I exposed you before kings, to feast their eyes on you. By the multitude of your iniquities, in the unrighteousness of your trade you profaned your sanctuaries; so I brought fire out from your midst; it consumed you, and I turned you to ashes on the earth in the sight of all who saw you. All who know you among the peoples are appalled at you; you have come to a dreadful end and shall be no more forever.'" (Ezek. 28:11-19)

There are other Scriptures that speak of Satan's fall as well as the angels' fall (see Luke 10:18; Jude 6; Rev. 12:3-4). Why the rebellion? Why did the other angels choose to follow Satan? Why did God allow this to occur in the first place? These are the kinds of questions that we will just have to speculate upon until we get to heaven. What we do know is that Satan was a created being, and is not God. He is subservient to God and is allowed to exercise limited power and authority only. His followers are fallen angels called demons who hate God, Christ, and His church. They know they will ultimately be assigned to an eternal hell, so they are actively and aggressively seeking to deceive and take as many humans to hell with them as possible. I know, not a good situation!

Satan and the demonic world not only hate and oppose the Lord Jesus, but they also hate and oppose anyone who belongs to Christ, His kingdom, or any organization that represents and advances His cause. Satan has an agenda and it is not pretty. Notice how Jesus describes our enemy's agenda compared to His: "The thief comes only to steal and kill and destroy. I came that they may have life and have it abundantly" (John 10:10).

Satan's goal is always destruction, never life. He is the leader of a host of diabolical creatures. During Jesus' earthly ministry, He had several encounters with demons and they knew to surrender and obey His commands. Whenever Jesus came upon those who were afflicted, oppressed, or possessed by a demon or demons, He always rebuked them and cast them out (see Matt. 8:28-34). He had absolute authority over them. They were no match for the Son of God. As His children, we too have authority over them and the power to overcome their influence in our lives. The apostle John tells us that one of the reasons why Christ came was to defeat Satan and his works: "Whoever makes a practice of sinning is of the devil, for the devil has been sinning from the beginning. The reason the Son of God appeared was *to destroy the works* of the devil" (1 John 3:8, emphasis mine).

In Matthew's gospel we read about a direct encounter that Jesus had with Satan following His baptism (see Matt. 4:1-11). Satan tempted the Lord Jesus three different times, but Jesus was victorious each time. Jesus would not submit to Satan's temptations and Satan eventually left Jesus. This must have been extreme warfare, since Jesus was all alone in this confrontation. It was not until after the temptations that angels came and ministered to Jesus. Clearly, this was an agonizing and tormenting experience. Nonetheless, Jesus won the victory and was strengthened to continue His earthly ministry.

SPIRITUAL WARFARE DEFINED

How do we define spiritual warfare? David Devenish in his excellent book, *Demolishing Strongholds*, gives the following definition of Spiritual Warfare:

> The reality that the advance of the gospel and the building of
> the church involve us in attacking and experiencing counter-
> attack in relation to real cosmic forces under the control of
> Satan who is also described as the god of this world.[1]

In studying the subject of spiritual warfare, I think it is critical that we understand we are in a spiritual battle fighting invisible creatures who exist in a realm described as the "powers of darkness," operating under the direction of Satan, the archenemy of God. As we read the Bible about spiritual warfare and the demonic realm, many of us have a tendency to view the Scriptures through the eyes of western rationalism, limiting our understanding of the reality of spiritual warfare. We tend to treat what we cannot see as if it does not exist because of our 'scientific' or 'rational' worldview. We often marginalize the possibility of supernatural activity.

However, there are many places in the world where people have a different worldview and a deeper awareness of demonic powers. It is not that demonic power or activity is any more prevalent in other places in the world, it is just more obvious and recognized.

There are *two potential dangers* in our response to spiritual warfare. First, we can be influenced by a rationalistic worldview into disbelieving spiritual warfare issues. Or second, we can swing too far the other way and develop an unhealthy preoccupation with the demonic. When people develop an unhealthy preoccupation with the demonic and the powers of darkness, they offer the enemy an opportunity to oppress them with fear by shifting their attention away from the power, the authority, and the victory we have in the resurrected Christ.

Satan and his demons are defeated enemies; but they do operate and have limited power within the system of our world. They will continue to do so until the consummation of the end of this age. Notice the title the apostle Paul gives to Satan: "In their case *the god* of this world has blinded the minds of the unbelievers, to keep them from seeing the light of the gospel of the glory of Christ, who is the image of God" (2 Cor. 4:4, emphasis mine).

Let me make clear that Satan is not a god with a capital G, "God," but he does possess *limited* power. The clear implication is that he has significant power and authority in our current world's system, but only to the extent that God permits. As the "god" of this world, he definitely has power and influence and is doing everything he can do to thwart the advancement of God's kingdom, including attempts to deceive, destroy, and undermine God's people – we who are believers. He will lie, deceive, and bring temptations in our life to detour and sabotage God's plans for our lives and His church. He wants to undermine our faith and he will use every means possible in his efforts to create doubt and confusion in our minds. His ultimate goal for believers' lives is to lead them away from their faith and trust in God.

Don't ever underestimate his schemes. Tragically, many have fallen and have been taken captive through his tactics, including people in full-time ministry positions with considerable success in their ministries. The apostle Peter gives a vivid warning: "Be sober-minded; be watchful. Your adversary the devil prowls around like a roaring lion, seeking someone to devour. Resist him, firm in your faith, knowing that the same kinds of suffering are being experienced by your brotherhood throughout the world" (1 Pet. 5:8-9).

If an alert went out that there was a lion prowling around in my neighborhood, I can assure you that I would lock the doors, board up the windows, keep my .38 revolver close by, and not go outside until I was positive he had been captured! In other words, I would take every possible precaution to ensure that he and I had no contact—period! Likewise, in the spiritual realm, Peter is saying that this is our reality. Satan is lurking in darkness, under cover, looking for any opening that he can lunge at and attack.

To consider Satan, demons, and spiritual warfare just as some make believe fantasy belonging to another era in history is foolish and spiritually naïve. To underestimate him is asking for heartache and spiritual disaster. But unfortunately, there are millions of Christians who wake up every day and never once give any serious consideration to the reality of this dark, devious, and destructive realm of existence.

Spiritual Warfare is Real

Consider the following. Throughout my educational journey, I received a bachelor's degree in religious studies, a master of divinity degree, and a doctor of ministry degree, but I never had one course or read one book concerning the subject of spiritual warfare. As I reflect on this, I find that the lack of material and teaching on the supernatural is not only astounding, but almost incredulous. If Satan exists and the demonic world is a reality, why wouldn't I have taken at least one course and read one text book that dealt with the subject?

In thinking about this, I cannot come up with any other reason except for the fact that spiritual warfare is not taken seriously. How can spiritual warfare be taken seriously if theological students are never instructed or prepared for the subject? Yes, I did take systematic studies in theology in which I read chapters that dealt with the origins of sin, evil, the devil, and demons. But I was never given a course or instruction on how to approach the subject of spiritual warfare, or the importance of developing a strategy to defend myself in battle.

Being the practical person that I am, now that I have studied spiritual warfare, I think it is almost malpractice not to equip theological students with the arsenal to engage in battle—and engage they will! Listen to Paul's admonition to the saints in Ephesus:

> Finally, be strong in the Lord and in the strength of his might.
> Put on the whole armor of God, that you may be able to stand
> against the schemes of the devil. For we do not wrestle against
> flesh and blood, but against the rulers, against the authorities,
> against the cosmic powers over this present darkness, against
> the spiritual forces of evil in the heavenly places. Therefore
> take up the whole armor of God, that you may be able to with-
> stand in the evil day, and having done all, to stand firm. Stand
> therefore, having fastened on the belt of truth, and having put
> on the breastplate of righteousness, and, as shoes for your feet,
> having put on the readiness given by the gospel of peace. In all
> circumstances take up the shield of faith, with which you can
> extinguish all the flaming darts of the evil one; and take the
> helmet of salvation, and the sword of the Spirit, which is the
> word of God, praying at all times in the Spirit, with all prayer
> and supplication. To that end keep alert with all perseverance,
> making supplication for all the saints... (Eph. 6:10-18)

Sounds like pretty serious words to me! These are not just words for good sermon materials or theological discussions. This is literally a call to arms to every born again child of God to get ready for battle. Paul is saying, "Wake up! Get dressed! Prepare yourselves because you're in a battle!"

I said at the beginning of this chapter that there are two things to avoid in our approach to spiritual warfare: being influenced by a rationalistic worldview into disbelieving spiritual warfare issues, or swinging too far the other way and developing an unhealthy preoccupation with the demonic. There must be a balance. I have read several books on spiritual warfare and encountered many different thoughts and opinions. I firmly believe that as we approach spiritual warfare and its reality, we must do so with balance and never forget that we are on the winning side. Satan and his followers were defeated at the cross!

> And you, who were dead in your trespasses and the uncir-
> cumcision of your flesh, God made alive together with him,

172

having forgiven us all our trespasses, by canceling the record of debt that stood against us with its legal demands. This he set aside, nailing it to the cross. He disarmed the rulers and authorities and put them to open shame, by triumphing over them in him. (Col. 2:13-15)

The Expositor's Commentary says the following about this passage:

Paul goes on to say that Christ, having thus disarmed the powers and authorities, "made a public spectacle of them." That is to say, he exposed them to public disgrace by exhibiting them to the universe as his captives. The added words, "triumphing over them by the cross," expand this idea. The picture, quite familiar in the Roman world, is that of a triumphant general leading a parade of victory. The conqueror, riding at the front in his chariot, leads his troops through the streets of the city. Behind them trails a wretched company of vanquished kings, officers, and soldiers — the spoils of battle. Christ, in this picture, is the conquering general; the powers and authorities are the vanquished enemy displayed as the spoils of battle before the entire universe. To the casual observer the cross appears to be only an instrument of death, the symbol of Christ's defeat; Paul represents it as Christ's chariot of victory.[2]

The apostle Paul declares that Satan and his demonic hosts are fully aware of their inevitable demise, but their final destruction is not until the end of the age. Knowing that they are defeated and doomed, they are doing everything within their power to blind people from the truth of the gospel and cause as much pain, suffering, chaos, and destruction in the world as possible.

In these last days, the Bible says that Satan will increase his activity knowing his end is inevitable and approaching: "Therefore, rejoice, O heavens and you who dwell in them! But woe to you, O earth and sea, for the devil has come down to you in great wrath, *because he knows that his time is short!*" (Rev. 12:12, emphasis mine)

Jesus' death and resurrection sealed the eternal fate of rulers, authorities, cosmic powers over this present darkness, and against the "spiritual forces of evil in the heavenly places", and our victory is certain (see Eph. 6:12). Christ's victory has delivered a decisive blow to them, but again, we must never underestimate their schemes or influence. At the appointed time, Christ will return and soundly defeat all of His enemies. But until then, they do still wield power. Never let your guard down. We are in battle. We may not see our enemies with our physical eyes, but I can assure you that they are present and watching for the slightest opportunity to attack.

It is imperative that we dress for battle, and as Paul said in his epistle to the Ephesians, "Put on the whole armor of God, that you may be able to stand against the schemes of the devil" (Eph. 6:11). The following are the steps Paul outlines that we must take to ensure victory and to avoid spiritual injuries.

1. Believe in the reality of spiritual warfare

If you do not choose to embrace the reality that you are in spiritual warfare, you will fail to prepare. Imagine being a soldier who has intelligence that the enemy is about to attack but instead of preparing, you choose to ignore the information and refuse to prepare. You leave your body armor in your room, your weapon not loaded, and your radio not charged. No soldier in his or her right mind would think of ignoring the message. Yet, this is what many people do even though they have clear, reliable, accurate information from the inspired Word of God that attacks are inevitable.

Attacks will come. Again, don't allow living in the twenty-first century and all its technological advancements lure you into believing that the spiritual world doesn't exist. If Satan can deceive you into believing that this is simply myth or fantasy, then he already has a huge edge on you in planning and implementing your defeat. Why? Because unless you believe that Satan, demons, and spiritual warfare are real, I can assure you that you will not take the steps to ensure your readiness.

2. Remember your source of strength

Paul begins this section on spiritual warfare with these words: "be strong in the Lord and in the strength of his might" (Eph. 6:10). He wants us to understand upfront that our strength and ability does not reside within our *natural* ability. We can never defeat the enemy on our own. We are dealing with a powerful foe and we must look to the Lord our God for strength. This battle is in the spiritual realm and requires the employment of spiritual power. This is one of the key reasons we need to be baptized in the Holy Spirit. The baptism in the Holy Spirit endues us with the necessary power we need (see Luke 24:49; Acts 1:8).

To attempt to battle in the spiritual realm in our flesh will only lead to disappointment. It is only when we stay filled with the Spirit, relying on the Spirit, that we find the power to face the various temptations, ploys, and onslaughts of the enemy. You may try your best to muster up enough willpower and resolve to battle the enemy on your own; but I can assure you that you will only be left disillusioned, wounded, and defeated.

We must look to our source, and when we do, we will find that He is more than able and willing to provide us all that we need to be victorious. "Now to him who is able to do far more abundantly than all that we ask or think, according to the power at work within us" (Eph. 3:20).

3. Prepare daily for spiritual warfare

Those engaged on the battlefield not only prepare, but they also remain in a state of readiness and alertness 24 hours a day, 7 days per week. They do not have the luxury of taking a break or ignoring the enemy. They always prepare and are armed in case there is a surprise and unexpected attack. If our enemy, the devil and his demons are constantly on the prowl and waiting for the opportunity to take advantage of us, then it is imperative that we too prepare daily and remain in a state of readiness.

In Ephesians chapter six the apostle Paul tells us to "put on the whole armor of God." Just as we get dressed physically on a daily basis, we must dress spiritually. The following is the armor checklist that Paul states we must put on so that prepared and ready for battle:

- The belt of truth
  Ephesians 6:14
  The belt of truth provides the foundation for guidance and stability. This piece of armor affects every dimension of life. Truth in this context does refer to the truth of the gospel, but also includes all truth pertaining to God, His kingdom, and all of the inspired Scriptures. The Greek word for "truth" refers to an honesty of heart and purity of motive. When we know the truth and walk in the truth, we enjoy stability, integrity, and character, which synchronize with every other dimension of our lives. The opposite of truth is hypocrisy and lies, which always lead to deception and derailment of God's blessings and favor in our lives.

  We cannot win spiritual battles if we are lying to ourselves, deceiving ourselves, and running from the conviction of the Holy Spirit. But when truth pervades our innermost being, the spiritual compass of our lives will be charted to fulfill God's purpose and destiny for our lives.

- The breastplate of righteousness
  Ephesians 6:14
  Here Paul is speaking about *practical* righteousness rather than *positional* righteousness. Positional righteousness refers to our standing before God. We were given positional righteousness – right standing before God – when we accepted Christ as our Lord and Savior. Christ's righteousness was transferred to us by our faith in His sacrificial death on the cross for our sins. In Ephesians 6:14, Paul is referring to *practical* righteousness. When we are both standing and acting in truth, righteousness will become our breastplate.

  The Roman soldier's breastplate covered everything from his shoulders to his loins, and its main purpose was to protect him from a life-threatening wound to the heart. In God's armor, the breastplate of righteousness protects

175

the spiritual condition of our hearts, helping us remain pure, devoted, and loyal to the Lord Jesus. Practical righteousness is living out and practicing our faith on a daily basis. We cannot do this on our own.

But we can cooperate with the Holy Spirit, allowing Him to lead us into a life of obedience to the Word of God. Righteousness is living in obedience to God and His Word as we yield to the empowering presence of the Holy Spirit.

- Shoes on your feet
  Ephesians 6:15
  The spiritual shoes Paul is referring to are given for the purpose of "having put on the readiness given by the gospel of peace" (Eph. 6:15). The Roman soldier wore a very distinctive shoe in battle. These shoes were called "caligae," heavy-soled hob-nailed military boots. They resembled modern sandals, but they were strapped up the ankle. These boots with hob-nails in their soles provided traction and stability, which helped in their readiness for battle. They were also an effective weapon for kicking.

  In this context, it is important to distinguish the phrase "gospel of peace" from "the gospel." Paul is not talking about spreading the Gospel specifically; but rather he is pointing out one of the benefits of the gospel—the peace of God. When the peace of God envelops your life, it settles, strengthens, and stabilizes. How can we stand if our feet are injured? Physically, our feet provide balance to our entire body and are a major component of our ability to move from one place to another. When our feet are injured, our entire body is affected. Have you ever stepped on a nail? Had a spur or thorn in your foot? The pain immediately immobilizes us.

  When I was growing up in Miami, Florida, I used to play in a field behind our house. At certain times of the year, sandspurs would grow in the field and create small but extensive patches throughout the field. Because I liked to play barefoot, on more than one occasion, I would often run into a patch of these sandspurs. They stopped me instantly, and I would have to sit down and pull them out of my feet, which created another problem—my bottom! I usually had jeans on, so the sandspurs did not penetrate too far through the jeans, but my feet were another matter. They required slow, painful extraction.

  Not having God's peace in our lives can lead to anxiety, fear, and a lack of faith. This will impair our readiness to engage in spiritual battles. We need to wake up every morning knowing that we have made peace with God and that His peace is abiding in our lives. This will give us courage, faith, and the needed boldness to face our adversaries. Notice the following Scriptures (emphasis mine) and how often "peace" is used.

Peace I leave with you; my peace I give to you. Not as the world gives do I give to you. Let not your hearts be troubled, neither let them be afraid. (John 14:27)

I have said these things to you, that in me you may have *peace*. In the world you will have tribulation. But take heart; I have overcome the world. (John 16:33)

For to set the mind on the flesh is death, but to set the mind on the Spirit is life and *peace*. (Rom. 8:6)

For the kingdom of God is not a matter of eating and drinking but of righteousness and *peace* and joy in the Holy Spirit. (Rom. 14:17)

May the God of hope fill you with all joy and *peace* in believing, so that by the power of the Holy Spirit you may abound in hope. (Rom. 15:13)

But the fruit of the Spirit is love, joy, *peace*, patience, kindness, goodness, faithfulness, gentleness, self-control; against such things there is no law. (Gal. 5:22-23)

And the *peace* of God, which surpasses all understanding, will guard your hearts and your minds in Christ Jesus. (Phil. 4:7)

God's peace is a source of great strength and security in the midst of battle. Any *lack of peace* should alert us that we are off the path and heading toward the devil's quicksand. It is God's peace that will lead us back to the safety of His will. Peace keeps us in alignment with God's purpose, plan, and destiny for our lives. Concentrate on these passages of Scripture and ask the Holy Spirit to allow His peace to rest upon you.

- Shield of faith
  Ephesians 6:16
  The Christian life is commenced by faith and is won by faith. You are saved by faith and you win the battles of life by faith. Faith is absolutely critical in every dimension of your spiritual life. It is faith that brings the divine pleasure and favor of God to rest, to abide, and to surround your life. The famous nineteenth century British preacher Charles Haddon Spurgeon said, "A little faith will bring your soul to heaven; a great faith will bring heaven to your soul."

The writer of the book of Hebrews says: *"And without faith* it is impossible to please God, because anyone who comes to him must believe that he exists and that he rewards those who earnestly seek him" (Heb. 11:6, *NIV*, emphasis mine).

If you ever doubt just how critical faith is and the importance of exercising faith in your daily walk with Christ, just remind yourself of the numerous and frequent number of times the Lord Jesus referenced faith in the life of His followers. He commended people for their faith and even marveled at the centurion's faith. "When Jesus heard this, he was astonished and said to those following him, 'I tell you the truth, I have not found anyone in Israel with *such great faith'"* (Matt. 8:10, *NIV*, emphasis mine).

Jesus marveled at people's unbelief (their lack of faith) as well. He appeared disappointed and even exasperated when people had no faith, such as when His disciples had a lack of faith in the midst of a storm.

He got up, rebuked the wind and said to the waves, "Quiet! Be still!" Then the wind died down and it was completely calm. He said to his disciples, "Why are you so afraid? Do you still have *no faith?"* (Mark 4:39-40, *NIV*, emphasis mine).

Jesus told many who were healed that they experienced their healing because of their faith.

Jesus stepped into a boat, crossed over and came to his own town. Some men brought to him a paralytic, lying on a mat. When Jesus *saw their faith,* he said to the paralytic, "Take heart, son; your sins are forgiven." (Matt. 9:1-2, *NIV*, emphasis mine)

Then the woman, seeing that she could not go unnoticed, came trembling and fell at his feet. In the presence of all the people, she told why she had touched him and how she had been instantly healed. Then he said to her, "Daughter, *your faith* has healed you. Go in peace." (Luke 8:47-48, *NIV*, emphasis mine)

Then he touched their eyes and said, *"According to your faith* will it be done to you;" and their sight was restored. (Matt. 9:29-30, *NIV*, emphasis mine)

Then Jesus answered, "Woman, *you have great faith!* Your request is granted." And her daughter was healed from that very hour. (Matt. 15:28, *NIV*, emphasis mine)

The Bible even says that Jesus could not perform many miracles in His home town because of the people's unbelief, their lack of faith. "And he did not do many miracles there *because of their lack of faith*" (Matt. 13:58, *NIV*, emphasis mine).

The shield of faith then is a part of God's armor that we dare not neglect if we desire to experience an overflow of the supernatural presence and favor of God in our lives.

The Greek word *thureos* translated "shield" refers to the larger shield that the Roman soldier used in battle. It was big, well constructed, and it fully protected the warrior in battle. It was about the size of your front door. Because it was the first piece of armor that came in contact with the enemy, it had to be strong and formidable. When the enemy attacks, it is our faith that will meet him and defeat him!

In Paul's day, soldiers often dipped their arrows in combustible fluids and lit them so that their arrows would burn whatever they hit. I am sure Paul was thinking about these "fiery arrows" when he mentions here "the flaming arrows of the evil one." When soldiers saw that their enemies were using fiery arrows, they immediately prepared their shields, which were made of an iron frame covered with several layers of leather. They would soak their shields in water so that when a fiery dart hit, it would fizzle out in a puff of smoke. How do we as believers soak our shields of faith? What do we use to soak our shields? We use water. Throughout the Scriptures, water is a symbol for the Word of God. "To make her holy, cleansing her by the washing with *water through the word*" (Eph. 5:26, *NIV*, emphasis mine).

Paul says that faith grows, matures, develops, and gains strength in us when we read, study, meditate on, and live the Word of God. "So then faith *comes* by hearing, and hearing *by the word of God*" (Rom. 10:17, *NKJV*, emphasis mine).

If we expect to be victorious in our spiritual battles, it is imperative that we soak and saturate our hearts and minds in the Word of God. It is faith in God's Word and knowing God's Word that gives us an unshakeable confidence and trust in what God says. Faith provides us the ability to quench all the fiery darts that come our way. The more we read the Word of God, the more we will think the Word of God, feel the Word of God, and respond to the Word of God.

The more our faith grows, the more our lives will reflect the Word, be grounded in the Word, and be in complete alignment with the Word. Whatever the enemy shoots our way isn't going to sting if we know the Word of God because our faith is entirely in the Lord Jesus Christ who is the living Word of God.

Remember, the shield of faith has mobility. It travels with you and surrounds you. There is no place or situation where the devil can place you that your faith can not rise up and win the victory. The book of Ephesians, from which we get this teaching on spiritual armor, was written by a man sitting in a prison cell. Yet his faith did not wane or diminish. Instead it rose up and filled the author Paul to exhort us by reminding us of the marvelous riches we possess in the Lord Jesus Christ.

Paul wrote from a Philippian jail cell, "For to me to live is Christ, and to die is gain" (Phil. 1:21)! Nothing could rob Paul of his faith and nothing could cause him to lose His faith. He also wrote from that jail cell, "Not that I speak in regard to need, for I have learned in whatever state I am, to be content" (Phil. 4:11, *NKJV*). It was his undaunted and uncompromising faith that carried him through any and all situations he encountered—and it will do the same for you!

- The helmet of salvation
Ephesians 6:17
Some parts of the soldier's armor were elaborate and expensive because they were designed to make a statement of indomitable strength and authority. This was true of the helmet. Other than the large shield, the helmet made the biggest impression. It covered the head entirely, including cheek pieces, and it was made of bronze with ornate carvings and etchings. It was extremely heavy and only the sharpest ax or heaviest hammer could pierce it.

To help the soldier bear the weight of the helmet, it was lined with a soft, spongy material. Without this kind of protection, the soldier would quickly lose his head. But the helmet also had the most flamboyant feature: a tall plume was extremely striking and made the soldier look as much as two feet taller than he actually was.

By calling this piece of armor the "helmet of salvation," Paul could not have made a more powerful statement about our redemption. When we truly understand that we are eternally, perfectly, and absolutely saved; cleansed and forgiven by the precious blood of the Lord Jesus; and that we are completely reconciled to God, we suddenly find ourselves standing 10 feet tall!

Because the helmet covers our heads, I believe a key truth Paul is emphasizing is that our minds must at all times be stayed and fixed on one basic truth. It is because of our faith in the Lord Jesus that we are saved. We must keep this reality in the forefront of our thinking. Many of us today spend the bulk of our praise time rejoicing over the fact that the Lord has given us power and authority. We are thanking Him for baptism in His Holy Spirit and all the gifts we receive through His anointing and empowerment in our lives.

This is good, it is exciting, and it should be part of our praise; but we need to remember what Jesus said to His disciples when they came back rejoicing that even the demons were subject to them. "Nevertheless do not rejoice in this, that the spirits are subject to you, but rather rejoice because your names are written in heaven" (Luke 10:20, NKJV).

The disciples had just returned from casting out demons and healing the sick all over the country. But notice that Jesus pulls them back to the center by reminding them that none of this was possible without salvation. He is saying that none of the blessings of life or supernatural manifestations in life come close to comparing to the forgiveness and eternal life we have received from the Lord Jesus.

We need to rejoice that we are saved and have eternal life. Rejoice that our sins have been cast as far from us as the east is from the west and our slate and our souls have been wiped clean. We have no reason for guilt and no reason for shame. You can remind the devil of that fact when he tries to bring up your past.

No matter what he says to you, you just say right back, "Satan, I am saved, and you cannot touch me, you cannot deceive me, and you cannot defeat me. Jesus died on the cross for me and I have been forgiven and covered with His blood and have received His righteousness and I am heaven bound. I am a child of God and nothing you can do can change that fact. So devil, get out of my life! Be gone in the name of the Lord Jesus!"

Putting on the helmet of your salvation means dwelling on your salvation, meditating on your salvation, and constantly reminding yourself that you are a child of the living God and a joint heir with the Lord Jesus. The devil cannot upset or distract a mind that is focused on the blessed reality of knowing that we are saved and have been given eternal and abundant life!

- The sword of the Spirit
Ephesians 6:17
Our belt of truth, our breastplate of righteousness, our gospel shoes providing peace, our shield of faith, and our helmet of salvation are all defensive pieces of our armor. But now we must put on the one piece of offensive armor we are given: "the sword of the Spirit, which is the Word of God." When we hear the word sword, we might immediately think of pirates, Robin Hood, or Zorro wielding their swords that have fancy handles. But the Greek word Paul uses for "sword" in this verse is *machairan*, which refers to a dagger. By using *machairan*, Paul is indicating that we fight spiritual battles at close range.

The Bible says: "For the word of God *is* living and powerful, and sharper than any two-edged sword, piercing even to the division of soul and spirit, and of joints and marrow, and is a discerner of the thoughts and intents of the heart" (Heb. 4:12, *NKJV*).

The word "living" is *zoon,* which means "life." The Word of God is alive, powerful, and sharp. It has pinpoint accuracy to determine exactly what is going on in our lives. This is why many unbelievers are so offended by the Bible. It paints a clear picture of their life and they get offended and angry when they are confronted with their sin and rebellious lifestyle. When we enter spiritual warfare, we come nose to nose with the devil and every bit of wickedness in this world's system. Therefore, it is imperative that we have a weapon capable of rendering the enemy powerless.

When Jesus was confronted by Satan, He used the Word of God as His weapon. Again and again when faced with temptation, Jesus said, "It is written" and Satan finally gave up and left Him alone.

To wield the Word of God in battle, we must not only be acquainted with the Word of God but we must also *know* the Word of God. We cannot just memorize it and give it mental ascent. It must be hidden deep within our hearts. The only way for that to happen is to read it, study it, hear it—and keep reading it, studying it, and hearing it until we know it! The Psalmist said, "Your word I have hidden in my heart, that I might not sin against You" (Ps. 119:11, *NKJV*).

The Word of God must be "quick" or "alive" within our hearts and minds. Then when we speak it in a time of crisis or spiritual battle, it will be powerful to defeat the enemy. God's Word should be the first and automatic response to every challenge of life. If the situation incites praise and thanksgiving, then a word of praise and thanksgiving should come alive in our hearts and minds, subsequently flowing in power from our lips. If the situation is rooted in falsehood or guilt and shame, then a word of truth should activate in our minds and hearts and trigger an outpouring of powerful words being spoken. If you really want to disarm the devil and his demonic hosts, just start quoting and declaring the Word of God. They will not be able to remain in your presence!

Remember, Jesus said that the enemy is "the father of lies" and that "there is no truth in him" (John 8:44). Satan despises to hear or listen to the truth, so remind him of it and do so often – he will flee from your presence!

- Praying in the Spirit
  Ephesians 6:18
  The last thing that Paul mentions in this book concerning spiritual warfare is prayer: "praying at all times in the Spirit, with all prayer and supplication" (Eph. 6:18). When we pray, we need to ask the Holy Spirit to fill us and intercede through us as we pray. I believe Paul is speaking about praying both in

our prayer language and in our native tongues. The Holy Spirit can guide and empower our words. When we don't know exactly how to pray about a situation, He intercedes for us according to God's will (see Rom. 8:26).

Notice Paul says, *"praying at all times."* Paul writing to the Thessalonians said, "Pray without ceasing" (1 Thess. 5:17). We are to be in an attitude of constant prayer. Prayer is a weapon that we can use in any given situation. Let's pray and let's pray often!

The purpose of getting fully dressed is to be fully prepared. A soldier would never go into battle partially protected. To do so would mean not only being seriously injured, but it would also significantly raise the possibility of receiving a mortal wound. Paul's reasoning for "putting on the full armor of God" is to enable us to "stand," "withstand," and once again "stand" (Eph. 6:11,13-14). The Pillar New Testament Commentary says the following about being fully clothed:

> The goal for which the readers are clothed with the divine armour is so that (pros) they 'might be able to stand against the schemes of the devil'. Four times over ... the apostle uses the language of standing, standing firm, or withstanding (various forms of the verb to describe the readers' overall objective in this spiritual warfare). The first reference to 'standing' involves resisting or holding their position against the devil's 'insidious wiles' (see on v. 14) so that they do not surrender to his evil opposition but prevail against it. This term invariably carries a bad sense, and here the plural suggests attacks that are constantly repeated or of incalculable variety. The varied nature of the diabolic attack is brought out again in v. 16, albeit in slightly different language: the 'evil one' launches his 'flaming arrows' against the saints. These differing expressions suggest not only inner temptations to evil but also 'every kind of attack and assault of the "evil one."'[3]

This ability to stand involves resisting and deflecting any and every devious attack the enemy sends our way. Satan and his minions are experienced and crafty, and Satan is the ultimate expert in his field. He knows our weakness and our points of vulnerability. Remember, his experience ranges over several thousands of years. Putting on the full armor of God protects and provides us the ability to "stand against" the various "schemes" of the devil (Eph. 6:11).

Look at this insight about the word for "schemes:"

> The Greek word "schemes" refers to the various methods or strategies Satan employs in his efforts to deceive. *Methodia*

(**schemes**), from which comes the English *method*, carries the idea of craftiness, cunning, and deception (see also Eph. 4:14). The term was often used of a wild animal that cunningly stalked and then unexpectedly pounced on its prey. Satan's evil **schemes** are built around stealth and deception.[4]

Schemes are not obvious, they are subtle. Another commentator describes them this way: "Mention of the 'schemes' of the devil reminds us of the trickery and subterfuge by which evil and temptation present themselves in our lives. Evil rarely looks evil until it accomplishes its goal; it gains entrance by appearing attractive, desirable, and perfectly legitimate. It is a baited and camouflaged trap."[5]

Spiritual warfare is serious and nothing to play around with or approach lightly. This is a lifelong battle. As we develop and advance in our faith, we will become better equipped to effectively win the engagement. The good news is that the Bible promises us that we are indeed well-equipped and we have the advantage. Let me remind you once again of Paul's words to the Corinthians: "For the weapons of our warfare are not of the flesh but have divine power to destroy strongholds" (2 Cor. 10:4). When we prepare, depend on the Lord's strength, stay filled with the Spirit, and get fully dressed, we will win and win decisively!

4.   Never let your guard down

When I was a boy, my dad and I used to enjoy watching boxing. I remember one fight between Muhammad Ali (formerly known as Cassius Clay) and George Foreman. At the time, Foreman was the heavyweight champion and everyone was predicting that Foreman, who was a power puncher, would knock Ali out in just a few rounds. But Ali implemented what he later called his Rope-A-Dope strategy, in which he would lay against the ropes while his opponent flailed massive blows only hitting his body and arms.

As Ali stayed covered up with his arms and hands, Foreman continued pounding blow after blow, never stopping, but doing limited damage. After a few rounds like this, Foreman's arms began to tire to such an extent that he had trouble keeping his arms and hands up to protect his head. When that happened, Ali came off the ropes and went into a flurry of punches to the head. By round eight, Foreman had tired himself out. Unable to adequately defend himself, Foreman was knocked out in the eighth round!

If our enemy can get us to drop our guard, we become vulnerable to his attack. One of the most dangerous times of vulnerability is when we have just won a major spiritual battle and we are on a spiritual high. We feel strong and victorious. Be careful. It is often after winning a significant battle that we are tempted to let our guard down. We feel somewhat invincible. This is commonly when the enemy returns for another assault. He is constantly looking for the opportunity of vulnerability and when we least expect it—he attacks. Do not become careless. Keep and maintain your guard at all times.

5. Establish and maintain boundaries

Every person has areas of weakness. I can assure you that our enemy is aware of them. I read once that we need to draw boundary lines and stay 10 feet behind them! Unfortunately, some people like to see how close they can get to the fence before crossing it. The objective is not to see how close you can get but to stay at a safe distance, far behind the boundary line. For instance, if you are dieting, it would be in your best interest to stay away from pizza, fried chicken, and ice cream. (I am speaking from personal experience!) When you know you have a weakness in a specific area, you must make every effort to avoid placing yourself in the context of an environment that would lead to temptation.

Let me give another example. One of the growing addictions of men today is pornography. Because of the Internet, the availability and seduction of this industry has invaded our homes in a way that was not possible just a few years ago. If men know they are tempted in this area, it is critical that they place a filtering system on their computer to keep them from having the opportunity to view it. They can also ask their prayer partner to keep them accountable to maintain their purity in this area.

Another example of an opportunity to cross the boundary lines is social networking. This has become a means of people developing relationships in which they have no business getting involved. If you're married, it is totally inappropriate to be chatting or messaging with anyone of the opposite sex. I have seen people who are struggling in their marriages turn to chatting with a "friend" of the opposite sex because they are not communicating with their spouse. Or they begin looking on social networking to find someone of interest to build a relationship. As a pastor, I have witnessed several breakups in marriages because of the availability of this new media outlet.

Living in the twenty-first century has opened up a multiplicity of new avenues for the enemy to come in and attack. Boundaries must be established. Not to do so will only lead to heartache, pain, and undermining and damaging one's faith.

6. Don't ever lose focus that sin has consequences

People often yield to temptation, thinking it will provide them happiness and fulfillment. But its end always leads to ruin at some level in your life. The lie of Satan is that you will be happier when you disobey the Word of God. That was his strategy in the beginning with Eve. His temptation was presented in such a way that God was seen as withholding something of value that would lead to a heightened sense of satisfaction than what He had already provided.

> But the serpent said to the woman, "You will not surely die.
> For God knows that when you eat of it your eyes will be

opened, and you will be like God, knowing good and evil."
So when the woman saw that the tree was good for food, and
that it was a delight to the eyes, and that the tree was to be
desired to make one wise, she took of its fruit and ate, and
she also gave some to her husband who was with her, and he
ate. Then the eyes of both were opened, and they knew that
they were naked. And they sewed fig leaves together and made
themselves loincloths. (Gen. 3:4-7)

Satan not only deceived her, but also what he told her was exactly the
opposite of what God had said. She took of the forbidden fruit and ate it, fully
expecting that she would achieve a higher level of pleasure and fulfillment.
Yet, when she and her husband ate the fruit, they both knew that something had
drastically changed – not necessarily for the better – and they sought to cover
their nakedness and hide themselves from God.

Regardless of how appealing and alluring the temptation is, never forget
that yielding to temptation will bring consequences. Paul writing to the
Galatians said, "Do not be deceived: God is not mocked, for whatever one
sows, that will he also reap. For the one who sows to his own flesh will from
the flesh reap corruption, but the one who sows to the Spirit will from the Spirit
reap eternal life" (Gal. 6:7-8).

In other words, mark it down. The law of the harvest says when you sow
you will reap. I once heard a preacher refer to the laws of the harvest by saying,
"You always reap what you sow, more than you sow, and later than you sow."
If we only had the ability to see the consequences prior to the temptation, we
would never yield. We have ample examples in the Scriptures to warn us of the
consequences of sin. Writing to the Corinthians, Paul says the following:

Now these things happened to them as an example, but they
were written down for our instruction, on whom the end of
the ages has come. Therefore let anyone who thinks that he
stands take heed lest he fall. No temptation has overtaken you
that is not common to man. God is faithful, and he will not let
you be tempted beyond your ability, but with the temptation
he will also provide the way of escape, that you may be able
to endure it. (1 Cor. 10:11-13)

I can assure you, it would be far better to learn from the failures of those
who have come before us than to learn from our own. The Scriptures are replete
with examples of those who did not consider the consequences of their sins.
Since we know there will always be consequences to sinful behavior let's determine to never yield to the schemes of the enemy.

7. Choose your friends wisely

The relationships we build *will* influence our lives either positively or nega-tively. How we think, the priorities we develop, our ambitions, our theological perspectives, and even our worldview can be influenced by the friendships we develop. Godly friends who are committed to the Lordship of Christ and have a passion for the things of God will keep you on track and encourage you in your personal faith. Godly friends have the ability to strengthen and edify your life. The writer of Proverbs says, "Iron sharpens iron, and one man sharpens another" (Prov. 27:17).

This is what happens when we surround ourselves with the *right* kind of friends. Our spiritual skill sets are developed and honed to assist in advancing us to the next level within the kingdom. This is especially true of those friends who are zealous for the Lord. Their contagious spirit will rub off on us and challenge us to move deeper in our faith.

The right friends are those who are willing to hold us accountable. They are willing to correct us when needed. They will speak truth into our lives when needed. Notice this verse: "An open rebuke is better than hidden love! Wounds from a sincere friend are better than many kisses from an enemy" (Prov. 27:5-6, *NLT*).

A true friend is willing to do this. Friends who care about us are willing to confront us if they see us heading off track. They are willing to hold us account-able. We just need to give them permission to hold us accountable. We all need accountability!

Godly friendships also provide reinforcement in our lives. There are times when we need good counsel, advice, and someone to stand beside us - times when we need someone to come beside us and give us extra strength, sup-port, and encouragement. It may be the need for combined prayer when we are dealing with a particular issue or situation we are facing. We just don't want to face it alone.

Notice the words from Solomon, the wisest man who ever lived on the planet (except for Jesus):

> A person standing alone can be attacked and defeated, but two
> can stand back-to-back and conquer. Three are even better, for
> a triple-braided cord *is not easily broken*. (Eccl. 4:12, *NLT*,
> emphasis mine)

The right friends will join you in your struggles and challenges in life. They will undergird you with prayer and words of encouragement. We all need friends, and we must choose them wisely. This is why the Bible warns us about the danger of choosing the *wrong* friends. When people choose to surround themselves with the wrong kind of friends, they will be negatively impacted. If you choose friends who lack passion for God and the things of God, you will find yourself being drained of spiritual vitality. Instead of building you up in the faith, they will tear down your faith. Instead of finding yourself being filled with faith, you will find yourself being filled with doubts and unbelief. Never underestimate the influence of those with whom you choose to associate. Notice these verses of Scripture:

> The righteous choose their friends carefully, but the way of the wicked *leads them astray*. (Prov. 12:26, *NIV*, emphasis mine).

> Don't fool yourselves. Bad friends *will destroy you*. (1 Cor. 15:33, *CEV*, emphasis mine)

> Make no friendship with a man given to anger, nor go with a wrathful man, *lest you learn his ways* and entangle yourself in a snare. (Prov. 22:24-25, emphasis mine)

Satan knows exactly how to use those around you to influence you negatively. He knows the very words, thoughts, and ideas that will have an effect on you. If you choose friends who are worldly, materialistic, and void of biblical values, your mindset and perspective will be affected by them. This is why Paul writes these words to the Corinthians:

> Do not be unequally yoked with unbelievers. For what partnership has righteousness with lawlessness? Or what fellowship has light with darkness? What accord has Christ with Belial? Or what portion does a believer share with an unbeliever? What agreement has the temple of God with idols? For we are the temple of the living God; as God said, "I will make my dwelling among them and walk among them, and I will be their God, and they shall be my people. Therefore go out from their midst, and be separate from them, says the Lord, and touch no unclean thing; then I will welcome you, and I will be a father to you, and you shall be sons and daughters to me, says the Lord Almighty. (2 Cor. 6:14-18)

At first glance, these words may sound harsh, but there is a principle here that is unavoidable. Believers in Christ have nothing in common with unbelievers. There is a huge chasm between the way we think and view the world and the way unbelievers see the world. We view things through different prisms. Paul is *not* saying that we cannot have friends that are non-Christians. If this was the case, how could we ever win people to Christ? Rather, he is forbidding *close attachments* with nonbelievers. He forbids developing *intimate* friendships with nonbelievers because he knows they will have an influence on us that can undermine our faith.

I am simply saying that when we consider spiritual warfare, we need to consider the extent to which relationships play a significant part in the battles we face and the temptations we encounter. We need to choose our friends wisely and cautiously. Spiritual warfare is challenging enough on our own. Let's choose friends who will help us in the midst of battle, not those who can potentially drag us down and sabotage our faith.

Conclusion

There are so many other things I would like to share on this subject, but I hope these truths will help you to take the necessary steps to walk in victory. Along with the things I have mentioned, incorporate the spiritual disciplines shared in chapter eight. Let me leave you with an encouraging word from the apostle John:

> "You, dear children, are from God and *have overcome* them, because
> the one who is in you is greater than the one who is in the world."
> (1 John 4:4, *NIV*, emphasis mine)

Discussion Questions

1. How often throughout the week do you think about the subject of spiritual warfare? How often should you?

2. What are Satan's goals?

3. How do you define spiritual warfare?

4. What are two potential dangers when approaching the subject of spiritual warfare?

5. Who does the Bible refer to as *the god of this world*, and how much authority and power does he have? What evidence is there of his activity?

6. What is the danger of ignoring the enemy?

7. Why do you think many Christians never think of spiritual warfare?

8. Since the Bible tells us that we are in a spiritual battle, what does Paul exhort us to do in Ephesians chapter six?

9. What does Paul list as our spiritual armor? How do we spiritually get dressed?

10. What are some key steps we can take to ensure that we are ready for spiritual battle?

11. How does Satan attack the church?

12. As members of a local body, how can you help in protecting your church?

Chapter Eleven

The End Times

veryone is fascinated with teachings on the subject of the end times. The theological term for the study of end times is called *eschatology*. Throughout the centuries, Christians have carefully sought to understand the Scriptures concerning the end times, also referred to as *the last days*, meaning those few years just prior to the return of Christ.

I am sure that believers in every generation looked for the Lord's return. Even in the first century, Paul had to write to the church in Thessalonica because there were some who had mistakenly thought that Christ had already returned (see 2 Thess. 2:1-2). Paul assured them that this had not happened, and that there were several things that had to take place before Christ's Second Coming.

I think it is safe to say that we all would love to be living when the Lord returns so that we can avoid experiencing physical death. This may be the reason why many study the end times, hoping that they will be alive during His return. Throughout the generations, there have been multiple predictions concerning the year when the Second Coming of Christ would take place, but no one knows when it will happen except God.

Concerning His coming and the consummation of the age, Jesus said, "But concerning that day and hour *no one knows,* not even the angels of heaven, nor the Son, but the Father only" (Matt. 24:36, emphasis mine). Jesus emphatically says that *no one*, no pastor, no preacher, no scholar, and no prophet knows the date when Jesus will return to bring judgment upon the earth and establish His eternal throne.

So there is no way to pinpoint the exact timing of the Lord's return, but Jesus did say that there will be signs that will provide insight concerning His coming. In this chapter, we will identify some of the signs that Jesus mentioned, but it is vital that you do not allow anyone to mislead you concerning when the Lord is going to return. There have been many predictions, even in my life-time concerning the timing of this event—but they have all been wrong. I have heard of people selling their homes and quitting their jobs because they were convinced the Lord would return on a certain date. Yet, Jesus said no one knows precisely when it will take place. So don't be deceived!

Even though no one knows the timing of the Second Coming of Christ, I can confirm from the Scriptures that we are living in the last days. Again, the phrase *last days* refers to those years just prior to the Lord's return. Not only are we living in the last days, but also we have been in the last days since the day of Pentecost. On the day of Pentecost, when the early church was birthed and the disciples were baptized in the Holy Spirit, the apostle Peter had to explain the phenomenon that was taking place. They were all speaking in other tongues, praising God and magnifying the works of God. Many were confused, so Peter stands and addresses the crowd with these words:

> But Peter, standing with the eleven, lifted up his voice and addressed them: "Men of Judea and all who dwell in Jerusalem, let this be known to you, and give ear to my words. For these people are not drunk, as you suppose, since it is only the third hour of the day. But this is what was uttered through the prophet Joel: 'And in the *last days* it shall be, God declares, that I will pour out my Spirit on all flesh, and your sons and your daughters shall prophesy, and your young men shall see visions, and your old men shall dream dreams; even on my male servants and female servants in those days I will pour out my Spirit, and they shall prophesy. And I will show wonders in the heavens above and signs on the earth below, blood, and fire, and vapor of smoke; the sun shall be turned to darkness and the moon to blood, before the day of the Lord comes, the great and magnificent day. And it shall come to pass that everyone who calls upon the name of the Lord shall be saved'" (Acts 2:14-21, emphasis mine).

Notice in Peter's explanation of what was taking place that he specifically states, "But this is what was uttered through the prophet Joel: '*And in the last days...*'" (Acts 2:16-17, emphasis mine). The apostle Peter definitely says that the pouring out of the Holy Spirit on the day of Pentecost is the fulfillment of what the prophet Joel said would happen in *the last days*. So the reality is that we have been in the end times since the day of Pentecost.

You may be asking, "How can Pentecost be considered part of the last days when it happened nearly 2,000 years ago?" Remember the words of Peter in his second epistle: "But do not overlook this one fact, beloved, that with the Lord one day is as a thousand years, and a thousand years as one day" (2 Pet. 3:8). In God's timetable, years are not viewed like ours. He doesn't measure time the way we do. The apostle Peter clearly says we have been living in the last days at least since the day the church was birthed and empowered with the presence of the Holy Spirit.

Why does any of this matter? Why should you be concerned with the Second Coming of Christ? Primarily because Christ's Second coming is taught extensively in the Scriptures and Jesus Himself had much to say about it. It is not my purpose to give you all the theological theories concerning Christ's Second Coming or the various views concerning eschatology, though I will share a few basic concepts. My focus is to share the practical applications that are taught in the Scriptures concerning Christ's Second Coming and what this means to you and me.

People write books upon books on various theories of the end times, so there is no way I can give you an extensive study explaining all the numerous views. But I do want you to be familiar with a few terms and concepts concerning eschatology, so I will share them before we get into the practical application of living in the last days.

SOME BASICS

Let me first comment on the phrase, *the Second Coming of Christ*. Many evangelicals view the Second Coming of Christ as happening in two phases. First, some use this term in referring to the *rapture*, when Christ returns for His saints, takes them to heaven, and the world enters a period referred to as "the tribulation period." Second, Christ returns at the end of the tribulation period, referred to as "the revelation of Christ," in which He returns, sets up His kingdom, and judges the world.

Even though the word *rapture* is not used in the Bible, it is commonly used to refer to Christ momentarily appearing in the heavens and literally transporting all believers into heaven to be with Him eternally. There is definitely going to be a "catching up," the meaning of the word *rapture*, which is going to take place; but it is the timing of this event that is debated. This "catching up" or rapture is described by Paul in 1 Thessalonians:

> But we do not want you to be uninformed, brothers, about those who are asleep, that you may not grieve as others do who have no hope. For since we believe that Jesus died and rose again, even so, through Jesus, God will bring with him those who have fallen asleep. For this we declare to you by a word from the Lord, that we who are alive, who are left until the coming of the Lord, will not precede those who have fallen asleep. For the Lord himself will descend from heaven with a cry of command, with the voice of an archangel, and with the sound of the trumpet of God. And the dead in Christ will rise first. Then we who are alive, who are left, will be caught up together with them in the clouds to meet the Lord in the air, and so we will always be with the Lord. Therefore encourage one another with these words. (1 Thess. 4:13-18, emphasis mine)

In the above text, Paul describes two things that will happen when Christ returns. First, the bodies of all dead saints will experience resurrection and be united with their souls and spirits. Second, all believers who are living at this time will be caught up into heaven and simultaneously given their new heavenly bodies. The term "asleep" is a metaphor in the Bible for physical death. Paul is saying that the physical bodies of those who have died *prior* to the Second Coming of Christ will be resurrected, transformed and fit for heaven, and then united with their souls and spirits.

Let me point out that at the *very moment* a Christian dies, his or her spirit and soul immediately goes to heaven. There is no teaching in the Bible about "soul sleep" or "purgatory." Writing to the Corinthians Paul says: "So we are always of good courage. We know that while we are at home in the body we are away from the Lord, for we walk by faith, not by sight. Yes, we are of good courage, and we would rather be *away from the body* and *at home with the Lord*" (2 Cor. 5:6-8, emphasis mine).

Notice the phrase, "away from the body and at home with the Lord." Paul clearly states that when we die, our spirit and soul goes instantly to heaven and rests in the very presence of the Lord. He confirms this in writing to the Philippians: "For to me to live is Christ, and to die is gain. If I am to live in the flesh, that means fruitful labor for me. Yet which I shall choose I cannot tell. I am hard pressed between the two. My desire is to depart and be with Christ, for that is far better" (Phil. 1:21-23).

Paul had uncertainty about his future. Because of persecution, there was the possibility that he could be martyred for his faith. If he didn't die as a martyr, he would continue to minister to the Philippians. He was content with either situation – living or dying. He acknowledges that he was pulled between the two options. If he lived, he could continue to minister and spiritually impart into the Philippians' lives. But if he dies, or "departs," he will be with Christ, which he says would be "far better." The apostle definitely believed that when a person takes his last breath on the planet, he goes to be with Jesus!

So when Paul writes about the return of Christ and says, "The dead in Christ will rise first," he is speaking about *the bodies* of Christians who have died being raised from their graves and meeting their souls and spirits in heaven. The souls and spirits of all those who have died in Christ will receive a brand new glorious body that is fit to live in heaven throughout all eternity!

Notice the passage from Thessalonians that I quoted earlier: "For since we believe that Jesus died and rose again, even so, through Jesus, God *will bring with him* those who have fallen asleep" (1 Thess. 4:14, emphasis mine). God will *bring with him* every soul and spirit that has *been with Him* in heaven in order for them to receive their new and glorified body. If Christ brings the souls and spirits to earth with Him when He returns, that means they have *already* been with the Lord.

The question is "When does the rapture take place?" When Christians are raptured, what happens to all the people who are on the earth? These are the kinds of questions that have led to a diversity of answers.

Three Interpretations of the Tribulation Timeline

As I previously stated, many evangelicals believe that the event in 1 Thessalonians (the rapture) will be followed by what is referred to as the Tribulation period. According to this theory, Christ appears briefly in the heavens (unnoticed except to believers) and takes all living saints up with Him in heaven, which will be followed by a seven year period leading to the consummation of the age. During the first half of the Tribulation period, a person will rise to world power and authority and become the supreme leader of the world. The Bible refers to this person as the Antichrist. He will posses supernatural powers to deceive the world and the world will follow his leadership. In the first three and a half years of his leadership, the world will experience unprecedented peace and prosperity. This world leader will have the ability to establish a peace covenant with the nation of Israel and other nations.

But in the middle of this seven year period, the Antichrist will break the covenant with Israel and the world will experience a time of tribulation like no other time in history. The Antichrist will demand to be worshipped, and all who refuse to worship him will be killed. At the end of this seven year period Christ will again return and destroy His adversaries in a battle called Armageddon. Then He will set up an earthly kingdom for one thousand years in which He will rule and reign forever and ever.

For one thousand years there will be peace on the planet under the sovereign rule of Christ. This thousand year period is referred to as the "millennium." At the end of the millennium, Christ will remake the entire heavens and the earth. The creative order will be totally restored as God had intended and we as His people will serve Him throughout all eternity.

Most evangelical Christians would agree that there is a rapture, but again, it is the *timing* of the rapture where there is disagreement.

Some feel the rapture will take place at the *beginning* of the seven year period. This would prevent believers from experiencing the persecution from the Antichrist and unbelievers, and preserve them from the cataclysmic upheavals on the planet caused by the wrath of God that will be poured out against unbelievers in the last three and one half years. (This wrath and God's judgment is described in the book of Revelation.) The theological position that holds that all believers will be taken to heaven at the beginning of the Tribulation period is called *pre-tribulation*. According to this position, believers will be spared the trauma of persecution and God's judgment being poured out on the nations of the world.

Another view says that believers will be present on the earth the first three and one half years of the seven year Tribulation period. In the middle of the seven years, before the severity of God's judgment takes place, all believers will be raptured. This is called the *mid-tribulation* position. In this perspective, believers may experience *some level* of persecution before they are taken into heaven, but will be protected from God's wrath being poured out on unbelievers.

One final view sees the rapture taking place at *the end* of the seven year period, thus the *post-tribulation* position. According to this view, Christians will go through *the entire* Tribulation period and at the end of the seven years, Christ returns; believers are caught up to heaven; Christ ends the rebellion of the Antichrist and the demonic realm; and Satan, demons, and unbelievers are judged and sent to an eternal hell.

There are many books written representing these three theological positions. One's position concerning the timing of these events certainly should not be a litmus test for theological soundness or biblical integrity. All these positions have a biblical foundation and each one has a level of speculation. We will just have to wait and see!

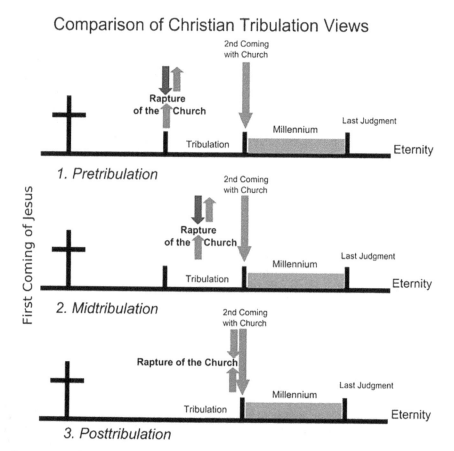

Figure 1: Comparison of Christian Tribulation Views[1]

Three Views of the Millennium

As mentioned above, the "millennium" represents the thousand year reign of Christ on the earth. As with the question concerning the timing of the rapture of believers, there are three distinct views concerning the millennium: Pre-millennialism, Post-millennialism, and Amillennialism positions. Here's a brief description of these positions. The *Pre-millennialism* position believes that *after* Christ returns there will be a literal thousand year period in which Christ and His people will reign with Him on the earth. The *Post-millennialism* position believes that Christ will return at *the end* of a thousand year period, which may be symbolic for just a long period of time. This position holds that the church age will flourish, most people and nations will become Christians, and this will usher in the return of Christ and His kingdom in which Christ will judge the world and set up His kingdom.

The *Amillennialism* position believes in the Second Coming, but rejects the idea of a literal thousand-year reign on earth. Some see Christ's reign beginning at the time of His resurrection. Here's how one author describes the millennium:

> The current age is the "Millennium" in that Christ rules in His Church and in the hearts of Christians, though the world becomes increasingly evil.... It is identified with the present spiritual reign of Christ at the right hand of God, where by faith His people are raised and seated with Him; thus there will be no literal millennial Kingdom. Christ's advent will be *after* the Millennium (or church age).... Amillenialists view the Kingdom promises to Israel as symbolic and apply them either to the Church age or to eternity.[2]

My theological persuasion concerning the millennium is the *Premillenialism* position. I believe the Bible teaches that the millennium will not begin *until* the return of Christ. Though there are those who view the millennium as only a symbolic representation of an undesignated period of time, I personally believe it *does* represent a literal thousand year period. This goes back to my view of interpreting Scriptures. Unless there is a clear reason not to interpret a word or phrase literally, it should be interpreted literally.

There is also a pattern in the Scriptures concerning length of the millennium. Scriptures mention the thousand year reign six times in chapter 20 of the book of Revelation, never hinting that it is symbolic. Thus I consider it to be a literal thousand year period (see Rev. 20:1-10). I do not see any reason to take the millennium as symbolic. The Scriptures seem to indicate that when Christ returns after the rapture and brings judgment upon the world, He will establish an earthly kingdom, and we His saints will rule and reign with Him for a thousand years on the earth. Many Bible scholars see the millennium period being described in the book of Isaiah:

But with righteousness he shall judge the poor, and decide with equity for the meek of the earth; and he shall strike the earth with the rod of his mouth, and with the breath of his lips he shall kill the wicked. Righteousness shall be the belt of his waist, and faithfulness the belt of his loins. The wolf shall dwell with the lamb, and the leopard shall lie down with the young goat, and the calf and the lion and the fattened calf together; and a little child shall lead them. The cow and the bear shall graze; their young shall lie down together; and the lion shall eat straw like the ox. The nursing child shall play over the hole of the cobra, and the weaned child shall put his hand on the adder's den. They shall not hurt or destroy in all my holy mountain; for the earth shall be full of the knowledge of the Lord as the waters cover the sea. In that day the root of Jesse, who shall stand as a signal for the peoples—of him shall the nations inquire, and his resting place shall be glorious. (Isa. 11:4-10)

This description clearly refers to something quite remarkable and futuristic. The millennium will be a time of universal peace and tranquility (see Isa. 2:4). God's glory and presence will be pervasive throughout the whole earth. We will have access to His temple and His presence at all times. It will be a glorious reign!

I wish I could say, "And now, we will live happily ever after." But this is not the case. The Bible teaches that Satan will be released for a period, will deceive nations, and lead a rebellion in defiance of God. I will not offer an explanation for Satan's release as it would be mere speculation. It doesn't appear that the revolt will last too long. At the end of this period, Satan and all demons will be assigned to the lake of fire and brimstone and be eternally tormented (see Rev. 20:7-10). After Satan's ultimate defeat, there will never be another rebellion and God's design for mankind and our enjoying His presence and serving Him will last forever. No more sin, no more pain, no more suffering, and no more death. Hallelujah and glory to God in the highest!

Sometime after the millennium, God will recreate a new heavens and a new earth. We will be able to behold the glory of it all. I don't know what it will be like, but I can assure you that it will be awesome!

I hope I have not confused you too much, but I thought it necessary to give you some theology concerning end time events. You may be frustrated and thinking, "Since there are so many different positions (Pretribulation rapture, Mid-tribulation rapture, Post-tribulation rapture, Premillennialism, Postmillennialism, and Amillennialism) what can we really know about the end times?" This is where the practical teaching comes in and there is no dispute on the meaning of Scripture and our response. Onward we go!

TEN FACTS CONCERNING THE END TIMES

1. Jesus will return

Jesus promised that He will take us to heaven to be with Him. The timing of His Second Coming is only known by God the Father, but He is coming, and it is going to be spectacular and glorious! (see Matt. 24:36)

Notice the words of Jesus: "Let not your hearts be troubled. Believe in God; believe also in me. In my Father's house are many rooms. If it were not so, would I have told you that I go to prepare a place for you? And if I go and prepare a place for you, I will come again and will take you to myself, that where I am you may be also" (John 14:1-3).

Many people wish they could know when the Second Coming of Christ will take place. But I think the uncertainty of when it will happen has been designed to ensure that every generation anticipates it. But as sure as Jesus was raised from the dead and is alive today, He is coming back! When He comes, He will take us to be with Him, as the Scripture above says. Jesus says that He is preparing a place for us. He is building a city and homes for our security, well-being, and for our life in heaven. The best thing about heaven is that we will be in the presence of Jesus throughout all eternity. Imagine constantly being in His presence, the presence of the One who gives us joy, peace, and eternity in heaven with Him as His children. It will be amazing beyond our imaginations!

The apostle Paul confirms the Second Coming of Christ in his letter to the Thessalonians:

> But we do not want you to be uninformed, brothers, about those who are asleep, that you may not grieve as others do who have no hope. For since we believe that Jesus died and rose again, even so, through Jesus, God will bring with him those who have fallen asleep. *For this we declare to you by a word from the Lord,* that we who are alive, who are left until the coming of the Lord, will not precede those who have fallen asleep. For the Lord himself will descend from heaven with a cry of command, with the voice of an archangel, and with the sound of the trumpet of God. And the dead in Christ will rise first. Then we who are alive, who are left, will be caught up together with them in the clouds to meet the Lord in the air, and so we will always be with the Lord. Therefore encourage one another with these words. (1 Thess. 4:13-18, emphasis mine)

Paul says that what he is writing concerning Christ's Second Coming has been directly confirmed to him by the Lord. We are to find encouragement in this promise, knowing that regardless of what happens in this life, our future is secure and eternal in the heavens. One day He will come, take us home, and we will never again be separated from the presence of our Lord or our loved ones who are also in God's family.

In the very beginning of the book of Acts, Luke affirms the promise of the Second Coming of Christ: "And when he had said these things, as they were looking on, he was lifted up, and a cloud took him out of their sight. And while they were gazing into heaven as he went, behold, two men stood by them in white robes, and said, 'Men of Galilee, why do you stand looking into heaven? This Jesus, who was taken up from you into heaven, will come in the same way as you saw him go into heaven.'" (Acts 1:9-11)

Luke affirms that exactly as Jesus ascended up into the clouds, He will return in the clouds at His Second Coming. Jesus will return literally and physically.

The apostle Peter writes this concerning the promise of the Second Coming of Christ:

> But do not overlook this one fact, beloved, that with the Lord one day is as a thousand years, and a thousand years as one day. The Lord is not slow to fulfill his promise as some count slowness, but is patient toward you, not wishing that any should perish, but that all should reach repentance. But the day of the Lord will come like a thief, and then the heavens will pass away with a roar, and the heavenly bodies will be burned up and dissolved, and the earth and the works that are done on it will be exposed. (2 Pet. 3:8-10)

Peter is exhorting us not to become impatient or discouraged. Though it may seem to us as if His coming is never going to happen, He assures us that it will. Part of His delay is because of His patience in waiting for people to come to Christ for salvation. He wants all people to repent, turn from their sins, and experience the forgiveness and eternal life He offers. And even though it may seem like forever to you and me, a day to the Lord is like a thousand years. So be patient, live in expectation, and be sure that in His time He will surely come!

2. His return will be sudden and unexpected

Have you ever had anyone come to your house unexpectedly? The doorbell rings, you look through the peep hole in your door, and a friend or relative has shown up without giving you any notice? Sometimes you're glad that your unexpected guest dropped by, but other times, you're not so happy to see them!

200

Jesus states that His return will be similar to that of a thief. When you least expect it—He comes! "But know this, that if the master of the house had known in what part of the night *the thief was coming*, he would have stayed awake and would not have let his house be broken into." (Matt. 24:43, emphasis mine)

A thief isn't going to call you on the phone, or email or text you that he's coming! No, the thief's modus operandi is the element of surprise, coming at an unexpected time, the precise time designed to catch you off guard. Jesus is saying that when we least expect it, when we are busy doing something else, that suddenly—He comes!

Paul writes: "Now concerning the times and the seasons, brothers, you have no need to have anything written to you. For you yourselves are fully aware that *the day of the Lord will come like a thief in the night*. While people are saying, 'There is peace and security,' then sudden destruction will come upon them as labor pains come upon a pregnant woman, and they will not escape." (1 Thess. 5:1-3, emphasis mine).

Paul says people will be thinking to themselves that everything is going fine, there is no need to worry, and we are living in times of peace and security. But suddenly, without notice, Jesus will come, and with His coming everything will be radically changed. Notice the words of Peter:

> *But the day of the Lord will come like a thief*, and then the heavens will pass away with a roar, and the heavenly bodies will be burned up and dissolved, and the earth and the works that are done on it will be exposed. Since all these things are thus to be dissolved, what sort of people ought you to be in lives of holiness and godliness, waiting for and hastening the coming of the day of God, because of which the heavens will be set on fire and dissolved, and the heavenly bodies will melt as they burn! But according to his promise we are waiting for new heavens and a new earth in which righteousness dwells. (2 Pet. 3:10-13, emphasis mine)

How do you prepare for a thief? With today's technology, many of us have alarm systems that alert us to an intruder. But when it comes to the Second Coming of Christ, there is no way to know exactly when He will come. Suddenly and unexpectedly we will hear a loud shout and the sound of a trumpet—and the next thing you know—He's come. Ready or not, you discover the Lord Jesus has come. So how do you prepare? Be ready every hour of the day, every day of the week, which brings me to my next point.

3. Constant readiness is the only way to prepare

When I was a child, one of the games I loved to play was a game called, "Hide and Seek." Whether there were two or more people playing, it was exciting and fun! The way you played the game was that one person would cover their eyes and count to ten. While they were counting, you would run to find a place to hide. When the person got to the count of ten, they would yell out, "Ready or not, here I come!" Being ready meant that you were in your hiding place by the time the person counted to ten.

If there is one undisputable and clear teaching that Jesus stressed concerning the end times it is this: we must remain in a state of constant readiness. He stressed that we should always be ready for His sudden appearance. He could come today, tonight, tomorrow, next week, or next month—and since we don't know His timing, we must be ready for His coming!

In chapters 24 and 25 of Matthew's gospel, Jesus focuses on the events of the end times. In chapter 25, He shares two parables with His disciples: the parable of the ten virgins and the parable of the ten talents. In both of these parables, Jesus stresses the need to prepare and be ready. He tells them they need to be watching (remaining in a state of readiness) and to stay busy in serving and advancing the kingdom. Notice His words at the end of His teaching on the ten virgins: "Watch therefore, for you know neither the day nor the hour." (Matt. 25:13)

As believers, though we will be somewhat surprised, we should not be *overtaken* with surprise when Jesus comes. Jesus and the Scriptures give us various signs and certain indicators that will point to the fact that the end is drawing near. Notice what He says in Matthew 24:

> And Jesus answered them, "See that no one leads you astray. For many will come in my name, saying, 'I am the Christ,' and they will lead many astray. And you will hear of wars and rumors of wars. See that you are not alarmed, for this must take place, but the end is not yet. For nation will rise against nation, and kingdom against kingdom, and there will be famines and earthquakes in various places. All these are but the beginning of the birth pains. Then they will deliver you up to tribulation and put you to death, and you will be hated by all nations for my name's sake. And then many will fall away and betray one another and hate one another. And many false prophets will arise and lead many astray. And because lawlessness will be increased, the love of many will grow cold. But the one who endures to the end will be saved. *And this gospel of the kingdom will be proclaimed throughout the whole world as a testimony to all nations, and then the end will come*." (Matt. 24:4-14, emphasis mine)

Sounds like the twenty-first century! Yes, many of these types of things have happened throughout the centuries, but there is one sign that until recently has not been a possibility. Notice in the last verse of the passage above, that I italicized, *"And this gospel of the kingdom will be proclaimed throughout the whole world as a testimony to all nations, and then the end will come."* (Matt. 24:14) Modern technology has accelerated the spread of the gospel as in no other generation. The age of mass media has brought about the spread of the gospel through radio, television, and now the Internet to regions of our world that would have been impossible to reach just a few years ago. The proclamation of the gospel is rapidly taking place, and with it I pray the Second Coming of Christ is drawing near!

Another key sign of His coming that He mentions is the moral condition within the world. At age 61, I am seeing the disintegration of morals and values to such a degree that I thought would never happen in my lifetime. Yet even as I write this chapter, things in America are rapidly changing. For instance, as a result of the 2012 election, the states of Washington, Maine, Maryland, and Minnesota have endorsed same-sex marriage. For the first time in their history, the Democratic Party's platform included same-sex marriage. The states of Colorado and Washington have voted to legalize marijuana for recreational use.

Even though I knew our nation was increasingly becoming a nation characterized by moral relativism, I must say I am appalled at the rapidity of our moral collapse. Many other nations have adopted and promoted same-sex marriage for some time, but I was caught off guard at the acceleration of this movement in the United States.

Our culture has jettisoned morality and embraced the philosophy of political correctness in which every ungodly behavior is to be accepted and tolerated. To differ is to be intolerant and bigoted. What used to be considered sinful, wrong, and an abomination in God's sight is now accepted and quickly becoming the norm. What was considered moral and right is no longer palatable by society.

Jesus told us that in the end times the moral compass of the last generation would be off-course and out of sync with God's order and His Word. Concerning the moral condition of the end times He said, "Sin will be rampant everywhere, and the love of many will grow cold." (Matt. 24:12, *NLT*)

In the same chapter Jesus said. "From the fig tree learn its lesson: as soon as its branch becomes tender and puts out its leaves, you know that summer is near. *So also, when you see all these things, you know that he is near, at the very gates.* Truly, I say to you, this generation will not pass away until all these things take place. Heaven and earth will pass away, but my words will not pass away." (Matt. 24:32-35, emphasis mine)

Jesus reveals these details concerning His Second Coming to let us know when His coming is near, "at the very gates." The things He describes in Matthew 24 should alert us to His soon coming. We are not to be overtaken or surprised at His return.

Notice Paul's characterization of the end times:

> You should know this, Timothy, that in the last days there will
> be very difficult times. For people will love only themselves
> and their money. They will be boastful and proud, scoffing at
> God, disobedient to their parents, and ungrateful. They will
> consider nothing sacred. They will be unloving and unfor-
> giving; they will slander others and have no self-control. They
> will be cruel and hate what is good. They will betray their
> friends, be reckless, be puffed up with pride, and love pleasure
> rather than God. They will act religious, but they will reject
> the power that could make them godly. Stay away from people
> like that! *...But evil people and impostors will flourish.* They
> will deceive others and will themselves be deceived. (2 Tim.
> 3:1-5,13, *NLT*, emphasis mine)

These verses describe the moral condition of the *last days*. It doesn't take a
Ph.D. to come to the conclusion that we are living in the last days. The reason
I am including extensive Scripture passages under this point is because these
verses describe clear signs of the end of the last days and we are seeing them in
our generation. As believers, we should be able to discern the times and know
that His Second Coming is near. We should not be overtaken with surprise.
Notice these words of Paul:

> *But you are not in darkness, brothers, for that day to surprise
> you like a thief.* For you are all children of light, children of
> the day. We are not of the night or of the darkness. So then let
> us not sleep, as others do, but let us keep awake and be sober.
> For those who sleep, sleep at night, and those who get drunk,
> are drunk at night. But since we belong to the day, let us be
> sober, having put on the breastplate of faith and love, and for a
> helmet the hope of salvation. (1 Thess. 5:4-8, emphasis mine)

As believers, we have entered a new realm and kingdom. Our lives should
be a reflection of the life of Christ, lived in His light and in the truth of the
gospel. We are no longer bound in a state of unbelief or of walking in darkness,
but have been set free by the truth of the gospel. Our eyes have been opened, we
can see clearly, and we have the Holy Spirit providing spiritual understanding
and illumination. Let's stay awake, stay alert, and be ready for His coming—at
all times!

The apostle Peter, foreseeing the consummation of the ages tells us how we
should live: "Since all these things are thus to be dissolved, *what sort of people
ought you to be in lives of holiness and godliness,* waiting for and hastening the

coming of the day of God, because of which the heavens will be set on fire and dissolved, and the heavenly bodies will melt as they burn! But according to his promise we are waiting for new heavens and a new earth in which righteousness dwells" (2 Pet. 3:11-13, emphasis mine).

Notice the descriptive words "holiness and godliness." As we wait for His coming, these are the attributes that should be active in our lives. We are to live pure, holy, unblemished, and godly lives. We don't have to be theologians to know what these words mean. The Holy Spirit within us constantly speaks to us and leads us into a life that is characterized by these traits as we yield and surrender to Him.

Peter continues this line of exhortation concerning how we should live, knowing the possibility of the imminent return of the Lord. He writes:

> Therefore, beloved, since you are waiting for these, *be diligent to be found by him without spot or blemish, and at peace*. And count the patience of our Lord as salvation, just as our beloved brother Paul also wrote to you according to the wisdom given him, as he does in all his letters when he speaks in them of these matters. There are some things in them that are hard to understand, which the ignorant and unstable twist to their own destruction, as they do the other Scriptures. You therefore, beloved, knowing this beforehand, take care that you are not carried away with the error of lawless people and lose your own stability. *But grow in the grace and knowledge of our Lord and Savior Jesus Christ. To him be the glory both now and to the day of eternity. Amen.* (2 Pet. 3:14-18, emphasis mine)

Again, Peter's emphasis is on living a pure and holy life and focusing on *growing in the grace and knowledge of our Lord and Savior Jesus Christ*. Let's press onward, deeper, and higher in our personal relationship with the Lord. Then, when He appears, we will be ready to meet the Lord in the air!

4.   There will be a rapture of believers and of bodies of deceased saints

Though we can dispute the timing of the rapture, there is no question that a rapture will take place. When Jesus returns, the dead bodies of believers will be raised and all believers who are alive at His coming will be taken up with Jesus into heaven. It will happen in an instant, what Paul referred to as a "twinkling of an eye" (1 Cor. 15:52). Earlier, I quoted Paul's letter to the Thessalonians. Notice again his words:

> For the Lord himself will descend from heaven with a cry of command, with the voice of an archangel, and with the sound

of the trumpet of God. And the dead in Christ will rise first. Then we who are alive, who are left, will be caught up together with them in the clouds to meet the Lord in the air, and so we will always be with the Lord. (1 Thess. 4:16-17)

I mentioned earlier in this chapter that when believers die, they go immediately into the presence of the Lord. But what happens to their bodies? Paul says that when Christ returns, the dead bodies of believers whose souls have already joined Christ will be raised to unite with their souls and spirits in heaven and receive new bodies. Those who are living will be instantly caught up in heaven to be with Jesus. This is going to be a great time of reunion, as we will see loved ones who had gone on before us and we will never be separated again!

5.   A world leader referred to as the Antichrist will arise

The Bible teaches that at the very end of the age, a world leader will rise who will capture the world's attention. He will be intellectually brilliant, charismatic, and have the ability to lead the entire world, who will indeed follow his leadership and eventually worship him. The Bible refers to him as the "Antichrist," the "man of lawlessness," and the "son of destruction." Here is the apostle Paul's description of this man:

> Now concerning the coming of our Lord Jesus Christ and our being gathered together to him, we ask you, brothers, not to be quickly shaken in mind or alarmed, either by a spirit or a spoken word, or a letter seeming to be from us, to the effect that the day of the Lord has come. Let no one deceive you in any way. For that day will not come, unless the rebellion comes first, and *the man of lawlessness* is revealed, *the son of destruction*, who opposes and exalts himself against every so-called god or object of worship, so that he takes his seat in the temple of God, *proclaiming himself to be God*. Do you not remember that when I was still with you I told you these things? And you know what is restraining him now so that he may be revealed in his time. For the mystery of lawlessness is already at work. Only he who now restrains it will do so until he is out of the way. And then the lawless one will be revealed, whom the Lord Jesus will kill with the breath of his mouth and bring to nothing by the appearance of his coming. The coming of the lawless one is by the activity of Satan with all power and false signs and wonders, and with all wicked deception for those who are perishing, because they refused to love the truth and so be saved. Therefore God sends them a

strong delusion, so that they may believe what is false, in order
that all may be condemned who did not believe the truth but
had pleasure in unrighteousness. (2 Thess. 2:1-12)

Here's what we learn from the above text: The Antichrist is no ordinary
man. He will be empowered by Satan himself to perform "false signs and wonders." And because of this power, he will have the ability to deceive the masses.
He will be similar to a Hitler, but far more diabolical. He will have the power to
deceive not only a nation, but also the entire world. The world will look to the
Antichrist with awe and eventually give him their devotion.

He is the antithesis of the Christ. He will come along with a message of
peace but lead the world into chaos and destruction. Ultimately, he will proclaim himself to be God, demand to be worshipped, and oppose anyone worshipping anyone but him. His appearance will definitely be a clear sign that the
end of the age as we know it is but only a few years away.

The spirit of the antichrist is already at work in the world. It is a spirit that
is against Christ, His message, and His kingdom. It is a spirit that is in opposition to godliness, holiness, and any moral restraint. The apostle John writing
about the coming antichrist says, "Children, it is the last hour, and as you have
heard that antichrist is coming, so now many antichrists have come. Therefore
we know that it is the last hour" (1 John 2:18). John is saying that there are
people living today who represent antichrist and who are propagating the spirit
of antichrist. Yet, there will be one specific man that will rise as the world
leader who will be the embodiment of all that Satan desires to accomplish in
this world.

Prophecy often has a *present* context and a *future* context. There are many
prophecies in the Old Testament that had dual application. For instance, a
prophecy could address the present situation directly applicable to the historical context while also pointing to a future event that would happen hundreds
of years later. Many theologians see the Antichrist predicted in prophecies
from this dual characteristic perspective. In *Bible Doctrines from a Pentecostal
Perspective*, the writer says the following about the Antichrist:

Although there are biblical allusions and characterizations
of Antichrist throughout the Old and New Testaments,
the clearest representation of this foe of God is given in 2
Thessalonians 2:3-9. He is pictured as the embodiment of
lawlessness (cf. Dan. 7:24-25; 2 Thess. 2:3, 8-9). He claims
to be deity (2 Thess. 2:9-10). It is probable that the Beast
referred to in Revelation 13 is another name for Antichrist,
for this monster is pictured as having authority ascribed only
to Antichrist. Antichrist will unmask his apparent beneficence
toward the state of Israel by perpetrating an act of sacrilege,
showing himself to be a great deceiver and an enemy of God.

This sacrilege that he will perform is called in Daniel "the abomination that causes desolation" (cf. Dan. 11:31; 12:11; Matt. 24:15; Mark 13:14). The desecration of the temple by Antiochus IV, Epiphanes, a Syrian ruler in 168 B.C. is probably the immediate fulfillment of Daniel's prophecy, but that it has a longer-range eschatological significance is borne out by New Testament references to this term "abomination of desolation" – which Jesus saw as still future.[3]

The bottom line is that the Scriptures are clear that a final person, empowered by Satan, will rise up in the end times and lead a worldwide rebellion. He appears to be personified as the Beast in the apostle John's description of the apocalypse:

And I saw a beast rising out of the sea, with ten horns and seven heads, with ten diadems on its horns and blasphemous names on its heads. And the beast that I saw was like a leopard; its feet were like a bear's, and its mouth was like a lion's mouth. And to it the dragon gave his power and his throne and great authority. One of its heads seemed to have a mortal wound, but its mortal wound was healed, and the whole earth marveled as they followed the beast. And they worshiped the dragon, for he had given his authority to the beast, and they worshiped the beast, saying, "Who is like the beast, and who can fight against it?" And the beast was given a mouth uttering haughty and blasphemous words, and it was allowed to exercise authority for forty-two months. It opened its mouth to utter blasphemies against God, blaspheming his name and his dwelling, that is, those who dwell in heaven. Also it was allowed to make war on the saints and to conquer them. And authority was given it over every tribe and people and language and nation, and all who dwell on earth will worship it, everyone whose name has not been written before the foundation of the world in the book of life of the Lamb who was slain. (Rev. 13:1-8)

This is a frightening description! Satan, through his instrument, the Antichrist, in these last days will do everything within his power to bring about deception and destruction. But I can assure you that his demise is certain! He and those who align with him will be decisively destroyed just prior to the inauguration of Christ's kingdom. (see Rev. 19:20; 20:10)

As believers, we need to rest assured that God is sovereign, in complete control, and that these end times will lead to total victory and the entrance of God's eternal kingdom. We as believers will be with Christ and will rule and reign with Him!

6.   Believers on the planet will be persecuted - The Great Tribulation
The Bible teaches that under the authority and rule of the Antichrist, that there will be a time called the "great tribulation." Jesus describes this period:

> So when you see the abomination of desolation spoken of by the prophet Daniel, standing in the holy place (let the reader understand), then let those who are in Judea flee to the mountains. Let the one who is on the housetop not go down to take what is in his house, and let the one who is in the field not turn back to take his cloak. And alas for women who are pregnant and for those who are nursing infants in those days! Pray that your flight may not be in winter or on a Sabbath. For then there will be *great tribulation*, such as has not been from the beginning of the world until now, no, and never will be. And if those days had not been cut short, no human being would be saved. But for the sake of the elect those days will be cut short. (Matt. 24:15-22, emphasis mine)

This period in history will be like none other that has ever occurred on the planet. Those who become believers at this time will be faced with unprecedented persecution. The apostle John says that under the leadership of the Antichrist, people will be required to receive *his mark*, a sign that they belong to him and are submitting to his authority. We are not sure what type of mark this will be, but its placement will be on the "right hand or forehead" (Rev. 13:16; 20:4). If you refuse to take his mark, you will be unable to purchase anything, including food, clothing, and other needed items (see Rev. 13:16-18). Ultimately, those who refuse to take the "mark of the beast" or worship the beast will be decapitated (see Rev. 20:4).

This period seems to be limited to a very brief period, but it will be the worst time of chaos and evil the world has ever seen.

If the pre-tribulation rapture position is correct, we as believers will be in heaven during the Antichrist's reign. This period is called the "great tribulation." I believe the majority of John's Revelation, and his description of his vision of the events on the planet describe this period. If the post-tribulation theory is correct, those living during this time will have to experience it.

You may be thinking to yourself, "What if the pre-tribulation position is wrong? What happens if we as believers have to go through the tribulation period?" I would agree that this is a frightening thought, but I am convinced that God will give us the grace and strength to endure. The key is to be ready, be filled with faith, empowered by the Spirit, and know that regardless of what happens, we will be victorious in the end!

7. Cataclysmic events will take place in the heavens and on the earth

As we have learned from Scripture, the apostle Peter stated that Pentecost commenced the last days. Peter said the outpouring and empowerment of the Holy Spirit is the beginning of the last days as predicted by the prophet Joel. But he also mentioned other cataclysmic signs that are yet to take place.

> But this is what was uttered through the prophet Joel: "And in the last days it shall be, God declares, that I will pour out my Spirit on all flesh, and your sons and your daughters shall prophesy, and your young men shall see visions, and your old men shall dream dreams; even on my male servants and female servants in those days I will pour out my Spirit, and they shall prophesy. And I will show wonders in the heavens above and signs on the earth below, blood, and fire, and vapor of smoke; the sun shall be turned to darkness and the moon to blood, before the day of the Lord comes, the great and magnificent day." (Acts 2:16-20)

The "wonders in the heavens above and signs on the earth below" have not happened and will not happen until the very end of the last days. Jesus said, "For nation will rise against nation, and kingdom against kingdom, and there will be famines and earthquakes in various places. All these are but the beginning of the birth pains" (Matt. 24:7-8). These kinds of things have been happening and are part of end day events.

In my lifetime, there seems to be an increase in the number of earthquakes. We have witnessed the 2004 Indian Ocean earthquake which triggered a series of tsunamis along land masses of the Indian Ocean, killing a staggering 230,000 people in 14 countries. The National Geographic Society reports that it is the most damaging tsunami on record, hitting Indonesia, then Sri Lanka, India, and Thailand.[4]

The events described by Jesus have been happening since He predicted them. But notice Jesus said, "All these are but the beginning of the birth pains" (Matt. 24:8). In recent years the Middle East has had an escalation in "nations rising against nation" and it appears that God is orchestrating world events for the final battle the Bible calls Armageddon, which leads me to my next point, the Battle of Armageddon.

8. Jesus will conquer His enemies in a battle called Armageddon

The period known as the last days will end with a great battle called Armageddon with the Antichrist leading the nations of the world. "And they assembled them at the place that in Hebrew is called Armageddon" (Rev. 16:16), which is the Mount of Megiddo, next to the Jezreel Valley. How fitting that this battle will be in the Holy Land of His people Israel. This is the battle of God against the Antichrist, the demonic world, and the nations under his control. The nations of the world will come against the nation of Israel, and Christ will come and defeat His enemies and throw Satan, the Antichrist, and his demons in hell.

The Bible says that Christ will return with His saints, defeat His enemies, and establish His kingdom. Depending on the timing of the rapture, this is the literal Second Coming of Christ to the planet. If the rapture precedes this event, Christ doesn't actually come to the earth but appears in the air to call His saints home. In the actual Second Coming, we will join Christ at His return as He swiftly puts an end to those in opposition to Him and establishes His kingdom. This is what will happen:

> Then I saw heaven opened, and behold, a white horse! The one sitting on it is called Faithful and True, and in righteousness he judges and makes war. His eyes are like a flame of fire, and on his head are many diadems, and he has a name written that no one knows but himself. He is clothed in a robe dipped in blood, and the name by which he is called is The Word of God. And the armies of heaven, arrayed in fine linen, white and pure, were following him on white horses. From his mouth comes a sharp sword with which to strike down the nations, and he will rule them with a rod of iron. He will tread the winepress of the fury of the wrath of God the Almighty. On his robe and on his thigh he has a name written, King of kings and Lord of lords. Then I saw an angel standing in the sun, and with a loud voice he called to all the birds that fly directly overhead, "Come, gather for the great supper of God, to eat the flesh of kings, the flesh of captains, the flesh of mighty men, the flesh of horses and their riders, and the flesh of all men, both free and slave, both small and great." And I saw the beast and the kings of the earth with their armies gathered to make war against him who was sitting on the horse and against his army. And the beast was captured, and with it the false prophet who in its presence had done the signs by which he deceived those who had received the mark of the beast and those who worshiped its image. These two were thrown alive into the lake of fire that burns with sulfur. And the rest were slain by the sword that came from the mouth of him who was sitting on the horse, and all the birds were gorged with their flesh. (Rev. 19:11-21)

After this battle, God will establish His kingdom on this planet for a thousand years. Earlier I mentioned this period called the millennium. For a thousand years, we will join Christ and assist Him in His rule and reign on the earth. It is going to be spectacular and glorious! Again, I wish I could say that everyone lives happily ever after. For us who are God's children, this is true. We will have our new bodies, have access to heaven and the earth, and be in the presence of Jesus for all eternity. But for some reason, at the end of the one thousand year reign of Christ on earth, Satan will be released for a brief period and many will once again fall under his deception. Look at the following passage from the book of Revelation:

> And when the thousand years are ended, Satan will be released
> from his prison and will come out to deceive the nations
> that are at the four corners of the earth, Gog and Magog, to
> gather them for battle; their number is like the sand of the
> sea. And they marched up over the broad plain of the earth
> and surrounded the camp of the saints and the beloved city,
> but fire came down from heaven and consumed them, and
> the devil who had deceived them was thrown into the lake
> of fire and sulfur where the beast and the false prophet were,
> and they will be tormented day and night forever and ever.
> (Rev. 20:7-10)

Why? I have no idea! I wish the Lord would keep Satan and his demons locked up forever, but the answer as to why is found only in the sovereign wisdom of God. One thing that does seem clear is that during this thousand year period, multitudes will once again fall under his deception and be led to revolt. But Satan's attempt will be decisively defeated as God sends fire down from heaven and dispatches them into the lake of fire to be punished for all eternity, never again to have any influence on the earth or the heavens.

9. There will be a final judgment

For those who have never received the forgiveness found in Christ, there will be a judgment. Following the thousand year reign of Christ, the unsaved dead will be resurrected. Though their spirits and souls had already been confined to hell, they will be resurrected to stand at what the Bible calls the Great White Throne of Judgment. This judgment is only for those who have rejected Christ. At the Second Coming of Christ, *only the saved*, born again believers will be resurrected. The unsaved will not be resurrected until the end of the thousand year reign of Christ, and then only to stand before God for their judgment. This is why the apostle John writes the following:

> Then I saw thrones, and seated on them were those to whom
> the authority to judge was committed. Also I saw the souls
> of those who had been beheaded for the testimony of Jesus
> and for the word of God, and those who had not worshiped
> the beast or its image and had not received its mark on their
> foreheads or their hands. They came to life and reigned with
> Christ for a thousand years. *The rest of the dead did not come
> to life until the thousand years were ended.* This is the first res-
> urrection. Blessed and holy is the one who shares in the first
> resurrection! Over such the second death has no power, but
> they will be priests of God and of Christ, and they will reign
> with him for a thousand years. (Rev. 20:4-6, emphasis mine)

Once the millennium ends, the *unsaved non-believers* will stand before
God, be judged for not having received Christ, and be assigned to everlasting
torment in hell. Notice this frightening description:

> Then I saw a great white throne and him who was seated on it.
> From his presence earth and sky fled away, and no place was
> found for them. And I saw the dead, great and small, standing
> before the throne, and books were opened. Then another book
> was opened, which is the book of life. And the dead were
> judged by what was written in the books, according to what
> they had done. And the sea gave up the dead who were in it,
> Death and Hades gave up the dead who were in them, and they
> were judged, each one of them, according to what they had
> done. Then Death and Hades were thrown into the lake of fire.
> This is the *second death*, the lake of fire. And if anyone's name
> was not found written in the book of life, he was thrown into
> the lake of fire. (Rev. 20:11-15, emphasis mine)

Let me share several truths from this Scripture. First, physical death does
not end it all. There is a *second death* that assigns the unbeliever to a place
the Bible calls hell. Unbelievers, following their physical death, still exist as
eternal spirit beings and will be resurrected to face God's judgment. Second,
you will be judged according to what you have done, according to your works.
Those who have rejected Christ have no other basis for judgment. No one's
works will get them into heaven.

But before God assigns them to hell, He opens one more book to make sure
their name is not there. It is called the Lamb's book of life where all names of
believers have been placed (see Rev. 21:27). When their name is not found, they
are thrown into hell's lake of fire as punishment for their rejection of God's free

gift of life through Jesus. Third, there is no indication that there is ever again any other opportunity to come to Christ. This judgment appears final.

I know that some people ask, "How can a loving God assign anyone to hell for all eternity?" I answer this question with the following statement: God doesn't send anyone to hell. Each person individually determines his or her own destiny depending on the choice he or she made concerning Christ. If you receive Him, you are forgiven of your sins and given the gift of eternal life. If you reject Him, you will spend eternity in a place called hell. It's your choice.

Others ask, "Is there really fire in hell? Do you experience torment in hell?" I know that there are some pastors and theologians who try to explain hell away, but the Bible is clear. There is a hell, and Jesus spoke about it often (see Matt. 5:22,29-30; 10:28; 18:9; 23:33; Luke 12:5). Are we to discount the words of Jesus? If Jesus was wrong concerning the reality of a place called hell, how could we believe Him about a place called heaven? Jesus said, "And do not fear those who kill the body but cannot kill the soul. Rather fear him who can destroy both soul and body in hell" (Matt.10:28).

If hell was just the act of experiencing death and once you die, you are annihilated, why would He ever make this statement? Jesus spoke of hell as a real place "where their worm does not die and the fire is not quenched" (Mark 9:48). He says it is a place where there will be *"weeping and gnashing* of teeth" (Matt. 13:42, emphasis mine). Does this sound like a place of annihilation?

His most graphic description of hell is found in His story about the rich man and Lazarus. In it He describes the rich man in hell and says this:

> The rich man also died and was buried, and in Hades, being in torment, he lifted up his eyes and saw Abraham far off and Lazarus at his side. And he called out, "Father Abraham, have mercy on me, and send Lazarus to dip the end of his finger in water and cool my tongue, for I am in anguish in this flame." But Abraham said, "Child, remember that you in your lifetime received your good things, and Lazarus in like manner bad things; but now he is comforted here, and you are in anguish. And besides all this, between us and you a great chasm has been fixed, in order that those who would pass from here to you may not be able, and none may cross from there to us." And he said, "Then I beg you, father, to send him to my father's house—for I have five brothers—so that he may warn them, lest they also come into this place of torment." (Luke 16:22b-28)

Was Jesus mistaken about this place called hell? Was He just trying to terrify us and use fear to make people believe in Him? I would submit to you that it is impossible to believe that Jesus was God in the flesh, the Son of the living God, and that He was either mistaken or purposely misleading us in His description of hell. As believers we have no other option but to believe that hell is a real place, a place of eternal torment, and a place where unbelievers will spend eternity because they have rejected the salvation that God offered through Christ. There is no possible way to do justice to the words of Jesus and explain away the reality of hell. As much as we find the subject unpalatable to our minds and emotions, we have no other choice but to take Jesus at His word. There is a hell!

Does this let believers off the hook? Yes and no. As believers, we are the children of God. We have been clothed in the righteousness of Christ and our entrance into heaven is based solely on our faith in His substitutionary death for our sins on the cross. We as His sons and daughters will not face the Great White Throne of Judgment described in Revelation 20:11-15. But we will stand at what is referred to as *The Judgment Seat of Christ*. This judgment is not for the purpose of determining our entrance into heaven but is rather a judgment that will determine our rewards in heaven. Notice these passages in Corinthians:

> Now if anyone builds on the foundation with gold, silver, precious stones, wood, hay, straw—each one's work will become manifest, for the Day will disclose it, because it will be revealed by fire, and the fire will test what sort of work each one has done. If the work that anyone has built on the foundation survives, he will receive a reward. If anyone's work is burned up, he will suffer loss, though he himself will be saved, but only as through fire. (1 Cor. 3:12-15)

> For we must all appear before the judgment seat of Christ, so that each one may receive what is due for what he has done in the body, whether good or evil. (2 Cor. 5:10)

These two passages speak of the same judgment. The purpose of that judgment is to determine what rewards should be received or lost. What are we doing in our service for the Lord? For instance, if we sing in the choir on a worship team, teach a class, serve as a greeter or usher, or any other capacity in the church—what is our motivation for serving? Is it because we want recognition? We like to be seen by others? We want prestige or power? Exactly why do we do the things we do for the kingdom?

The other question many may ask is "Why didn't we do more for the kingdom?" Examples of "doing more" could be sharing our faith with others, inviting a family to church, doing acts of kindness for others without expecting anything in return, serving in the church in some capacity (nursery, usher, greeter, teacher, in leadership), and the list could go on.

In saving us, God has certain expectations of us, His children. He didn't say to just sit back and wait for His coming. He wants us actively serving in and advancing His kingdom whatever way that we can. I am not sure of all the things by which the Lord will give out rewards or by which we will lose rewards, but it is clear that all believers will stand in this judgment. There is a day of accountability. I don't think we should fear this day, but simply do our best to serve the Lord with awareness that He does have expectations for our lives.

One question I often ask my congregation is, "What are you doing in your life that has eternal significance and value?" The reason I ask this is because if we are not careful, we will come to the end of our lives knowing that we made very little contribution for Christ and His kingdom. Let's *be intentional* about serving Him. Why not make a list of spiritual and kingdom goals each year and determine to make an eternal difference? If we do, we will be blessed indeed!

10. There will be a new heavens and a new earth

I love our planet! I never cease to be amazed at the wonder and awesomeness of God's creation. Pam and I feel so blessed by living near the Gulf of Mexico here in Sarasota, Florida. We love walking on the beach and watching the various species of birds and other marine life. Just watching the sunset on the beach is an incredible site to behold that shouts the glory and majesty of our omnipotent God.

The Hubble telescope has given us a peek into the beauty and vastness of our universe and the grandeur of God's glory. Some of the colors and designs are breathtaking. Yet the Bible tells us that at the end of the thousand year reign of Christ, God is going to create a new heavens and a new earth! Notice the following Scriptures:

> But the day of the Lord will come like a thief, and then *the heavens will pass away with a roar, and the heavenly bodies will be burned up and dissolved, and the earth and the works that are done on it will be exposed. Since all these things are thus to be dissolved*, what sort of people ought you to be in lives of holiness and godliness, waiting for and hastening the coming of the day of God, because of which *the heavens will be set on fire and dissolved, and the heavenly bodies will melt as they burn! But according to his promise we are waiting for new heavens and a new earth* in which righteousness dwells. (2 Pet. 3:10-13, emphasis mine)

> Then I saw a new heaven and a new earth, for the first heaven and the first earth had passed away, and the sea was no more. And I saw the holy city, new Jerusalem, coming down out of heaven from God, prepared as a bride adorned for her

husband. And I heard a loud voice from the throne saying, "Behold, the dwelling place of God is with man. He will dwell with them, and they will be his people, and God himself will be with them as their God. He will wipe away every tear from their eyes, and death shall be no more, neither shall there be mourning, nor crying, nor pain anymore, for the former things have passed away." (Rev. 21:1-4)

The new heavens and earth will be filled with the glory of God without any stain of sin or sin's destruction. Suffering, sickness, disease, pain, death, and grief will never again exist in the new heavens and new earth. This is one reason we call it heaven. It is a place that seems so unbelievable and awesome that we can only dream about it—and yet it is real! God's perfect design for the universe, His creation, and mankind will be restored.

We will forever remain in the very presence of our Creator and our God and enjoy His presence throughout eternity. We will serve Him in His kingdom, without ever experiencing the threat of violence, fear, worry, anxiety, loneliness, discouragement, or depression. There will be no wars, but only universal peace being executed under the Lordship of Christ. I know - sounds too good to be real. But believe me my friend, it is as real as the eyes you are using to read these words.

This is the promise of the Scriptures, the promise of the Lord Jesus, and God's ultimate plan and purpose for His creation. We will live together in harmony with the nations of the world, have fullness of joy, and for all eternity join with all creation giving praise, adoration, and worship to our incredible God. I can't wait! Glory to God in the highest!

Conclusion

As this chapter comes to a close, you still may have many questions about the end times. There are countless numbers of books you can read, but remember that they are filled with speculation. These ten things I mentioned we know. They are facts where evangelical believers find agreement. Stop worrying about the things you don't know and begin rejoicing in the things you do know. It is going to be okay—far more than you can imagine!

Discussion Questions

1. What is wrong with setting a date for the return of Christ? Why would people set a date and what are the dangers of date setting?

2. What is the Scriptural evidence that we are living in the *last days*?

3. What will happen to the bodies of those who have died and the bodies of those who are alive at the Second Coming of Christ?

4. Where are believers presently who have died? Why is this important to know?

5. What are three theological views concerning the tribulation period?

6. What are three theological views concerning the millennium?

7. What is the rapture and when will it take place?

8. Why should we have an interest in the teachings concerning the Second Coming of Christ?

9. What can we know for sure concerning the Second Coming of Christ?

10. How do we prepare for the Second Coming of Christ?

11. What would be the result of not preparing for the Second Coming of Christ?

12. If you knew Christ's return was some point in the next seven days, what changes would you make and why?

Chapter Twelve

Apostasy Versus Eternal Security

T he subject of apostasy is controversial and emotional. Even at the present I experience tension when seeking to understand these two topics theologically. The word apostasy refers to "the act of rebelling against, forsaking, abandoning, or falling away from what one has believed."[1] I would venture to say that almost everyone – pastors, theologians, and lay people – have strong opinions on this topic.

Apostasy is a highly sensitive subject because it concerns the eternal destiny of the soul. When we discuss the possibility of believers apostisizing their faith, we are talking about the potential of believers forfeiting (losing) their salvation. Any discussion on apostasy has the potential of becoming emotionally explosive.

Among evangelicals, there are two main theological positions. One position is called *eternal security*, or what some refer to as *once saved, always saved*. This position teaches that once a person becomes a Christian, he or she is eternally secure in his or her salvation. That is, there is nothing one can ever do, no sin or sins one can ever commit, that will sever one's relationship with Christ. Thus, believers are eternally secure and can never lose their salvation.

The other position is the belief in *apostasy*, that people can apostatize (lose their faith), walk away from their relationship with Christ, and eventually come to a point of unbelief, severing their relationship with Christ and losing their salvation.

As I shared earlier, I served in the Southern Baptist Convention for most of my ministry. As a Baptist pastor for 23 years, I preached and defended the doctrine of the eternal security of the believer, which is a cardinal doctrine of the Baptist faith. As such, I have a firm grasp and understanding of the position. I never questioned it and I was totally convinced that the security of the believer was clearly taught in the Scriptures. But when I experienced the baptism in the Holy Spirit, I began to reevaluate my theological position on eternal security. I thought to myself, "If I could be wrong on the doctrine of the baptism of the Holy Spirit, could I also be wrong about the subject of eternal security?"

I began a diligent study of the Scriptures, read several books from *both* positions, and came to the conclusion that apostasy *seems* plausible. In saying this, let me say *if* it is possible for a person to lose their salvation, it is not the norm, – but there are more than a few Scriptures that seem to imply this possibility. It is important that when we look at the Scriptures, we need to examine them as if we have not already determined our theological presuppositions and ask, "What is the *natural* meaning of the text?" By just reading the text, what jumps out as the *obvious* meaning, the intent that the writer is seeking to convey? I am convinced that when we approach the subject of apostasy versus eternal security, and look for the obvious meaning of the Scriptures without any theological presuppositions, you *can* build solid cases for both positions. I know this will not make people on either side of the topic happy, but I want to be honest with you and say from my perspective, there remains theological tension as to which position is correct. This is why I will share biblical teaching for both positions, seeking to provide balance in this discussion.

The Apostasy Position
Evidence from Hebrews

I will give argumentation from various Scriptures to demonstrate the position of apostasy, but I, would suggest that if you approached the subject by just reading the book of Hebrews alone, without any other proof text from any other book of the Bible, you would be forced to conclude that the author does seem to present the *potential* for a person to apostatize his or her faith.

One scholar who points out the value of Hebrews to the subject of apostasy is the late Dr. Dale Moody, a Southern Baptist theologian who served as senior professor at the Southern Baptist Theological Seminary and received his Ph.D. from Oxford University. In his book, *The Word of Truth, a Summary of Christian Doctrine Based on Biblical Revelation* he wrote a section titled, "Salvation and Apostasy." He clearly believes that a person can apostatize his or her faith. He makes a case that the doctrine of the "perseverance of the saints," later to be called "eternal security" can be traced back in church history to the Catholic theologian Augustine, followed by theologian John Calvin. Concerning the numerous warnings of apostasy in the book of Hebrews, he states the following:

> If one follows the teachings of Hebrews all the other teachings on apostasy in the New Testament present no problems. It is when one tries to twist Hebrews to fit a traditional system based on false philosophy and dogma that difficulties arise. Few passages in the New Testament have been twisted with more violence than the five warnings on apostasy in Hebrews.[2]

This is a challenge for both positions. I am suggesting that to support either position, in my opinion, theological gymnastics are required. That is, some

Scriptures have to be "twisted" from, what appears to be, their natural and obvious meanings to fit into either of these doctrines. Scriptures that seem to support apostasy are too numerous to simply ignore.

Before I go any further in my discussion, let me say that I respect and appreciate both theological positions on the subject. As I have stated, I do believe that both positions have biblical credibility. If they didn't, there would not be a theological divide among Bible-believing, conservative evangelicals. Both sides affirm the inerrancy of the Scriptures and are sound theologically on the major tenets of the Christian faith. Regardless of ones position on this subject, I do not want to characterize either of these positions as heretical, and we should respect one another irrespective of where we land theologically.

There is an abundance of Scripture that allows one to build a biblical case.At this point, let me correct an accusation often aimed at those who believe in eternal security. Throughout my years as a Baptist, I have heard people say the following: "Baptists teach that once you're saved, you can live however you want, because you will never lose your salvation." Having pastored most of my ministry as a Baptist, I can assure you that neither I nor any other Baptist pastor I've known would ever approach the subject of eternal security with that mindset.

My position along with others was that if people said they were Christians but approached their Christian life in this flippant manner, they really weren't saved. I had always taught and preached that if people continue sinning and having an attitude that chooses to live however they want because they believe they are eternally secure, then they are not saved in the first place. So in fairness to those who hold to the position of eternal security, I believe that they would never approach living in sin or habitually committing sinful acts with the viewpoint that once a person is saved one can live however one pleases. Such a description is a misnomer that misrepresents those who believe in eternal security.

Having said this, I am *not* suggesting that is doesn't matter what position one takes. I do feel it is extremely important as one's position can affect people's attitudes about sin and can potentially lead people down a very precarious path. This is the very reason why I have included a chapter on apostasy. There is one additional comment that I want to make before presenting the biblical case for apostasy. If apostasy is possible, I *do not* believe that there is a sin or any particular sin or sins that cause a person to apostatize his or her faith, but rather a series of *progressive* acts of disobedience that slowly chip away at a person's faith, eroding it to such an extent that he or she becomes agnostic and subsequently loses faith. Thus ultimately, it is *a loss of faith* that causes a person to lose his or her salvation. We are saved by faith, continue to be saved by faith, and maintain our salvation by faith in Christ—and faith alone. If apostasy is possible when a person reaches a point of losing one's faith that one forfeits one's salvation.

The following diagram illustrates this point.

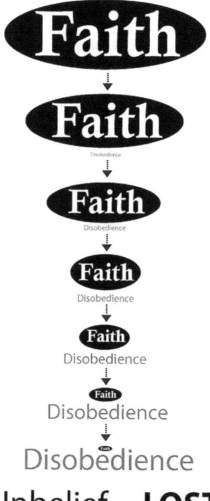

Unbelief = **LOST**

When a person continues to disobey God, that disobedience *does* affect that person's level of faith. The more we live in disobedience without repenting of our sins, the more our faith is undermined, becomes diluted, and is vulnerable. If we continue living in this state of disobedience, we are more susceptible to a marginalization of our faith and the question becomes, "Can we continue in sin to such a point that our faith evaporates and unbelief sets in?" If this is possible, this doesn't happen overnight it evaporates and unbelief sets in. Again, this doesn't happen overnight or because of one particular sin or sins—but is a *progressive process* in which a person's disobedience takes him or her down a path that ultimately leads to unbelief.

Some may argue that sounds like a salvation earned by works. That is, a person can perform certain behaviors that will earn entrance into heaven. I am absolutely not saying this! Apostasy would only become a reality when one reaches a point of *unbelief*—having *no faith*—that a person will lose his or her salvation. Living a godly life and not living in sin is definitely key to maintaining and stabilizing our faith. But no works of righteousness that we perform will ever merit our entering heaven and having a right standing with God. It is only our faith and trust in Christ.

My point is that I believe there is sufficient support in the Scriptures that implies that a person's faith can be eroded by continual acts of disobedience, which could ultimately lead to apostasy. The church of Laodicea certainly had a carnal faith (see Rev. 3:14-21). Ultimately it will be a *lack of faith* (unbelief) that keeps people out of heaven, not their performance of good works. What I am saying is that good works definitely has an effect on one's faith and its stability and development, or lack therein.

Good works and spiritual disciplines are designed only to edify and strengthen one's faith and never to be justification for entrance into heaven. Let's begin our study of the Scriptures that seem to support the position of apostasy. We will begin with the words of Jesus.

1. The words of Jesus

Did Jesus ever say anything that would imply the possibility of a person coming to faith, believing in Him, but then walking away from that faith? Did He ever say anything about people following Him for a certain period of time, and then falling away? I believe He did. Examine the following words of Jesus:

And you will be hated by all for my name's sake. But the one who *endures to the end will be saved.* (Matt. 10:22, emphasis mine)

And then many will fall away and betray one another and hate one another. And many false prophets will arise and lead many astray. And because lawlessness will be increased, the love of many will grow cold. But the one who *endures to the end will be saved.* (Matt. 24:10-13, emphasis mine)

In these passages, Jesus implies that it is an *enduring* faith that secures one's salvation. He isn't referring to one's physical life being saved, because He says some will be *put to death.* Jesus must be speaking about an *enduring* faith that continues to trust and believe in Him regardless of the trials and persecutions in life.

The synoptic gospels (Matthew, Mark, and Luke) all record Jesus' teaching called, the Parable of the Sower. The focus of the parable is people's responses to hearing the Word of God. People responded differently when they heard the Word. But notice particularly Jesus' interpretation of the Word that falls *among the rocks.*

> And the ones on the rock are those who, when they hear the word, *receive it* with joy. But these have no root; *they believe for a while*, and in time of testing fall away. (Luke 8:13)

Notice His words, "they believe for a while." Jesus definitely states that some received the Word and believed—*but then fall away*. They even received the word with joy, but then after experiencing a time of testing, they fall away, the implication being they no longer believe. If we take His words at face value they certainly seem to imply that they once had faith, but lost it. Concerning this passage, Dale Moody wrote:

> There are several warnings in the Synoptic Gospels about the danger that disciples may fall away, but perhaps the plainest passage is Luke's interpretation of the Parable of the Sower (8:9-15). Some only hear the word of God without believing it, but those in a second group "believe for a while and in a time of temptation fall away" (8:13). A.T. Robertson comments: "Ostensibly they are sincere and have a real start in the life of faith.[3]

One of the most convincing passages of Scripture that appears to validate the position of apostasy is Jesus' teaching about Him being the vine and we the believers as the branches. Read these words and ask yourself, "What would be the obvious, most natural interpretation of the text without having any theological presuppositions?"

> Abide in me, and I in you. As the branch cannot bear fruit by itself, unless it abides in the vine, neither can you, unless you abide in me. I am the vine; you are the branches. Whoever abides in me and I in him, he it is that bears much fruit, for apart from me you can do nothing. *If anyone does not abide in me he is thrown away like a branch and withers; and the branches are gathered, thrown into the fire, and burned.* (John 15:4-6, emphasis mine)

To abide in Christ presupposes that we are *already abiding in Christ, having been connected to Him.* That is, we have already entered and established a relationship with Him because of our faith. Jesus is teaching that *abiding in Him,* staying connected to Him, and following His teachings enables us to experience a productive and meaningful life. He is our source of strength and the only reason for our productivity.

He makes it clear that apart from Him we "can do nothing." But then He goes on to say that if anyone chooses *not* to abide in Him, that "he is thrown away like a branch and withers; and the branches are gathered, thrown into the fire, and burned." Some interpret this passage as Jesus speaking exclusively about being chastised or disciplined, not referring to losing one's salvation. But to me, the natural understanding of this text implies that if you are no longer connected to Him and you are "thrown into the fire and burned," then you no longer *belong* to Him or have *any part* with Him. The severity of the judgment appears to be rather permanent. One has to develop a very creative interpretation of this passage in order to avoid seeing the possibility of apostasy.

When I was in seminary, I had a New Testament professor named Dr. William Coble. I remember in one particular class we were discussing John chapter three, where Jesus and Nicodemus converse about the New Birth. Dr. Coble made a statement in reference to John 3:16, a verse many of us know by heart. In that verse, Jesus said to Nicodemus, "For God so loved the world, that he gave his only Son, that whoever *believes* in him should not perish but have eternal life" (John 3:16, emphasis mine). He proceeded to say that the word "believe" in the Greek was a present tense verb, implying continued action. He was saying the person who *continues* to believe has eternal life.

Being a young theological student who was always ready to defend the faith, I instantly raised my hand to ask a question. When I was called on, I asked, "Dr. Coble, are you saying that a person can believe and then stop believing, in other words, lose their salvation?" I was accused of trying to put words in his mouth and then assured that he was simply saying that the word believe is written in the present tense, meaning a continued belief.

To me and several other students that I talked with, it seemed as if Dr. Coble was saying that one's salvation was dependent upon one's *continued* act of believing. Many years later, I have come to believe that Dr. Coble was right and that this is the teaching of the Scriptures. The one who *continues* to believe that Jesus is God's Son, who died for one's sins and was resurrected from the dead has forgiveness of sins and possesses the free gift of eternal life.

Dr. Dale Moody says many people use John 10:28 as a proof text for eternal security. He writes the following:

> Eternal life is the life of those who continue to follow Jesus. No one can retain eternal life who turns away from Jesus. John 10:28 is frequently used as a security blanket by those who ignore many of the New Testament warnings about going back or falling away, but a literal translation of John 10:27-28, all of the sentence, hardly needs explanation, for it is a promise to those who continue to follow Jesus. Not for one moment do I doubt this literal translation: "My sheep keep on hearing my voice, and I keep on knowing them, and they keep on following me and I keep on giving them eternal life, and they shall never perish, and no one shall snatch them out of my hand." Some read the passage as if it says, "My sheep heard

my voice, and I knew them, and they followed me, and I gave to them eternal life." The verbs are present linear, indicating continuous action by the sheep and by the Shepherd, not the punctiliar fallacy of the past tense.[4]

Moody's point here is that believers must continue believing in Jesus and obeying His commands. As you will notice in this chapter, many of the verses that I will cite concerning salvation talk about salvation in a conditional light, meaning, our salvation is conditional, based on our continued belief and faith in Christ. Notice these words of Paul: "Keep a close watch on yourself and on the teaching. *Persist* in *this*, for by so doing you will save both yourself and your hearers." (1 Tim. 4:16, emphasis mine)

2. Warnings about apostasy

Another key argument concerning apostasy has to do with Scriptural warnings about our salvation. If a warning has no consequences, then why give one? In other words, why give warnings about the consequences of a particular action or behavior if the consequences or repercussions are not real? It would simply be lying. And God does not lie.

Earlier, I said that the book of Hebrews alone gives us sufficient warnings that a person *could* potentially apostatize his or her faith. But other books in the Bible including the words of Jesus are replete with warnings that imply apostasy. I don't think the Scriptures, written under the inspiration of the Holy Spirit, give us warnings that are meaningless. Why would the Holy Spirit give us warnings if there was never any intention of administering consequences for those who ignore the warnings?

I believe the warnings given to us in Scripture must be taken seriously and taken at face value. I also believe that ignoring the warnings will bring about dire consequences. It is an injustice to the Scriptures to read a warning and conclude, "They really don't mean what they seem to be saying." I want you to read the warnings in the following Scriptures and ask, "What is the obvious meaning of these words?"

> So then, brothers, we are debtors, not to the flesh, to live according to the flesh. For if you live according to the flesh *you will die*, but if by the Spirit you put to death the deeds of the body, you will live. For all who are led by the Spirit of God are sons of God. (Rom. 8:12-14, emphasis mine)

Is Paul speaking about physical or spiritual death in this passage? The recipients of his epistle are Christians, referred to as *brothers*. There are many people who live *according to the flesh* but still live a long life. It appears as if

Paul is speaking about spiritual, not physical death. Notice Paul's words in this passage:

> But if some of the branches were broken off, and you, although
> a wild olive shoot, were grafted in among the others and now
> share in the nourishing root of the olive tree, do not be arro-
> gant toward the branches. If you are, remember it is not you
> who support the root, but the root that supports you. Then you
> will say, "Branches were broken off so that I might be grafted
> in." That is true. They were broken off because of their unbe-
> lief, *but you stand fast through faith.* So do not become proud,
> but fear. *For if God did not spare the natural branches, neither
> will he spare you.* (Rom. 11:17-21, emphasis mine)

Here Paul is referring to the Jews who were "broken off" the branch of Christ because of their *unbelief.* He then refers to Gentiles who have been grafted into Christ because of belief, that is, faith. But notice that Paul then warns that if the Jews, who were natural branches, were still broken off because of *unbelief,* that the Gentiles must not become so arrogant or prideful that they assume it cannot happen to them. So he tells them to "stand fast in the faith." We must continue believing in Christ and in His salvation.

In this next passage, Paul is speaking about eating meat offered to idols. His message is that it doesn't technically matter if we eat meat offered to idols because idols are not really gods. But we still must be mindful of what we eat because of the potential damage we can cause to a "weaker brother." If they are not mature in their faith, there is the potential for them to be "destroyed." Notice:

> But take care that this right of yours does not somehow
> become a stumbling block to the weak. For if anyone sees
> you who have knowledge eating in an idol's temple, will
> he not be encouraged, if his conscience is weak, to eat food
> offered to idols? And so by your knowledge this *weak person
> is destroyed*, the brother for whom Christ died. (1 Cor. 8:9-
> 11, emphasis mine)

Again, Paul is speaking of a fellow Christian, *the brother for whom Christ died.* What does he mean when he says the disillusioned person with weak faith will be "destroyed?" Is Paul not speaking about the danger of under-mining a brother's faith, which can potentially cause this brother in Christ to be destroyed? How can this happen if a person can never lose his or her salvation?

When I first began studying the possibility of apostasy, I searched in a Bible concordance for the little preposition "if" in the New Testament. "If" means that certain conditions must be met in order for something else to be true. As I studied and tracked the various "if" uses, it became clear to me that our salvation was conditional upon my *continual* faith in Christ. Notice the following Scriptures in which I have underlined the word "if:"

> Now I would remind you, brothers, of the gospel I preached to you, which you received, in which you stand, and by which you are being saved, *if you hold fast* to the word I preached to you—unless you believed in vain. (1 Cor. 15:1-2, emphasis mine)

> And you, who once were alienated and hostile in mind, doing evil deeds, he has now reconciled in his body of flesh by his death, in order to present you holy and blameless and above reproach before him, *if indeed you continue in the faith, stable and steadfast, not shifting from the hope of the gospel that you heard*, which has been proclaimed in all creation under heaven, and of which I, Paul, became a minister. (Col. 1:21-23, emphasis mine)

> Now Moses was faithful in all God's house as a servant, to testify to the things that were to be spoken later, but Christ is faithful over God's house as a son. And we are his house *if indeed we hold fast* our confidence and our boasting in our hope. (Heb. 3:5-6, emphasis mine)

The following warning in Hebrews seems to conclusively suggest that there is the possibility of losing our salvation. Remember as you read these verses that the writer is speaking to Christians.

> Therefore we must pay much closer attention to what we have heard, *lest we drift away from it.* For since the message declared by angels proved to be reliable, and every transgression or disobedience received a just retribution, *how shall we escape if we neglect such a great salvation?* It was declared at first by the Lord, and it was attested to us by those who heard. (Heb. 2:1-3, emphasis mine)

> Take care, brothers, lest there be in any of you an evil, *unbelieving heart, leading you to fall away from the living God.* But exhort one another every day, as long as it is called "today," that none of you may be hardened by the deceitfulness of sin. For we have come to share in Christ, *if indeed we hold our original confidence firm to the end.* As it is said, "Today, if

you hear his voice, do not harden your hearts as in the rebellion." For who were those who heard and yet rebelled? Was it
not all those who left Egypt led by Moses? And with whom
was he provoked for forty years? Was it not with those who
sinned, whose bodies fell in the wilderness? And to whom did
he swear that they would not enter his rest, but to those who
were disobedient? So we see that they were unable to enter
because of unbelief (Heb. 3:12-19, emphasis mine).

For if we go on sinning deliberately *after receiving the knowledge of the
truth*, there no longer remains a sacrifice for sins, but a fearful expectation of
judgment, and a fury of fire that will consume the adversaries. (Heb. 10:26-27,
emphasis mine)

The above passages in the book of Hebrews seem to offer indisputable
proof that a person can potentially apostatize his or her faith. Again, the writer
is addressing believers (brothers) not unbelievers. He is warning us not to
develop an "unbelieving heart, leading you to fall away from the living God"
(Heb. 3:12-19). Again, by looking at the text for the natural, normal meaning
and intent of the writer, what would the average person conclude without any
predetermined theological presuppositions? What appears to be the obvious
meaning of the text? I would submit that to those who embrace eternal security,
these are extremely difficult passages to explain.

The apostle Peter warns about the importance of practicing, or living out
one's faith, which provides the believer the security of salvation. I think the
same is true of this passage:

For this very reason, make every effort to supplement your
faith with virtue, and virtue with knowledge, and knowledge
with self-control, and self-control with steadfastness, and
steadfastness with godliness, and godliness with brotherly
affection, and brotherly affection with love. *For if these
qualities are yours and are increasing*, they keep you from
being ineffective or unfruitful in the knowledge of our Lord
Jesus Christ. For whoever lacks these qualities is so nearsighted
that he is blind, having forgotten that he was cleansed from
his former sins. Therefore, brothers, be all the more diligent
to confirm your calling and election, *for if you practice these
qualities you will never fall*. For in this way there will be richly
provided for you an entrance into the eternal kingdom of our
Lord and Savior Jesus Christ. (2 Pet. 1:5-11, emphasis mine)

Again, when we see this little preposition "if," it speaks of a condition. For
example, following the condition that has been set forth will result in the stated

outcome. But if the stated condition is not followed, the stated outcome will not take place.

These Scriptures definitely seem to build the case of the potential of one's faith being eroded and become non-existent if one persistently lives in disobedience and unwillingness to submit one's life to the teachings of the Scriptures. Take a look at the following passages:

This charge I entrust to you, Timothy, my child, in accordance with the prophecies previously made about you, that by them you may wage the good warfare, *holding faith and a good conscience. By rejecting this, some have made shipwreck of their faith*, among whom are Hymenaeus and Alexander, whom I have handed over to Satan that they may learn not to blaspheme. (1 Tim. 1:18-20, emphasis mine)

For the love of money is a root of all kinds of evils. It is through this craving that some have *wandered away from the faith* and pierced themselves with many pangs. (1 Tim. 6:10, emphasis mine)

O Timothy, guard the deposit entrusted to you. Avoid the irreverent babble and contradictions of what is falsely called "knowledge," for by professing it some have *swerved from the faith*. (1 Tim. 6:20-21, emphasis mine)

My brothers, if anyone among you *wanders from the truth* and someone brings him back, let him know that whoever brings back a sinner from his wandering will *save his soul* from death and will cover a multitude of sins. (Jas. 5:19-20, emphasis mine)

Now the Spirit expressly says that in later times some will *depart from the faith* by devoting themselves to deceitful spirits and teachings of demons. (1 Tim. 4:1, emphasis mine)

You cannot "depart" from something that you never had. The Bible teaches that particularly in the last days, there will be some who will depart, leave, and forsake their faith in Christ. Not only will they depart from their faith, but they will also devote themselves to deceitful spirits and teachings of demons. That is a pretty radical turnaround to say the least!

One of the most convincing Scriptures for the position of apostasy is found in Hebrews 6:4-6. I never preached on this passage when I was a Baptist. I honestly did not know how to expound it and maintain consistency with my belief in eternal security. I had read numerous commentaries on these verses, but I was never content with their explanations. Their comments just weren't convincing.

For instance, they would often comment that this passage is just a hypothetical situation, something that really couldn't happen. If this is the case, why give the warning about the possibility? I would read the text and ask, "How does the writer want me to view his words as 'hypothetical?'" Look at the warning from the writer:

For it is impossible, in the case of those who have once been enlightened, who have tasted the heavenly gift, and have

> shared in the Holy Spirit, and have tasted the goodness of the
> word of God and the powers of the age to come, *and then have
> fallen away*, to restore them again to repentance, since they
> are crucifying once again the Son of God to their own harm
> and holding him up to contempt. (Heb. 6:4-6, emphasis mine)

Does the writer really intend for us to read these words and conclude that this kind of a situation can never happen? Are we to read these words and conclude that the writer isn't really speaking about true Christians? How can a person have "been enlightened, who have tasted the heavenly gift, and have shared in the Holy Spirit, and have tasted the goodness of the word of God and the powers of the age to come" and not be a Christian? I remember one particular pastor trying to explain this away by saying, "He has tasted; but it doesn't say he has eaten!" I don't think anyone can approach this passage with intellectual honesty and say the writer is referring to non-believers.

Yet this passage has been used to support a theology that says a person who has never accepted Christ can taste God's goodness and not accept it. The description of the people in this passage clearly speaks of those who have experienced the New Birth in Christ. I think this is one of the strongest passages in the Bible that refutes the doctrine of eternal security or *once saved always saved*.

I also believe that this passage teaches that whenever the person described crosses the line of no return, he or she has made a permanent choice. That is, that person will never again come back to the Lord. The decision is final. I do not believe that a person is saved, then lost, then saved, then lost, etc. If it is possible for a person to walk away from the faith to the point of unbelief, I feel this passage teaches that if they do, they can never come back.

Consider these words from the apostle Peter: "For if, after they have escaped the defilements of the world through the knowledge of our Lord and Savior Jesus Christ, they are *again entangled in them and overcome*, the last state has *become worse* for them than the first" (2 Pet. 2:20, emphasis mine).

One of my seminary professors said the "they" in this passage refers to false prophets who were never truly saved. But it appears to me that they *became* false prophets because the text definitely seems to imply that they at one time had "escaped the defilements of the world." Then it says, "they are again entangled." To me the natural meaning of the text seems to imply that they were once saved, but then left the faith and went back into the world, having become entangled *once again*. "Escaping" implies that they had been rescued, delivered, and liberated. The group of people mentioned here seem to be genuine believers who became teachers, who had embraced the gospel, but backslid, leaving their genuine faith and becoming false teachers.

Let me give you a few additional verses that I feel affirm the potential for apostasy, and then make a few concluding remarks.

Strive for peace with everyone, and for the holiness without which no one will see the Lord. *See to it that no one fails to obtain the grace of God;* that no "root of bitterness" springs up and causes trouble, and by it many become defiled. (Heb. 12:14-15, emphasis mine)

No one who denies the Son has the Father. Whoever confesses the Son has the Father also. *Let what you heard from the beginning abide in you.* If what you heard from the beginning abides in you, then you too will abide in the Son and in the Father. And this is the promise that he made to us—eternal life. (1 John 2:23-25, emphasis mine)

And if anyone takes away from the words of the book of this prophecy, God will *take away his share in the tree of life* and in the holy city, which are described in this book. (Rev. 22:19, emphasis mine)

The "tree of life" as described in the garden represents eternal life. I have heard some interpretations of this passage that says the judgment from God mentioned here is physical death. But again, I don't think one would naturally conclude that the judgment is physical death, unless one has an already established position on apostasy.

THE CASE FOR ETERNAL SECURITY

As I stated earlier, there are extremely strong feelings on this topic. I am sure that those who embrace eternal security would consider those who believe in apostasy as theologically heretical. The reverse position is also true. Again, I think this is where we need to be intellectually honest with one another. If either position was crystal clear, why would there be a divide among conservative, Bible believing, evangelicals on these positions, when they agree on ninety-eight percent of all the major doctrines of the Bible? This is why I feel there needs to be respect for both positions. The following would be Scriptures represented by those who hold to the eternal security of the believer.

John 5:24

> "Truly, truly, I say to you, whoever hears my word and believes him who sent me has eternal life. He does not come into judgment, but has passed from death to life."

The argument is made that as soon as a person inherits eternal life, it is just that: eternal. One might ask, "How can it be eternal if you can lose it?" So if eternal life is received upon the reception of Christ as Lord and Savior, yet there is a possibility to lose it, than it is not eternal life. Furthermore, the person who has accepted Christ "has passed from death to life." The implication seems to teach the passing from death to life is a *present* reality which is completed action. The transition has been made and completed.

John 6:37

"All that the Father gives me will come to me, and whoever comes to me I will never cast out."

These are the words of Jesus in which He definitely speaks of our security in Him. Jesus emphatically says "I will never cast them out." If Jesus is true to His word, the implication is that it is an impossibility to ever be cast out from Him since He says it will "never" happen. The counter argument from those who believe in apostasy would say, "But this verse does not say that a person on his or her own cannot walk away from his or her relationship with Christ." True. But if they walk away, how does the word, "never" fit into the equation?

Apostasy is not addressed in this verse. As long as we are exercising faith in Christ, we will never lose our relationship with Him. But if through disobedience, we walk away and lose our faith, it isn't Jesus casting us out, but us and our unbelief that has severed our relationship.

John 10:27-30

"My sheep hear my voice, and I know them, and they follow me. I give them eternal life, and they will never perish, and no one will snatch them out of my hand. My Father, who has given them to me, is greater than all, and no one is able to snatch them out of the Father's hand. I and the Father are one."

I definitely feel this is one of the strongest Scriptures supporting the position of eternal security. Not only does Jesus say we are secure in His hands, but we are secure within the Father's hands. The phrase "no one" not only refers to humans, but to any force or power whether human or demonic. The emphasis is on the power of Jesus to protect and keep you. If He is going to prevent others from snatching you from His hands, wouldn't He keep you from having the power to be snatched out of His hands? Why would you have this power and ability to take your soul from Him? For those who continue to believe in Christ, yes they are secure in the hands of Jesus. They have no worries of anyone or any power snatching them out of His hands. But the text does not address what happens if one's faith is eroded, or if the person chooses to walk away from the faith. This passage simply teaches that those who *continue* to have faith in Christ are safe and secure in His hands. (Read my comments earlier in this chapter on Dr. Dale Moody's discussion of the tense of these verbs.)

2 Corinthians 1:21-22; Ephesians 1:13-14; 4:30

I have put these passages together because of the unity of theme: the "seal" that is placed on believers when they exercise faith in Christ.

> And it is God who establishes us with you in Christ, and has
> anointed us, and who has also put his seal on us and given us
> his Spirit in our hearts as a guarantee. (2 Cor. 1:21-22)

> In him you also, when you heard the word of truth, the gospel
> of your salvation, and believed in him, were sealed with the
> promised Holy Spirit, who is the guarantee of our inheritance
> until we acquire possession of it, to the praise of his glory.
> (Eph. 1:13-14)

> And do not grieve the Holy Spirit of God, by whom you were
> sealed for the day of redemption. (Eph. 4:30)

These Scriptures are given to say that when a person believes in Christ,
that a "seal" of protection is given, securing that person's salvation until the
day Christ returns. Something definitely transpires when a person believes, but
what did Paul mean by the word "sealed?" There are differences of opinion.

Dr. Martyn Lloyd Jones, who served as senior pastor of Westminster Chapel
in London for nearly thirty years, believed in eternal security. In his excellent
commentary on Ephesians entitled, *God's Ultimate Purpose*, he describes being
"sealed" with the Holy Spirit as *the baptism in the Holy Spirit*. I am not saying
he is correct here, but he makes a good argument that being "sealed" is being
baptized in the Holy Spirit. I point this out to say that there are various interpretations of this verse. Let me share what a few other commentaries say on
these verses.

> In speaking of the Holy Spirit as a *seal* the notions of
> ownership and protection are in view. Cattle, and even
> slaves, were branded with a seal by their masters to indicate
> to whom they belonged. Owners thus guarded their property
> against theft; in this sense the seal was a protecting sign or a
> guarantee. In the Old Testament God set a sign on his chosen
> ones to distinguish them as his own possession and to keep
> them from destruction (Ezek. 9:4–6). The figure of sealing is
> used by Paul in relation to the Spirit at 2 Corinthians 1:22:
> 'God has made them his inviolable possession; the pledge
> of this is the Spirit of God in the heart'. By giving Gentile
> believers the Spirit, God 'seals' or stamps them as his own
> now, and he will protect them through the trials and testings
> of this life (cf. 6:10–18) until he takes final possession of them
> (cf. v. 14) on 'the day of redemption' (4:30).[5]

O'Brien continues to say:

> The Holy Spirit by whom the Gentiles were sealed when they believed the gospel is now called the *deposit guaranteeing our inheritance*. Behind this translation lies the word that signifies a 'down payment' or 'pledge', and which in the New Testament is used only in the Pauline writings and always with reference to the Spirit of God. Originally of Semitic origin, this word in Hellenistic Greek became the ordinary commercial term for a down payment or first installment. According to 2 Corinthians 1:22 the Corinthians received the 'down payment' of the Spirit to guarantee the consummation of their future salvation. Their longing for the heavenly dwelling (2 Cor. 5:1–5) results from the certainty that they have been provided with an advance installment of the Spirit (cf. Rom. 8:23). Here in v. 14 the Spirit received is the *deposit guaranteeing our inheritance:* in giving him to us God is not simply promising us our final inheritance but actually providing us with a foretaste of it, even if it 'is only a *small fraction* of the future endowment.'[6]

Here is one final excerpt from a commentary.

> Paul adds a further analogy: The Holy Spirit is a 'deposit (NIV) or an earnest—*arrabōn* (cf. 2 Cor. 1:22; 5:5). The word is borrowed from the commercial world and means a deposit or first installment in hire purchase. It is a token payment assuring the vendor that the full amount will eventually follow. It can also be applied to an engagement ring (MM, p 79). Paul regards the Holy Spirit as the first installment of the Christian's inheritance. At the end of the age God will redeem his pledge and open the treasuries of heaven to all who are his in Christ. Meanwhile, the Spirit gives us the assurance that these things will one day be ours.[7]

From the last comments on Ephesians 1:13-14 and 2 Corinthians 1:21-22, we can conclude the following. First, to be sealed by the Holy Spirit is a sign of identification. When we are saved, the Holy Spirit enters us and witnesses with our spirits that we belong to Christ (see Rom. 8:17). Second, it is a sign of ownership. The Spirit living within us is constantly reminding us that we belong to Christ. And he is showing us how our lives and our priorities should be a reflection of our new owner: The Lord Jesus. Third, the seal of the indwelling Spirit gives us the promise that our faith in Christ is authentic, that is, real.

The seal of the Spirit within us confirms that everything we believe about Christ and the promises of eternal life following our death is not based just on some hopeful whim, but is based on the reality of the experience of the New Birth and confirmed by His Spirit. This is what the Scriptures means when referring to "a guarantee", a deposit so to speak of the spiritual life we have inherited. We have been given a small deposit of what we will be receiving when we receive full redemption in heaven.

Fourth, as we look to and depend on His Spirit, He will watch over us, guide us and protect us. We have His continual presence and power fused within our spirits, giving us the assurance that we will gain the victory by exercising our faith in Christ.

I do understand why these verses mentioned are used to support eternal security. But these verses do not address the consequences of the person that falls into a life of disobedience. I have already conclusively demonstrated from the Scriptures that I listed in this chapter that we as Christians can disobey the Lord. We can become worldly and resort to living a life that is inconsistent with the teachings of Scriptures.

This is why there are so many warnings about the need to persevere in our faith and not be disobedient. The church I mentioned earlier in the book of Revelations, Laodicea, is a clear indication that we can develop a weak and tepid faith.

The question is, can our faith become so weak that after a while it vaporizes? That is, can we become agnostics leading to a state of unbelief? That is the question concerning this subject!

Let me share a few other arguments for the eternal security of the believer. One is that the sealing of the Spirit represents His ownership. The Bible clearly teaches that when we placed our faith in Christ that a transaction was made. We were purchased with the blood of Jesus and we became His. Paul writes:

> Or do you not know that your body is a temple of the Holy Spirit within you, whom you have from God? You are not your own, for you were bought with a price. So glorify God in your body (1 Cor. 6:19-20).

When we were bought with His blood, we were given a seal of ownership. Christ as our purchaser put down a down payment and sealed us with His Spirit indicating we are His. It was a guarantee that the transaction was real, that it had substance. We are no longer our own, we have become His unique possession!

Now, I must admit that when I consider that I am not my own, that I have been purchased by Christ's own blood, and sealed with the Holy Spirit, it doesn't make theological sense to me that my actions or conduct could rob Christ from what He paid such a dear price for. How can a puny, finite creature like me, have the power and ability to take back from Jesus what He died on the cross for and purchased with His own blood? To me this argument carries significant weight and is extremely difficult to refute.

Secondly, corresponding to this, as a result of the transaction of Christ purchasing me, I have been birthed into God's family. Upon receiving Christ, we become the sons and daughters of God. The Spirit has given us a spiritual birth to which we can now look to God and say, Abba Father. How can I be unbirthed as His child? Notice the following Scriptures:

> But to all who did receive him, who believed in his name, he gave the right to become children of God (John 1:12).

> Beloved, we are God's children now, and what we will be has not yet appeared; but we know that when he appears we shall be like him, because we shall see him as he is (1 John 3:2, emphasis mine).

The verse you just read says, "we are God's children now." If we are God's children now, how can we ever eradicate this relationship? Will He not protect and keep safe His very own children? Can His indwelling presence that birthed us really unbirth us? Would a loving Father ever cast out His children? I think these are good questions that would seem to favor the eternal security of every believer.

Then there is Paul's passage in Romans that is often quoted for eternal security:

> What then shall we say to these things? If God is for us, who can be against us? He who did not spare his own Son but gave him up for us all, how will he not also with him graciously give us all things? Who shall bring any charge against God's elect? It is God who justifies. Who is to condemn? Christ Jesus is the one who died—more than that, who was raised—who is at the right hand of God, who indeed is interceding for us. Who shall separate us from the love of Christ? Shall tribulation, or distress, or persecution, or famine, or nakedness, or danger, or sword? As it is written, "For your sake we are being killed all the day long; we are regarded as sheep to be slaughtered." No in all these things we are more than conquerors through him who loved us. For I am sure that neither death nor life, nor angels nor rulers, nor things present nor things to come, nor powers, nor height nor depth, nor anything else in all creation, will be able to separate us from the love of God in Christ Jesus our Lord. (Romans 8:31-39)

If God loved us prior to our salvation, how much more does He love us now that we belong to Him? Paul says nothing can separate us from the love of God. Doesn't that mean our sinful actions and behavior, or are these exceptions? Didn't God know before He saved us and took up residence within us what our future would hold? Why would He draw us to Him in the first place, purchase us with His blood, adopt us as His children, and fill us with the Spirit if He knew that we were going to walk away from him? Let me share three additional Scriptures for the eternal security of the believer. The first two are found in John's first epistle:

> They went out from us, but they were not of us; for if they
> had been of us, they would have continued with us. But they
> went out, that it might become plain that they all are not of
> us (1 John 2:19).

Here it appears there were certain people who were in the church with other believers, and they left the church. John seems to imply the reason they left is because they never really belonged to the body. If they had been genuine, they would not have left. In other words, John seems to be saying that those who have experienced a genuine conversion will not depart. Their departure indicates their faith was superficial, not real.

But some would question, "But what happens if someone continues to sin, live in disobedience, and remains in their state of rebellion? How can they be saved?" Those who believe in eternal security have an answer from John's first epistle:

> "No one born of God makes a practice of sinning, for God's
> seed abides in him; and he cannot keep sinning, because he
> has been born of God" (1 John 3:9).

Notice John says they "cannot keep sinning." The Greek here means who continually, habitually practice sinning. It cannot happen. Why? Because they have been "born of God." In other words, if you are really born of God, though you may fall into sin, and drift from the Lord, eventually you will return, because you have been born of God. In addition, "God's seed abides in you", which many would interpret to be the seed of the Holy Spirit. So those who embrace the doctrine of eternal security will say that if someone is genuinely converted, sooner or later they will repent and return to the Lord. They were out of fellowship with God, but not out of relationship.

The last Scripture that is often cited for the eternal security position is from Paul's letter to the Philippians:

> And I am sure of this, that he who began a good work in you
> will bring it to completion at the day of Jesus Christ (Phil. 1:6).

From this text it is deduced that if God saves you and breathes new life into you, He will complete what He started. He will finish what He has begun. He will not abandon His work but bring it to its final and glorious completion.

CONCLUDING REMARKS

First, as I said at the beginning of this chapter, I do respect and understand both positions. Anyone who is being intellectually honest would admit that both positions can put forth credible arguments based on the Scriptures. There is an undeniable tension in the Scriptures concerning the subject. I am not going to be presumptuous as to claim with absolute certainty which position is correct. At least for me, it is extremely difficult.

A few years ago I called Pastor Jim Cymbala and asked him concerning his position on the subject. I knew he used to believe in apostasy, but he recently had several Southern Baptist pastors speaking in his pulpit. So I called him and asked him point blank if he had changed his position. I cannot remember his exact words, but let me paraphrase his answer, "Dwain, I know you are wanting a clear answer but I am cloudy on this. Sometimes I lean one way, sometimes I lean the other. I just can't give you a definitive answer."

Second, I know that some people will conclude that even implying apostasy could be possible is teaching a works plus faith position. Let me state categorically that the only reason for my entrance into heaven is my personal faith in Christ. It is His righteousness alone, and not one thing I have done that merits my entrance into heaven. I can do good works every hour of the day on every day of the week yet never gain access to heaven. As Isaiah said, my righteousness is as filthy rags (Isa. 64:6).

I trust solely in the death of Christ on the cross, forgiveness through His shed blood, and the power of His resurrection that gives me life. It is only the righteousness of Christ applied to me when I repented of my sins and trusted in the all-sufficient sacrifice of Christ on the cross that gives me eternal life. The purpose of good works is to glorify God, to strengthen and stabilize my faith, but never for the purpose of earning admission into heaven. I do believe the Scriptures teach that our faith can in fact be undermined, sabotaged, and attacked by the enemy and the various circumstances in life. As we yield to the Holy Spirit and follow the teachings of the Scriptures, our faith remains strong and vibrant. It is our faith, and our faith alone that saves us and secures our entrance into heaven.

Third, some may say if you believe in apostasy that it can lead to legalism, a life filled with a bunch of do's and don'ts. I do agree that it could evolve into a works based theology leading to legalism. The reality is that people can take any theological system to extremes. The position of eternal security can also be taken to an extreme where people embrace a radical grace in which they feel they can live however they want. Paul had to address the misinterpretation that people could live in sin and receive more grace (see Rom. 6:15). In the same chapter he goes on to speak about the importance of obedience and yielding to the Holy Spirit. We cannot live for ourselves and live in obedience to the Holy Spirit. The bottom line here is balance. Both positions can be distorted if not kept in balance with other Scriptures.

Fourth, I have stated several times the importance of looking at the Scriptures holistically, not isolating a few passages to build one's theological position. Again, I don't think anyone can deny that there are extremely complicated Scriptures on both sides of this issue; but perhaps this is the intention of the Scriptures.

Finally, some people may ask, "How can you ever be sure you are saved if you think there is a possibility you can lose your salvation?" Let me say that in my study of this subject, I have never once, ever, doubted my security in Christ. The reason—I have never once doubted or questioned the genuineness of my faith.

Some will be asking "What then do you believe?" Which position is yours? Apostasy, or eternal security?" As Pastor Cymbala said to me, you may not like my answer but here it is. After weighing the totality of Biblical evidence, I lean toward eternal security, but I feel both positions can be supported by scripture. And though there are difficult passages of scripture, here is what I know: as long as I believe, and have faith in Christ, I am eternally secure. I cannot begin to imagine not believing in Christ, thus I have never had a doubt concerning my salvation. And every Christian should feel the same way. As long as a person has faith in Christ, there is never a reason to be concerned about or doubt ones salvation. We have no reason to live in fear, only to live in the assurance of our salvation. But, if a person begins living a life of disobedience and carelessness, with no conviction of the Holy Spirit, a yellow light should begin blinking as a warning and an indication that one is drifting in one's faith. Those who can continue to live in sin without the conviction of the Holy Spirit, and be comfortable in their sin, are in a dangerous position. They should at once renew their faith, forsake their sin, and recommit their lives to Christ.

I conclude this chapter with the first verse and refrain of a great hymn of the faith written by Edward Mote in 1834 called, "The Solid Rock."[9]

> My hope is built on nothing less
> Than Jesus' blood and righteousness;
> I dare not trust the sweetest frame,
> But wholly lean on Jesus' name.
> On Christ, the solid Rock, I stand;
> All other ground is sinking sand.
> On Christ, the solid Rock, I stand;
> All other ground is sinking sand,
> All other ground is sinking sand.

Discussion Questions

1. What is *apostasy*?

2. What is the meaning of the term *eternal security*?

3. Why are these two subjects controversial?

4. Among Bible-believing evangelicals, why is there a difference of opinion concerning the positions of apostasy and eternal security?

5. How much do you think prior doctrinal teachings affect one's opinion on theological conclusions concerning these subjects?

6. What does the author mean by the natural and obvious meaning of the text?

7. Which Scriptures seem to teach that Jesus taught that it may be possible to lose one's faith?

8. What are the Scriptures often cited that seem to teach the eternal security of the believer? How can they be rebutted?

9. What role do good works and living in obedience to Christ serve in relation to our faith?

10. What is the significance of a warning?

11. What are some of the warnings in Scripture that seem to imply a person can apostatize his or her faith?

12. According to the author, what is the danger of being dogmatic concerning the position of eternal security?

Further Reading

Paul: A Man of Grace and Grit, Charles Swindoll
Job: A Man of Heroic Endurance, Charles Swindoll
Elijah: A Man of Heroism and Humility, Charles Swindoll
David: A Man of Passion and Destiny, Charles Swindoll
Moses: A Man of Selfless Dedication, Charles Swindoll
Esther: A Woman of Strength and Dignity, Charles Swindoll
Fascinating Stories of Forgotten Lives, Charles Swindoll
The Greatest Life of All, Charles Swindoll
A Life of Power, Andrew Murray
Absolute Surrender, Andrew Murray
Andrew Murray on the Holy Spirit, Andrew Murray
Fresh Faith, Jim Cymbala
Fresh Power, Jim Cymbala
The Charismatic Century, Jack Hayford
Grounds for Living, Jack Hayford
Hayford's Bible Handbook, Jack Hayford
Living the Spirit Filled Life, Jack Hayford
The Person and Work of the Holy Spirit, R.A. Torrey
Spirit Rising, Jim Cymbala
Spirit-Filled, Jack Hayford
The Spirit-Filled Life, Charles Finney
The Spirit of Christ, Andrew Murray
Surprised by the Power of the Spirit, Jack Deere
The Way to Pentecost, Samuel Chadwick
The Holiness-Pentecostal Tradition, Vinson Synan
Apostasy, Dale Moody
Awakened by the Spirit, Ron Philips
Christ in You, A.B. Simpson
The Glorious Disturbance, Ernest Gentile
Holy Spirit Revivals, Charles Finney
The Holy Spirit, R.A. Torrey
The Holy Spirit, Billy Graham
The Holy Spirit Today, Dick Iverson
David Worshiped a Living God, Judson Cornwall
David Worshiped with a Fervent Faith, Judson Cornwall

Elements of Worship, Judson Cornwall
How to Worship Jesus Christ, Joseph Carroll
Real Worship, Warren Wiersbe
Worship as David Lived It, Judson Cornwall
Divine Healing, Andrew Murray
Healing, Francis MacNutt
The Nearly Perfect Crime, Francis MacNutt
Manifest Presence, Jack Hayford
Of God and Men, A.W. Tozer
Celebration of Discipline, Richard Foster
Forgotten God, Francis Chan
Freedom of Simplicity, Richard Foster
Life on the Highest Plane, Ruth Paxson
Spiritual Disciplines for the Christian Life, Donald Whitney
Spiritual Power, Dwight Moody
The Beginner's Guide to Spiritual Warfare, Neal Anderson and Timothy Warner
Demolishing Strongholds, David Devenish
Vanquishing the Enemy, Ron Phillips
Victory over the Darkness, Neil Anderson
The Beauty of Spiritual Language, Jack Hayford
The Essentials of Prayer, E.M. Bounds
Helps to Intercession, Andrew Murray
The Path of Prayer, Samuel Chadwick
Prayer, Richard Foster
With Christ in the School of Prayer, Andrew Murray
The Attitude of Faith, Frank Damazio
Humility, Andrew Murray
The Knowledge of the Holy, A.W. Tozer
Life in the Son, Robert Shank
Listen to Me, Satan! Carlos Annacondia
Man – The Dwelling Place of God, A.W. Tozer
The Mystery of God's Will, Charles Swindoll
The Practice of the Presence of God, Brother Lawrence
The Case for Christ, Lee Strobel
The Case for Faith, Lee Strobel
The New Evidence that Demands a Verdict, Josh McDowell
The Pursuit of God, A.W. Tozer
Total Forgiveness, R.T. Kendall
You Were Made for More, Jim Cymbala
Your Sons and Daughters Shall Prophesy, Ernest Gentile
Your Spiritual Gifts Can Help Your Church Grow, Peter C. Wagner

Endnotes

Chapter 1: The Bible: Our Authority

1. Josh McDowell, *The New Evidence that Demands a Verdict* (Nashville, TN: Thomas Nelson, 1999), p. 16.
2. Frank Harber, *Sherlock's Faith* (Keller, TX: HeartSpring Media, 2004), p. 64.
3. McDowell, *The New Evidence that Demands a Verdict*, p. 7.
4. Biblestudy.org
5. Answerbag.com
6. McDowell, *The New Evidence that Demands a Verdict*, p. 8.
7. Ibid., p. 9.
8. Harber, *Sherlock's Faith*, p. 69.
9. Ibid., pp. 65-67.
10. W A Criswell, *Great Doctrines of the Bible* (Grand Rapids, MI: Paige Patterson Publisher, 1982), vol. 1, p. 108.
11. McDowell, *The New Evidence that Demands a Verdict*, p. 10.
12. Ibid., p. 11.
13. Harber, *Sherlock's Faith*, p. 69.
14. Ibid., pp. 54-55.
15. William Menzies and Stanley Horton, *Bible Doctrines: A Pentecostal Perspective* (Springfield, MO: Logion Press, 1993), pp. 21-22.
16. W A Criswell, *Great Doctrines of the Bible* (Grand Rapids, MI: Paige Patterson Publisher, 1982), vol. 1, p. 106-107.
17. Jack Hayford, *Grounds for Living* (Ada, MI: Chosen, 2003), pp. 18-19.
18. McDowell, *The New Evidence that Demands a Verdict*, p. 14.
19. Harber, *Sherlock's Faith*, pp. 48, 50-52.
20. Ibid., pp. 73-74.
21. Ibid., pp. 76-77.
22. Ibid., p. 82.

Chapter 2: The Deity of Jesus Christ

1. Josh McDowell, *The New Evidence that Demands a Verdict* (Nashville, TN: Thomas Nelson, 1999), pp. 155-157.
2. Ibid., p. 159.
3. Ibid., pp. 159-160
4. Ibid., pp. 160-162
5. Ibid., pp. 162-163

Chapter 5: The Baptism of the Holy Spirit! Part 1: Introduction

1. T.M. McCrossan, *Christ's Paralyzed Church X-Rayed* (Rev. C.E. Humbard, 1937), p. 24.
2. Ibid., p. 25

Chapter 6: The Baptism of the Holy Spirit! Part 2

1. "Assemblies of God Fundamental Truths" General Council of the Assemblies of God, www.ag.org.
2. A. W. Tozer, quoted by Alan Redpath in "Christian Life," *Christianity Today*, vol. 29, no. 18.
3. Bill Bright, "7 Basic Steps to Fasting and Prayer" *Campus Crusade for Christ*, http://www.cru.org/training-and-growth/devotional-life/7-steps-to-fasting/index.htm (accessed September 2012).

Chapter 7: The Church: The Body of Christ

1. James Strong, *Enhanced Strong's Lexicon* (Bellingham, WA: Logos Bible Software: 2001).
2. J.B. Polhill, *Acts, The New American Commentary*, vol. 26 (Nashville, TN: Broadman & Holman, 1995), p. 119.
3. T. D. Lea and H. P. Griffin, *The New American Commentary: 1, 2 Timothy, Titus*, vol. 34 (Nashville, TN: Broadman & Holman, 1992), p. 107.
4. Ibid., p. 115.

Chapter 8: Spiritual Disciplines

1. James Strong, *Enhanced Strong's Lexicon* (Bellingham, WA: Logos Bible Software: 2001).
2. Ibid.
3. Ibid.
4. Ibid.
5. Ibid.
6. Ibid.
7. Ibid.
8. Ibid.
9. Ibid.
10. Donald Whitney, *Spiritual Disciplines for the Christian Life* (Colorado Springs, CO: Navpress, 1991), p. 17.
11. Richard Foster, *Celebration of Discipline* (New York: Haper Collins Publishers, 1998), p. 158.
12. *The Westminster Assembly's Shorter Catechism* (Philadelphia, PA: Presbyterian Board of Publication and Sabbath-School Work, 1888), p.7.
13. Joseph Carroll, *How to Worship Jesus Christ* (Chicago, IL: Moody Press, 1984), p. 11.

14. Oswald Chambers, *My Utmost for His Highest* (New York: Dodd, Mead & Co., 1935), p. 254.
15. Warren Wiersbe, *Real Worship* (Grand Rapids, MI: Baker Books, 2000), pp. 12-13.
16. Don McMinn, *The Practice of Praise* (Printed in US: World Music, 1992), p. 14.
17. G. Campbell Morgan, *The Westminster Pulpit*, vol. 18 (London: Pickering & Inglis, N.D.), p. 248.
18. Whitney, *Spiritual Disciplines for the Christian Life*, p. 18.
19. Ibid., pp. 13-14.

Chapter 9: Spiritual Gifts
1. Jack Hayford, *Hayford's Bible Handbook* (Nashville, TN: Thomas Nelson, 1998), pp. 359-360.
2. Jack Hayford, *The Beauty of Spiritual Language* (Nashville, TN: Thomas Nelson, 1996), p. 10.
3. James Strong, *Enhanced Strong's Lexicon*, (Bellingham, WA: Logos Bible Software: 2001).

Chapter 10: Spiritual Warfare
1. David Devenish, *Demolishing Strongholds* (Colorado Springs, CO: Authentic Media, 2001), p.25.
2. C. Vaughan, *The Expositor's Bible Commentary*, vol. 11 (Grand Rapids, MI: Zondervan, 1981), p. 202.
3. P. T. O'Brien, *The Letter to the Ephesians: The Pillar New Testament Commentary* (Grand Rapids, MI: Wm. B. Eerdmans Publishing Co., 1999), p. 463.
4. J. F. MacArthur, Jr., *Ephesians, MacArthur New Testament Commentary* (Chicago, IL: Moody Press, 1986), p. 338.
5. O'Brien, *The Letter to the Ephesians: The Pillar New Testament Commentary*, p. 464.

Chapter 11: The End Times
1. *Nelson's complete book of Bible maps & charts: Old and New Testaments* (Nashville, TN: Thomas Nelson, 1996).
2. Ibid.
3. Ibid.
4. William Menzies and Stanley Horton, *Bible Doctrines: A Pentecostal Perspective* (Springfield, MO: Logion Press, 2000), p. 222.
5. "Tsunamis: Facts About Killer Waves" *National Geographic News*, October 28, 2010. www.nationalgeographic.com/news (accessed November 2012).

Chapter 12: Apostasy

1. Trent Butler, ed., *Holman Bible Dictionary* (Nashville, TN: Broadman & Holman Publishers, 1991), p. 74.

2. Dale Moody, *The Word of Truth, A Summary of Christian Doctrine Based on Biblical Revelation* (Grand Rapids, MI: Wm. B. Eedrmans Publishing Co., 1981), p. 352.

3. Ibid., p. 349.

4. Ibid., pp. 356-357.

5. P.T. O'Brien, *The Letter to the Ephesians: The Pillar New Testament Commentary* (Grand Rapids, MI: Wm.B. Eerdmans Publishing Co., 1999), p. 120

6. Ibid., pp. 120-121.

7. A. S. Wood, *The Expositor's Bible Commentary*, vol. 11 (Grand Rapids, MI: Zondervan, 1981), p. 27.

8. Robert Lee Shank, *Life in the Son* (Minneapolis, MN: Bethany House, 1989), pp. 105-106.

9. Edward Mote, "The Solid Rock" Public Domain.

About the Author

D r. Dwain Kitchens has served as a senior pastor for 33 years. He currently serves The Tabernacle Church in Sarasota, Florida, as senior pastor. Though most of his ministry he served as a Southern Baptist pastor, his theology concerning the Holy Spirit was dramatically changed when he experienced the fullness of the Holy Spirit at a Fresh Wind Fresh Fire Conference under Pastor Jim Cymbala of the Brooklyn Tabernacle. Pastor Dwain holds a B.A. in Religious Studies from Southwest Baptist University, Bolivar, MO.; a Master of Divinity from Midwestern Baptist Theological Seminary, Kansas City, MO., and a Doctor of Ministry from Mid-America Baptist Theological Seminary, Cordova, TN. Dwain and Pam have two sons, Andrew and James, wonderful daughters-in-law, Stacie and Whitney, and four grandchildren, Lia, Judah, Kaylin, and Hunter.

CPSIA information can be obtained
at www.ICGtesting.com
Printed in the USA
FSHW011150090421

9 781625 096777